Praise for Vampira

"Scott Poole has the chops, the Hollywood savvy, and the horror genre's insider smarts to write a killer book on Vampira. I'll be first in line to grab a copy."

—JONATHAN MABERRY, multiple Bram Stoker Award winner and *New York Times* bestselling author of *Assassin's Code* and *Dust & Decay*

"Horror hostess, bondage goddess, Charles Addams cartoon come to life, Vampira was every first-generation fanboy's wet dream. Scott Poole takes us on an unforgettable ride through the overlapping underworlds of B+D magazines, Hollywood noir, and early political liberation movements that inspired actress Maila Nurmi to challenge a postwar culture bent on stifling women's, choices, bodies, and desires. This book is a subversive masterpiece."

—SHERI HOLMAN, author of *Witches on the Road Tonight* and *The Dress Lodger*

"W. Scott Poole's last book, *Monsters in America*, was a dazzling work of cultural history: smart, funny, subversive and wildly entertaining. He showed a special gift for playfully saying serious things. His new book is even more wonderful. The life of Maila Nurmi, better known as the late-night TV hostess Vampira, is a great, strange story in itself, but also allows Poole to explore our attitudes about sex, death, fear, and difference. 'The Lady of Horror' was famous in the 1950s, but she is a remarkable symbol who connects backward to Poe and forward to Goth. She is as American as the Statue of Liberty."

—CHRISTOPHER BRAM, author of *Gods and Monsters* and *Eminent Outlaws: The Gay Writers Who Changed America*

"Vampira is up there with Vincent Price for lovers of the macabre, an icon whose shadow and influence lingers long after death. She's not only important to modern children of the night for being the first TV horror host, but as the original 'Glamour Ghoul,' whose style has inspired generations of Goth Girls to adopt the sexy undead look as their own. But there is more to her story than her ability to look good screaming, and Scott Poole, whose writing on the dark side of popular culture has proven to be some of the smartest, sassiest commentary on American society around, is the man to tell it."
—Liisa Ladouceur, author of *Encyclopedia Gothica*

"An expert critic of pop culture, W. Scott Poole is one of the finest historians of all that is wicked, salacious, and sexy in America. By looking into the life and times of Maila Nurmi, the former stripper turned television's dark goddess of sex and death, Poole unveils a new side of midcentury America, which we too often forget the steamy, scary, and sensational."
—Edward J. Blum, author of *The Color of Christ: The Son of God and the Saga of Race in America*

"Vampira represents a way to talk about fifties culture, especially about its political and moral pressures. Scott Poole has shown how brilliantly he can unearth cultural fears and desires."
—James R. Kincaid, author of *Erotic Innocence*

VAMPIRA

VAMPIRA

Dark Goddess of Horror

W. Scott Poole

SOFT SKULL PRESS

"I got this graveyard woman . . . she's a junkyard angel"

—Bob Dylan, "From a Buick 6"

Library of Congress Cataloging-in-Publication Data

Poole, W. Scott, 1971-
Vampira : dark goddess of horror / W. Scott Poole.
pages cm
ISBN 978-1-59376-543-9 (paperback)
1. Vampira, 1921-2008. 2. Entertainers—United States—Biography.
3. Actresses—United States—Biography. I. Title.
PN2287.V315P66 2014
791.4502'8092—dc23
[B]

2014014147

Cover design by Charles Brock, Faceout Studios
Interior design by Domini Dragoone

Soft Skull Press
An Imprint of Counterpoint
2560 Ninth Street, Suite 318
Berkeley, CA 94710
www.softskull.com

Printed in the United States of America
Distributed by Publishers Group West

10 9 8 7 6 5 4 3 2 1

This book is dedicated to a teenaged Elizabeth Syrjaniemi and long, lonely afternoons in the 1930s with her comics and pencils, all her strange road before her.

And to Bogey and Bobo, devoted companions for the solitary.

CONTENTS

by Sheri Holman

FOREWORD

One summer night when I was seven years old, I snuck out of my bedroom and down the hall. My young, sexy parents were out doing what young, sexy parents did on Saturday nights in the 1970s, and my teenaged aunt had been left in charge. It was past midnight and the house was dark except for the flickering light coming from our black-and-white television in the living room. I'd had another of the nightmares that plagued me back then. Abduction. Unfamiliar cars in the driveway. Formless dread. I padded in to see my aunt and glanced at the TV. An old woman in a nightgown caressed a butcher knife and cooed, "You must die, die, my darling."

I was paralyzed with terror, but almost instantly the scene cut away to a backdrop dungeon where a fake vampire in a black unitard and scuffed sneakers strummed a ukulele. Perched on the edge of a prop coffin, Bowman Body told a handful of jokes too corny even for Bazooka bubble gum wrappers. And just like that, the horror was vanquished. I snuggled up next to my aunt—who was grateful for the company—and watched alternating clips of gore and slapstick until I fell back asleep.

This was my first glimpse of *Shock Theater*, Richmond, Virginia's answer to *Creature Feature*, in San Francisco, *Chiller Theater*, in Pittsburgh, Ghoulardi in Cleveland, Zacherley in New York. Until 1980 when cable swept away independent local television stations, every large to midsize market had its own late-night horror movie host. Dressed as ghouls and ersatz vampires, they introduced films from Universal Studio's "Shock!" package, a bundle of 52 movies that included everything from *Dracula* and *The Mummy* to *The Spider Woman Strikes Back*. I was one of millions of kids who stayed up late or snuck downstairs to be initiated into the adult world of sex and violence from the safety of my living room.

Thirty-odd years later, the devotion I felt toward my childhood horror host found its way into my fifth novel, *Witches on the Road Tonight*. In it, dying Eddie Alley, a.k.a. "Captain Casket," must reconcile his Appalachian witch mother and his 24-hour cable news anchor daughter. The novel is about a family that peddles fear and anxiety, with Eddie serving as the campy pivot between two generations of dark feminine power. More than anything, though, it's a book about why we crave being afraid—how we seek it out in love and sex and family dynamics; how we, as a society, create the very monsters we then feel compelled to destroy.

While researching this novel, I did a lot of reading on the Shock! package and the origins of horror hosting. To my surprise, I learned the first horror host was a hostess—a former bondage model turned starlet, Maila Nurmi, who created the character Vampira. *Dig Me Later, Vampira*, exploded onto Los Angeles local television in 1954. The intro to her show—a long slow walk down a fog-shrouded corridor and her piercing scream of horror and ecstasy—quickly became iconic. She was featured in *TV Guide, Newsweek*, and *Life* magazine. She had celebrity spots of *The Red Skelton Show* and Ed Sullivan's

Toast of the Town. Vampira was everywhere, then just as suddenly she was gone, canceled a year later at the height of her popularity.

I was instantly intrigued by her story. Most of my fiction has dealt with women who transgress and are roundly punished for it. Wannabe saints, prostitutes, women labeled witches. Maila Nurmi—the daughter of communist Finnish immigrants, a housewife who yearned to be an evangelist but made her living as a television black widow vampire, seemed to push all the right buttons. God, Sex, and Death all in one glamorous wasp-waist package. Sipping poisoned cocktails and hinting at a deviant off-screen sex life, Vampira became a touchpoint of postwar male desire and anxiety. And like most intensely sexy women who refused to play by male rules, she found herself first celebrated and then discarded.

While I was doing my own research on Vampira, historian Scott Poole was one-upping me by writing a whole book about her. But Scott didn't want to write a straightforward biography. Here was a woman whose show lasted only a year—a show for which almost no footage survives—and yet her reputation grows bigger every year. Her zombie alien turn in *Plan 9 from Outer Space* is one of the most iconic moments in the history of B-movies, yet in it, she doesn't utter a word. What about her, then, continues to spawn so many imitators and fan clubs and websites? With so little of her to hold on to (not to mention Nurmi's own intensely guarded life and history) Scott understood a book about Vampira would need to be as much, if not more, about the society that created her. Using Nurmi's transgressive character as a touchstone, he has written a book about camp and cult in midcentury America and the threat that Nurmi and others like her posed to 1950s postwar convention.

In her classic 1964 essay, "Notes on 'Camp'" Susan Sontag wrote: "Camp sees everything in quotation marks. It's not a lamp, but a "lamp"; not a woman, but a "woman." To perceive Camp in objects and persons is to understand Being-as-Playing-a-Role. It is the farthest extension, in sensibility, of the metaphor of life as theater."

In this new biography, Scott Poole invites us into the campy underworld that created Vampira. Here, the marginalized learn the importance of performance for survival. They understand themselves as different from the dominant power structure and know a direct challenge rarely ends well. So they role-play and subvert, often through the medium of anarchic humor. Maila Nurmi, the child of peripatetic, uncaring immigrant parents, who came of age during the Great Depression and spent much of her childhood as an outsider, learned this lesson early. She ran away from home in her teens and spent the late 1940s and early 50s hanging with Beatniks and posing for bondage magazines. By the time she came into her stunning beauty, she had imbibed the power dynamics of parents and children, men and women, oppressor and oppressed. In an era that sought to contain women safely in the home, "Vampira dripped sexual power and aggression." Scott writes, "She completely subverted the image of 50s housewife, turning her into a rebellious monster."

It was one thing for camp to have free rein in Greenwich Village and the bohemian neighborhoods of downtown Los Angeles, but the new medium of television was virgin territory. For a postwar society determined to heal by placing itself in the induced coma of *I Love Lucy* and *Leave It to Beaver, Dig Me Later, Vampira*, was outsider art accidentally allowed to go mainstream. For the first time, a woman brought horror directly into the domestic sphere. Unlike Lucille Ball and June Cleaver, Vampira's ghoulish housewife didn't read as comforting. She read as hypnotically dangerous.

Camp can provide a release valve—a way of channeling the dark absurdities of life so that they don't swallow one whole. But while Sontag characterizes camp taste as "above all, a mode of enjoyment, of appreciation—not judgment," Nurmi dared to take herself seriously. Young people recognized a rebelliousness in her that mirrored the attitude of her friend and contemporary James Dean. These actors did not portray transgression, they *were* the very thing they represented. They couldn't, or wouldn't, turn it off to make others comfortable. When the wildly popular Nurmi refused to allow syndication of her character, and her employers understood she couldn't be easily controlled, they pulled the plug and ended her career.

As a child suffering bad dreams, I appreciated the campiness of Bowman Body. As an adult who understands the horrors of society far exceed any cinematic representation, I've come to appreciate Vampira's determination to engage with the horror beyond the movies she showed. In an era that sought to heal the wounds of war with a false narrative of safety and prosperity, Nurmi's "homage to deSade by way of Betty Crocker" persona belied the white-knuckled normalcy of mainstream American television. By refusing to play along, Vampira became a reminder that though the war might be over, you were safe nowhere—Death was mocking you inside your own living room, she was soaking in your bathtub, waiting for you with a cocktail, ready to take you to bed. Hers was a scream of existential horror at the human condition, followed by a nihilistic laugh of inevitable surrender. This was not a message for children. But it is a message that demands to be acknowledged and remembered.

What defines a cult figure—what elevates her beyond mere camp—is the enduring devotion she inspires in her audience and how that audience performs its own active role in sustaining the legend. A cult object is never static. She draws her strength through interconnectivity—uniting genres and transcending time. For a figure to attain cult status, she must create a truth that is at once recognizable yet impossible to pin down. She must remind us that for all our efforts at control, the world will not hold, nothing is easily categorized or made safe. She must be knowing in her refusal to claim knowledge. Rarely do popular, successful performers form cult followings. Cult status is conferred through tragedy and failure, attempts by a vulnerable individual to challenge the status quo of a monolithic, tranquilized society.

To that end, Vampira speaks as loudly to our own fear-obsessed society as she did to the containment culture of midcentury America. We live in a world where horror is no longer relegated to Saturdays at midnight or the local drive-in. Man's inhumanity to man comes into our living rooms on a 24-hour news cycle, or is tweeted in real time, but now instead of campy or cult hosts and hostesses, the breaks are filled with commercials for Prozac and sleep aids. In a world defined increasingly by noise and numbness, I'm happy that this book has made its way to publication. It stands as one devotee's method of passionate engagement and reminds us of the enduring importance of camp figures like Nurmi and other strong women who dare to challenge mainstream ideas of security and the status quo. We can only celebrate those brave enough to hold the circus mirror up to America's false constructs of self-control.

Introduction
SCREAM!

> *"Whiplash girl-child in the dark"*
> **—The Velvet Underground, "Venus in Furs"**

She walked screaming out of the white smoke, a black-clad goddess of death, exuding aggressive sex. Her eyes held just a tinge of threat. Her nails, phallic daggers of implied violence. Waist shrunken to a ghastly circumference, her eyebrows archly painted, her long black hair swirling behind and around her, she shocked, titillated, angered, obsessed.

She called herself Vampira.

She introduced every show with a scream, a bloodcurdling extrusion that had to issue out of some cavern too big, dark, and lonely to live inside her impossible 36-17-36 figure. She screamed and looked directly at the camera, a goth Garbo who seized the eye of the audience, refusing to become a simple object of their regard. She seduced them with the offer of a night of B-movies, horror and sci-fi fare, mostly execrable, but seasoned with her spicy sweetness and her undertone of aggression that radiated underneath heavy white pancake makeup.

Nobody could turn off the TV. It was 1954.

Maila Nurmi screamed in a postwar America of chilling optimism, everyday repressions, and awkward silences. She was the child of Finnish immigrants, a runaway in the 30s who worked as an actor, a model for soft-core men's magazines, and a burlesque dancer. She had a taste for the macabre that led her to delve into the sediment of midcentury America until it yielded its dark treasures. A pin-up model who found herself turned into the 50s American middle-class housewife, she refashioned herself to escape the confines of cultural expectation.

Nurmi had explored the tangled underside of the country since the mid-1940s, an underground gothic land lived beneath the sunlit world of postwar America. As a young runaway, she performed in a New York horror/burlesque show known as *Spook Scandals* that had called for her to rise out of a coffin and scream. There she had begun to craft the character of Vampira, thinking about how the sexy and the horrific could intertwine, a dance between Eros and Thanatos.

By 1946, Nurmi stood on the verge of wider fame after being cast in a Howard Hawks production called *Dreadful Hollow* with a screenplay written by William Faulkner. This would have been Faulkner's first and only foray into the world of gothic horror; indeed, it would have become Faulkner's "vampire movie." The production collapsed in development, though it also became Nurmi's ride to L.A., a way to reach Hollywood and breathe the tinseled air full of fantasy and promise.

Walking through the glitzy caverns of mostly broken dreams, Nurmi discovered limited success in what the era called "modeling magazines." She appeared as a centerfold in *Glamorous Models*, blonde and voluptuous but with a hint of mystery. Even while crafting her "blonde bombshell" character, she made sure the shadowy aspect of her persona grew. In her modeling career, she experimented with an outrageous variety of looks that borrowed in equal parts from Lauren Bacall, pulp science fiction, B-movie horror, and the American tradition of burlesque.

Marriage to screenwriter Dean Riesner (who later scripted *Play Misty for Me* and *Dirty Harry*) provided her with some financial security. Marriage also transformed her into a housewife who worked part-time as a hatcheck girl. She was determined to find ways to break out of the bonds of domestic containment. In this period, she later claimed, she dreamed of becoming a traveling evangelist in the mold of the 30s religion and glamour diva Aimee Semple McPherson.

Nurmi hoped to unite the weirdness of America's religious underground with the increasingly marginalized carnival world of the sideshow. She planned to tour with a tent, call herself Sister Saint Francis, proclaim world peace, perhaps put on display some "psychic abilities," and make boatloads of cash. Unfortunately, such an endeavor required capital she didn't have. She had no idea what steps to take that would allow her to launch such an ambitious plan.

So she waited, stuck with Riesner in their common-law marriage that still managed to replicate the revival of domestic values so important to postwar America. She modeled for photographers, checked coats and hats, and waited.

Her break, she thought, came at a Halloween party in 1953. Dance choreographer Lester Horton (famous for his work in the Tarzan films of the 30s) invited her to his annual Halloween ball. For the occasion, Nurmi created an early version of Vampira, a prototype creature with long black hair and a black cocktail dress, a kind of bride of Dracula that owed something to Carroll Borland's fey vampire child in *Mark of the Vampire* and a bit to Gloria Holden's Sapphic seducer in *Dracula's Daughter.*

Horton's party, the Bal Caribe, was the hottest event of the year for avant-garde Hollywood. Horton, long part of golden age Hollywood's "gay mafia," created a spectacle of camp, drag, and dance. But even amid the subversive glitter, Maila stood out. She won the grand prize for best costume, and Hunt Stromberg Jr., a producer for Los Angeles's KABC-TV, had the idea that he could use the character in connection with a late-night horror show he hoped to create. Stromberg wanted to show horror and sci-fi films, B-pictures mostly, to late-night audiences. The pictures he could show without risking copyright infringement were mostly dreadfully shot and acted. He knew he needed a gimmick, a host to leaven the celluloid lump with humor, maybe a little sex and something indefinable that would give his wretched list of flicks some sizzle.

Dig Me Later, Vampira was like nothing that had yet appeared in television's brief existence. Premiering on April 30, 1954, it became an instant hit in the Los Angeles area. Then things exploded.

Vampira quickly reached a larger audience through a *Life* magazine photo shoot. She appeared on Red Skelton's popular show alongside Lon Chaney Jr. and Bela Lugosi. She hung out with James Dean and his entourage at Googie's restaurant, one of the few late-night spots in 1950s Hollywood. She became part of "the night watch," aspiring actors and directors that hovered around Dean, the strange and beautiful boy from Indiana who had yet to reach super-stardom in *East of Eden*.

Ratings for the *Vampira* show shot through the roof in the year to come and Nurmi seemed on the verge of major stardom. But KABC canceled her contract around the time of the death of James Dean. Despite her popularity, Vampira had spun a web of controversy that entangled her and the station: FCC warnings, a lawsuit by a starlet who thought her career had been ruined by the image of Vampira, and, finally, the end of Nurmi's marriage to Riesner, a blow to the station's public relations campaign that had attempted to portray her as a normal housewife who liked to play dress-up as a bit of "horrific whimsy." Dean's death, or at least the bizarre rumors that surrounded Nurmi in the aftermath of it, represented the final straw.

By the late 1950s, her television career was over; she lived with her mother while receiving unemployment benefits. She appeared in the Ed Wood–directed *Plan 9 from Outer Space* that, while later a cult hit, barely had any audience at all in the first years of its existence. True and lasting stardom never came calling again. By the 1960s, Nurmi supported herself as a tile contractor. Stories, patently untrue, circulated of roles in pornographic films. She became a figure of local legend in West Hollywood, part of a cast of peculiar characters who'd once been famous and now were not.

Vampira disappeared. But she thrived in the cultural underground. Maila Nurmi hung out with the punk/metal band the Misfits in the 80s at places like West Hollywood Vinyl Fetish. She also worked on a book she never finished, a memoir of the underside of a 50s Hollywood that stayed up late nights at Googie's restaurant, popped pills, and lived off the warm glow of stardom it stalked.

She died, alone, in 2008.

Perhaps this is all that we need know of her story. Perhaps it's more or less all that can be known. It's true that her influence has spread far and wide. There may not be a horror convention where her visage doesn't influence the tattooed seductress cos-players, not a horror host who doesn't owe something to her camp humor, no mistress of the night anywhere whose ultimate origin point can't be traced to this runaway, this late-night comedian.

Vampira borrowed from many of the ghosts that haunted American culture, elements never before brought together with the kind of sexual energy and threatening cultural pose that Vampira adopted. She described her character as a monster crafted out of the elements of American history, the terrors of the Great Depression, and the postwar style of the Beats. She raises questions about everything we think we know about the American 50s.

*****

Vampira rose out of the grave just as advertisements for various new styles of home appliances appeared in magazines such as *Good Housekeeping, House Beautiful,* and *Ladies' Home Journal.* The refrigerators and ovens the ads extolled came in pastel colors of pink, green, and blue and stood like quiet monuments on the showroom floor.

These ads created a fantasy space in which American women walked among the appliances as in a dream, maenads and hearth-goddesses that corrected, pleasured, and purified the home and its inhabitants. Ad copy promised women that not only would these lovely machines make "their lives brighter" but they would also make "their chores lighter." The bright colors would not just beautify, they would "glorify" their kitchen. Henry Adams's dichotomy of the Virgin and the Dynamo had reached its logical conclusion. The Virgin would live among the Dynamos, would transform their harsh, metallic groans into sweet cries of release. The woman in the home would tame these technological wombs so that they would pour forth clean laundry, sparkling dishes, and sumptuous meals for breadwinning men home from the office.

These candy-colored Dynamos, meanwhile, allowed the apron-wearing "Virgin" to open herself to an asexual fertility. Sex and reproduction itself had all the attributes of a kind of domestic industrial process since to women, according to a *Coronet* article in 1957, "sex is just one incident in a whole series of events—pregnancy, childbirth, lactation, and childcare." The assembly line of the fertile home did not slow down even for clitoral orgasm. But that really didn't matter, according to the article's male author, since women's responses to sex are "spread out over her whole body" and "more diffuse." The shadow of "sex problems" could not, should not, stop this productive generation of moms and dads, patriotic postwar midsections grinding away to the rhythm of washing machines.

The American dream became dreamscape, housewives floating ethereally above all that sex and all those babies and all that commerce. In most of the period's appliance ads, the American women who inspect these ovens and refrigerators are dressed in styles that suggest that this is no literal showroom floor but rather a mystical plane of consumerism where all levels of society mix freely. Women in pillbox hats and dresses of the newest Dior cut mingle with their proletarian sisters in plain smocks and hats that evoke the church picnic instead of the cocktail party. Here among the beautiful machines, America the consumer society is America the classless society. A democracy among those of varying social status made possible not by communist revolution, but by Frigidaire.

How did Vampira emerge in a world such as this? She seems to belong to the realm of David Bowie and Lou Reed, not the one that included Ozzie Nelson and Bobby Vee. How did she get here, and what did she mean? What did the culture have at stake in her? Why did it need to love her and then punish her for the feelings she so skillfully aroused? Why did American popular culture embrace her many imitators while leaving her to, literally, die alone? Why couldn't we always love Vampira as it seemed we did, for a moment, back in 1954?

In the last decade, historians have reconstructed the American 50s in much the same way that historiography has had its wanton way with every decade. The narrative for the postwar era, like most historical narratives, has lost its solidity. Books with titles like *The Other Fifties* and *Lost Revolutions* have rediscovered forgotten voices and experiences and are reclaiming the decade for social and cultural radicalism. It wasn't all about housewives and suburbia; maybe Vampira does belong to that 50s since it was the world of the Beats, new experimental jazz forms, the emerging civil rights movement, and the explosion of rock and roll.

Would the housewife agree? Can they speak to us at all? Are they simply symbols or actual human beings caught up in an incredibly viral cultural fantasy? They are re-represented in literally thousands of images in popular magazines, advertising bodied forth in a consumerist narrative of true Americanism instantly recognizable to the postwar generation. These are women delighted to find mechanical constructs that provide aesthetic pleasure, simplify

The middle class American housewife became an object of fascination, even obsession in the 1950s. Vampira sought to create a countermyth with her gothic revolution.

household labor, and even connect them to a larger network of appliance fetishists. This is an America of unparalleled economic prosperity, backyard barbeques, and loving Lucy (across the bedroom, in her separate, single bed).

We know such images by rote. And though historians really have sought to reframe the narrative, the standard representation of the 1950s, then and now, locates the white middle-class housewife at the center of its story. We know her by the ads that sought to appeal to her, by the way she was described, and now by the way she appears in *Mad Men*. We know what was expected of her. We think we know that there is terror at least behind her placid smile. We've seen her affectionately mocked. Betty Friedan explored her frustration that came without a name in the 1963 bestseller *The Feminine Mystique*. In the 1998 flick *Pleasantville*, she was made fun of yet again.

An endless source of irony, satire, political propaganda, and cultural meaning, this American housewife. She fascinated even Nikita Khrushchev. In 1959, during Vice President Richard Nixon's historic visit to the Soviet Union, he and the head of the Communist Party held an impromptu ideological debate at the opening of the American National Exhibition in Moscow. The debate centered on the merits of American appliances versus their Soviet counterparts. Ironically, the humorous though heated discussion shifted to a discussion of wives, households, and work.

Nixon asserted the superiority of the American system, its foundation in the middle-class home where labor-saving devices worked in tandem with the housewife as human automaton. Nixon supplied a definition of American democracy that sounds crafted by Sears, Roebuck. It's a society with "many different manufacturers and many different kinds of washing machines so that the housewives have a choice." Nixon's Cold War came down to an attitude toward consumer choice, a long twilight struggle whose true meaning could be found on the industrious wife's shopping list.

Khrushchev ignored Nixon's peculiar definition of democracy and instead took note of what he called the vice president's "capitalist attitude toward women." The future center of America's political scandal seems not to have understood the premier's point. Nixon literally waved Khrushchev's objections away and asserted that the men on both sides of the Cold War "want to make easier the life of our housewives." Surely a détente could be reached over masculine privilege?

Nixon's comments emerged out of a carefully ordered postwar construction of America, a velvet consensus that held the popular imagination like iron. Like most cultural constructions, it depended on the cooperation of the influencing machine of American media. It relied on History with a capital *H*, the willingness of the historical profession and its heavy cloth-bound textbooks to shape a narrative in which women had been at home in 1939, left to become Rosie the Riveter in 1941, and then happily returned, disappearing into domesticity, when the boys came home from war.

But this is not the whole story. Despite the significant amount of propaganda that suggested otherwise, women did not simply leave their jobs in the munitions plants and become 50s housewives composing shopping lists and mooning over new appliances. Historians of Cold War culture Peter Kuznick and James Gilbert argue that women remained in, and continued to enter, the workforce "despite the weight of advice, opinion, and propaganda that sought to prevent it." Women worked in the postwar textile mills of the southern Piedmont as they had done since the 1880s. African American women continued to work in large numbers, in positions ranging from domestic workers to public school teachers.

But the real lives of women mattered very little to the imagery of domesticity that carried so much cultural heft during the first phase of the Cold War. Indeed, the geopolitical struggle between the United States and the Soviet Union generated many of the images we connect with 1950s home life. Berlin walls and iron curtains were far from the only barriers being constructed in this period. An America both fearful and defiant, seeking to face down its recent ally, built what it thought were strong and permanent boundaries around its national identity.

What if panic over the very real possibility of atomic holocaust seized America? What if the American people could not live with what foreign policy experts called "nightmare scenarios" as the basis for American diplomacy? What if they refused to support the new war against communism?

Leaders in business, religion, media, and advertising sought to prevent panic by building boundaries around American women, children, and men, often sinking the foundations of walled enclosures right in the middle of their most intimate experiences. This effort sought to contain the possible horror of the postwar era, indeed to contain the lives of its own citizens in sealed bubbles of domestic pleasure. And more than a few Americans tried to live within this enclosure, assuming that containment meant safety, security, and happiness. Author Sydney Greenbie's book *Leisure for Living* suggested that the home could potentially become "a clubhouse for the family unit." In the postwar years, books appeared with titles like *The Family Fun Book* and *Planning Your Home for Play.*

Contained in their homes, middle-class Americans lived under a lethal aegis. The Truman administration first used the term "containment" to describe an attempted geopolitics, a vision of what the role of the United States in global history could and should be in the postwar era. Containment expressed itself in diplomacy, espionage, and military intervention. But it also should be understood as a titanic effort to control the meaning of the big story that every American was being asked to believe. Historian Alan Nadel has suggested that the immediate postwar period can be understood as an effort to construct a "national narrative" of struggle against the Soviets as a noble and ultimately victorious enterprise. According to Nadel, this narrative allowed policy makers and architects of public culture "to control the fear and responsibility endemic to possessing atomic power."

Fear of the threatening Soviet Other transmogrified into a fear of internal dissent. Increasingly, the culture of containment became a culture of surveillance (an early version of the digital mining of our private lives we experience today). J. Edgar Hoover's FBI shifted from fighting organized crime to fighting an alleged "underground maze" of communist activity in America. Hoover's book *Masters of Deceit* warned anxious Americans to keep an eye on their neighbors and to take a special interest in labor union members and women who displayed an excessive interest in issues of education. In the mid-1940s, Hoover wrote an article titled "Mothers . . . Our Only Hope" that suggested maternal neglect as a cause for both "crime" and "perversion."

Hoover's invocation of "perversion" illustrates how the emerging national security state became as interested in ferreting out sexual minorities as in finding communist infiltrators. Gay men became a particular target. This active persecution of the gay community grew not only from the belief that homosexuality made government agents easy prey for Soviet blackmail, but also because of the idea that a combination of heteronormative marriage and masculinity helped to shape strong Cold Warriors.

The so-called Lavender Scare of the early 50s consumed at least as much national energy, and perhaps reflected more anxiety, than the fear of commies. Historian Elaine Tyler May has described the period after 1945 as bringing "a wave of officially sponsored homophobia." A 1950 Senate report entitled "Employment of Homosexuals and Other Sex Perverts in Government" argued that "perversion . . . weakens the moral fiber" of the American government. In fact, the report asserted that "one homosexual" could corrupt an entire government agency. Gay men, generally referred to simply as "perverts," represented an archetypal anti-Americanism for the official American consensus.

Terror of alternative sexuality obsessed not only the Pentagon. Local municipalities gave the matter anxious attention, as surveillance and control of sexual minorities became part of the work of urban police forces. The Stonewall Rebellion in 1969 constituted, in part, a response to nearly two decades of regular and brutal harassment from special squads of "vice police" who raided bars and drag clubs and beat up, arrested, and jailed gay men. In Vampira's Los Angeles, politically active gay men such as Dale Jennings faced constant police harassment. The LAPD arrested Jennings, a leader in the early gay rights organization known as the Mattachine Society, in 1952 on trumped-up solicitation charges. His arrest and trial for "lewd and dissolute behavior" became part of a public discussion of homosexuality. Local governments replicated the attack on him and the Mattachine Society throughout the country, wherever efforts at creating the so-called homophile movement appeared.

Efforts to define and control deviant behavior also filtered out through the culture in less official ways. The term "sissy," though dating to the 19th century, came into common usage during the 1950s through the popularity of childcare manuals. Most of these guides encouraged readers to chisel young boys into strapping American men by teaching them to control their emotions and play sports. Meanwhile, media pundits and official police pronouncements urged women to stay close to the home and suggested that "sex perverts" hunted them relentlessly on America's new interstate highway system. And it was not only women who had to worry. In 1951, a popular exploitation paperback called *Terror in the Streets* told the story of "homosexual prowlers" that the author called "sex deviated versions of what is known as the wolf." Not only were gay men perverts—they were ravening beasts, stalking the innocent.

Lesbian and bisexual women remained mostly hidden from view, even in the rhetoric of sexual containment. Male journalists, novelists, and psychiatrists associated these women with crime and decadence. Historian Donna Penn writes that "medical, psychiatric, and legal authorities" usually assumed a cultural connection between lesbians and prostitutes. In this bizarre equation, women could not deviate their sexual desires so much that they could yearn for other women. Instead, they simply found themselves forced into secretive relationships with their fellow prostitutes, relationships born out of trauma instead of desire. Gay men might be "perverts" who chose a "lifestyle," but lesbians were simply confused and desperate for affection.

In the 1950s, the hidden lesbian only appeared in fictions of trauma, narratives in which women are forced into bed with other women and, seemingly with nothing better to do, give one another attenuated and ultimately unsatisfying pleasures. Pulp novels aimed at a male audience such as Ann Aldrich's *We Walk Alone: Through Lesbos' Lonely Groves* (1955) and Tereska Torres's *Women's Barracks* (1950) sought to confirm this fantasy. In the 1960s, the "women's prison film" genre took up these themes, displaying male fantasies of women in institutional bondage, trapped without men, and forced to turn to one another in their anxiety.

These stories are tales of the missing penis, exciting to men because they suggest that women are left in sweaty, erotic, but ultimately unsatisfying embraces without male genitalia. The genre did not celebrate or investigate or even wonder very much about the nature of female desire. It did not even make female desire the center of erotic titillation. Instead, these books and films highlighted male sexual prowess by suggesting that women are stranded, imprisoned, and enclosed without it. Grindhouse flicks and pulp novels about women locked away in prison, the girls' school, and the convent offered the secret pleasure of knowing that their unfortunate attempts at intercourse left them unfulfilled, hidden behind walls and bars, desperately in need of a man even as they are forced to settle for sapphic pleasure.

The experience of gay and lesbian people in this period reveals the 50s as a world of secret violence, a world where horrible things came out to play after the suburban streets fell silent and the shades came down. On TV, Ralph constantly threatened to punch Alice so hard that she'd be "off to the moon." Ads for coffee showed women bent over their husband's knee and being spanked for buying the wrong brand. But the threat of violence was joked about so frequently because it was very real, one of the dirty little secrets of American suburbia. High rates of institutionalization of women (and the frequent prescription of tranquilizers) locked independent women away and introduced them to the terrors of hydro-treatment and shock therapy.

African American women, facing the double bind of gender and race oppression, may have borne the brunt of male violence during this period. Danielle L. McGuire's extraordinary book *At the Dark End of the Street* lifts the veil on how racial and sexual violence intertwined in the period leading up to the civil rights movement and indeed throughout American history. McGuire's research has uncovered numerous stories of African American women in the 40s and 50s abducted, raped, and frequently murdered by white men who had little fear of getting caught or of a conviction were they to be.

Extraordinary violence came from a desire to exercise extraordinary control. But violence represented only one weapon in the era's arsenal of oversight and supervision. Perhaps more important became the notion of the expert, the authoritative advice giver, the voice of restraint, order, and happiness. Although scientific mandarins supported by a new and powerful national security state had helped create an apocalyptic weapon, public culture still affirmed the need to trust them. *Look* magazine, when urging its readers not to worry about the possibility of radioactive fallout, assured them that "the experts will tell you" when the time for anxiety arrives. Science fiction films, the era's most popular genre other than westerns, usually promised safety from alien invasions through an alliance of science and the military.

Even in more intimate areas of life, the expert held sway. Americans purchased marriage guides and child-rearing advice books by the tens of thousands. Expertise even came to dominate public religious life. Both Billy Graham and Bishop Fulton Sheen made their appearance in this decade. Sheen's broadcasts emphasized his authority by placing him in his most elaborate bishop's attire and giving him a chalkboard to scribble on as if the nation had become his parochial school classroom.

Truth remained on the side of respectability. White men with training, academic credentials, wealth, and position inherited from their mentors and supporters prescribed and proscribed the truth. In the sciences, in historical study, in politics, in theology, and in philosophy, the truth was most likely to be bound in a volume that had been written in the quiet, book-lined study of someone who held a significant position in American society. These guidelines explained how American capitalism worked, how religious faith interacted with civic life, how medicine proscribed the body and its yearnings, how gender roles must be performed, and how all the unappealing and unwanted devices and desires of human existence could be controlled.

New technology helped to extend the sway of the experts over American public opinion. Radio, television, and the boom in American publishing facilitated the rise of the experts, speaking on behalf of their fundamental racial, gendered, and class interests in such a way that they appeared to speak for the entire nation. Through these media, the male expert became the defender of American democracy, the ultimate Cold Warrior. Even the medical profession had something to say on behalf of an ordered, stable society. In 1950, Elmer L. Henderson, newly elected president of the American Medical Association, used his inaugural speech to lend his profession's considerable authority to the postwar

Red Scare. Major radio networks carried the speech in which Henderson asserted that "our affairs are no longer medical affairs" and argued that doctors must join the vanguard of those fighting to prevent America from becoming "a socialist state under the yoke of government bureaucracy."

The expert could even take religious faith, always in danger of accelerating into a roaring blaze of eschatological and apocalyptic flames, and safely relegate it to the domestic hearth and the boardroom. Popular books and television assured this outcome. Will Herberg, author in 1955 of the highly influential book *Protestant, Catholic, Jew*, made use of the "melting pot" metaphor to argue that, despite religious differences, unity could be found by assenting to the values of "the American Way of Life." Norman Vincent Peale suggested that religious faith was little more than belief in one's ability to achieve success in American society in his 1954 book *The Power of Positive Thinking*. Sheen's broadcast Catholicism downplayed sectarian belief in favor of offering middle-class Americans placid, and rather flaccid, guidelines for happiness in business and family life.

Television, as the example of Sheen shows, helped reinforce these dominant ideals. Indeed, in the enclosed space of the home, the television became the true influencing machine of the decade. By 1955, almost two-thirds of all American households owned a television set. Aggressive marketing campaigns in the late 1940s, as well as easy credit plans, put the tube in most American homes.

The television terraformed a new geography of family life, placed in a position of prestige within the family home. Popular magazines described TV as "the family pet" or part of "the family circle." *House Beautiful*, in a 1955 article, simply called it "a member of the family." Indeed, one General Electric ad in 1955 suggested that one TV was not enough by picturing mother and child sequestered in the kitchen in front of a small screen while father with his pipe enjoys the console model in the living room.

After an initial burst of creativity, the material presented on television became another ally of American social elites in their war on dissident weirdness. Early television included some incredibly innovative experiments in entertainment, from Red Skelton to Ernie Kovacs. However, TV quickly became sanitized with only the occasional and minor moment of subversion. As early as 1951, Richard Cushing, the archbishop of Boston, released a major statement about what he called "the perverted sense of humor" found in many television variety shows. In the same year, the National Association of Radio and Television Broadcasters published their own "Code of Ethics" meant to guide content for the American public.

Even *I Love Lucy*, sometimes held up as an example of low-intensity subversion because it placed a woman at the center of its narrative and an interracial couple in Manhattan instead of the suburbs, generally reinforced concepts of domesticity. Feminist cultural critic Andi Zeisler has noted that what makes the main character so "cringeworthy" is that she will have to answer to Ricky for even the smallest acts of independence and rebellion. For every independent action she will have "some 'splainin to do." Moreover, as the series hobbled to a close with increasingly poor ratings, Ricky and Lucy finally made the move to the suburbs that much of middle-class America had made by the 1960s.

*****

Vampira screamed. She screamed instead of cleaning the house, washing the dishes, or falling in love with appliances. She screamed rebellion, a challenge to the high walls of containment and a symbolic middle finger raised toward the popular representation of the housewife. Nurmi later explained the kind of cultural sap mining she hoped Vampira would carry out. "There was so much repression," Nurmi later remembered, "and people needed to identify with something explosive, something outlandish and truthful."

Maila Nurmi's Vampira was a ghoulish incarnation of a wave of rebellion. The idea that something could be both outlandish and truthful, that it had to be outlandish in order to be truthful, represented an idea just coming out of the American closet in the mid-50s. The Beats, and their white hipster followers, thought they had found this outlandish truth out on the road with Kerouac. William S. Burroughs became the junkie wizard of the genre. His bizarre behavior and mystical flights fueled by mountains of white powder seemed to promise that the doors of perception had swung open at last, indeed that they had blown off the hinges and left a gaping hole in human consciousness.

Burroughs's *Naked Lunch,* most importantly, served notice that the truth was perhaps not Lady Philosophy on a Doric column, but rather a drag queen junkie, wandering streets, alone and forgotten and horny. The "naked lunch," Burroughs explained with a metaphor guaranteed to ruin a *Good Housekeeping*–fueled family dinner, "is that frozen moment when everyone realizes what is on the end of every fork." Burroughs's exploration of American history, his excavation of the junk culture of the bohemian flophouses, and his wanderings into the alternative worlds of the Interzone constitute a series of surgical strikes on the postwar consensus. "America is not a young land," he wrote in *Naked Lunch*, "it is old and dirty and evil before the settlers, before the Indians. The evil is there waiting."

If the Beats had caught sight of something burning bright and deadly in the American night, so too had a new generation of postwar jazz musicians, represented and embodied in Charlie Parker. During the 30s and 40s, jazz had been America's pop music, especially in its whitened variation of swing. Louis Armstrong, Duke Ellington, Benny Goodman, and Artie Shaw had created an unstoppable rhythm, one that even they sometimes found fearful in its implications and direction.

Young musicians in the late 40s and 50s needed something more, hearing a beat that forced them to yield up their new, complex arrangements. Simple chord structures became a platform for all manner of experiment. Jazz became less the performance of a composition and much more the high-wire act of improvisation it had always been at its heart. New York City, especially Minton's on 118th Street in Harlem, became a hive for a new group of musicians who collectively created what critics called bebop, or simply bop.

Charlie Parker, Dizzy Gillespie, and Thelonious Monk created an anxious sound, a music that implied stress and tension as much as release and liberation. Joachim-Ernst Berendt famously referred to this new style, which was both spare and complex, as "a musical shorthand" that builds "ordered relationships from a few hasty signs." Like Vampira's scream, its nervous beat seemed to some like messages scrawled quickly on a wall, an erotic ache of a sound not quite able to find release. Bop became a message in a bottle, music that both caught the pace of modern life and syncopated its dark undertow and increasingly wanton desires.

These musical and literary subversions appealed to the young and the bohemian. They also reached a relatively small audience. Charlie Parker was dead by 1955 and bebop rose to prominence among a relatively small cult of admirers as jazz ceased to be America's popular music. *Naked Lunch* was available in the United States only after 1962 and only after a significant court battle in Massachusetts. "Beatnik" came to be a term of derision in the anxious middle class and a number of grindhouse films associated the term not only with drug use, but also with violence and mayhem and bad poetry.

Minor rebellions, sounds that created dissonance, yearnings that ended up in court, whispers in the dark. Meanwhile, all of the collective forces of medicine, law, politics, and religion assembled for the purpose of maintaining gender and sexual boundaries in American society. And yet, unexpectedly, these boundaries slowly became more elastic, refracted, easily held up to scorn in the years between the dropping of the bomb on Hiroshima and the 1960s.

Perhaps the greatest historic shift of the 20-odd years after the defeat of the Axis powers was the ability, the very real cultural ability, to laugh at these boundaries, to mix them up and let them bleed into each other. In short, to camp it the hell up.

Camp, a highly sophisticated public form of irony, can find expression in all kinds of aesthetic choices ranging from clothing styles to gender performance. Drag queens are camp, so was the 1960s *Batman* TV show. Susan Sontag began a debate now decades long about the meaning of camp when she defined it as an artifice highly favored in the gay community. In response, scholars have challenged the idea of camp as apolitical, suggesting that it creates a situation in which "certain groups and interests might be challenged, resisted, and modified." It can be political because it can become a place of satire, where media can be turned back on itself and made to mean something different from its original intention. The voice of the expert and the forces of order can be mocked. We can put them in drag.

Film star Mae West often used camp conventions dating back to the 1920s. West, who has been described as a "female female impersonator," had fallen to the cultural margins in the 1950s but made her comeback on the great tidal wave of camp that followed. When asked to define the meaning of camp in the early 70s, West responded, "It's when people try to act like me."

But maybe West took too much credit. Indeed, Nurmi herself created the dark side of camp. In creating Vampira, she managed something very difficult for 1954, and in a sense her success at it helps explain her larger failure. Her persona was, like West's, that of a "female female impersonator" that reimagined sex in relation to the American tradition of horror. From her plunging neckline to her scream of dark orgasm, she created a new way to be weird not fully realized until decades later.

The style Nurmi created, the style that America found deeply intriguing and ultimately repulsive, could best be described as gothic camp. It borrowed heavily from horror movies while blending that terror with the possibility of erotic excess, even sexual madness, which had long been part of the gothic tradition in literature. Mixing and matching these styles in ways that had never been attempted, Vampira dripped sexual power and aggression, completely subverting the image of the 50s housewife and turning her into a rebellious monster.

Vampira's scream is the best example. The scream of women in horror, from *King Kong*'s Fay Wray forward, had been the sound of abject terror. Vampira made her scream an effusion of pleasure and threat, a sound that at once obscured and revealed a world of secret desires. She was the first velvet underground, the whiplash girl-child who bid us to come into the dark. A graveyard woman, she was also a junkyard angel who built herself from the raggedy bits and bangles she found in the flea market of American history. The monster she made showed us that screams of terror and screams of orgasm could make the same sound.

Vampira belongs in the iconography of American 50s, beside Elvis, beside backyard barbeques, beside James Dean, beside the suburbs. Her image should complicate, or maybe simply smash, the imagery of the American housewife happy and satisfied with her appliances. Maila Nurmi was, like many women in the era, the runaway housewife, the woman who attempted to create something organic in an era that celebrated a stylized, plastic-and-steel consumerist futurism. She was a fetishist extraordinaire that hinted at the thriving world of leather, whip, and orgasm boiling just under the surface of the placid 50s housewife fantasies of order. All the naughty bits from Freud and Masters and Johnson in a fright wig, the terror of the 50s made incarnate as transgender desire.

Maila Nurmi gave America back its monsters. She did it at a time when the culture assured itself that the monsters were either not real or easily defeated. Her creation of gothic camp provides us access to a much larger world of shifting American sensibilities, embodied in everything from the artwork of Alberto Vargas, to the glam camp turn in rock music, to the emergence of the goth style in the 1980s. Her scream shook America's windows and rattled its walls, notifying the elites and the experts that the times were indeed a-changin'. The American housewife that Maila Nurmi had been became a startlingly seductive monster, a powerful creature of the night. American culture tried to contain her. Now it was payback time.

The sources for her story, and the kind of story she has to tell, do not allow for a traditional biography. Her fame flamed out quickly. She spent decades in the underground of American entertainment. She seldom spoke about her childhood and gave out very little information about her parents. When a moment of fame brought her enormous attention, she lied a great deal about her background. She lived as a virtual recluse, and the few times we hear from her in her last years, she worked hard to creatively reconstruct the meaning of her past. Mostly, no one paid attention to her until she was dead.

I haven't written a biography of Maila Nurmi. Her story emerges only in fits and starts, facts filtered through genealogical history, short newspaper accounts, occasional notices, the sometimes conflicting memories of fans, interviews close to the time of her death that usually focused on her relationship to James Dean or Ed Wood and not on her life. Other than one self-published fan tribute, no book about her exists.

It is as difficult to write a biography of Vampira, Maila's Frankenstein. Today she's a religion without a holy scripture. No original footage of her television show exists other than a short promotional kinescope. Archival footage unearthed by filmmaker R. H. Greene in 2011 has provided the only images we have of Vampira performing in front of a live audience, and these images are as brief as twilight shadows. It's a measure of her significance that, with such a slender portfolio, her image lives on in folk art,

Internet forums, Facebook pages, Tumblr tributes, horror conventions, and the imaginations of fans who have constructed a vernacular cult of Vampira as a dark goddess of horror, a patron saint for the children of the night.

Readers who go looking for Maila and her chiaroscuro creation in these pages will sometimes be disappointed that they don't learn more. I suspect that, at its best, it will be like attending a raucous party where everyone jabbers about a mysterious guest of honor. Revelers regale you with stories about her. Some, with very serious (if a bit tipsy) voices, try to explain her significance. Some are even dressed like her. She is just a face glimpsed through the press of people, a beautiful specter that disappears as someone drunkenly buttonholes you to tell you "just one more thing" about this mysterious woman whose image, once seen, will not leave your dreams.

If not a traditional biography, then this is the story of the world that made her and the world she made. It is a history of cultural representation. I make no claim to providing an interpretation of "the 50s," as if a single book could encompass a decade, and as if a decade has some essential identity with clear parameters that could be encompassed.

Nor is this meant primarily as what some avant-garde scholars like to call a "secret history." This term, used frequently by cultural historians, suggests that a given period or topic has an underground story, one that can be accessed to show us strange new delights. These hidden narratives may be subversive or staid but they offer a new angle of vision on our dry and desiccated textbook narratives.

I like the idea of the "secret history" very much, and in a certain sense, this exploration of the life and meaning of Vampira offers such a history. She was certainly interested in secret histories, but mostly in regard to keeping them a secret. Unfortunately, scholars who explore these forgotten chronologies usually see themselves as voyeurs of the disconnection, archaeologists that dig up the hidden event that illuminates the whole. Secret histories are detective stories that uncover the clue that solves the cultural crime.

That is not exactly what this book attempts. I believe that secret histories are made, not found. We don't make them out of our imaginations, but neither do we find them finished and complete, Rosetta stones of explanation and code-breaking. The work of cultural history involves listening to the confusing acoustics of the echo chamber and trying to discern something from the chaos.

In this case, the chaos asks: So what do we do with her? What do we have at stake in her story? How do we explain how a costume created for a Hollywood party reconfigured American cultural history? Why didn't we love her as much as she deserved? And a better question: Why didn't we realize how much we needed her?

Part I

BAD GIRL

"Different colors made of tears"
—The Velvet Underground, "Venus in Furs"

"She'd crawl into a coffin to climax a show."

This titillating tagline appeared over a profile of Maila Nurmi in the January 1955 issue of *People in TV.* Describing her as "a TV screen shatterer on platformed shoes" in a "deep V-Necked tattered black gown," the writer called her act a pantomime of "a girl vampire's social life."

But *People in TV* let the image go only so far, allowed her to shatter only certain kinds of screens and break through limited boundaries. While showing images of Maila as both a jet-black bewigged vamp and a blonde cavorting in a bikini, the magazine rushed to reassure its readers that the character of Vampira represented only a bit of "gruesome whimsy."

People in TV wanted readers to know that Los Angeles had not given a platform to a sexual and cultural renegade. The text of the profile explained away the headline about wanting to crawl into a coffin at the end of each show as something she wanted to do but also "her only frustration." Why couldn't she do it? "Because," the profile asserted, "her husband had put his foot down."

People in TV introduced Dean Riesner as "a quiet, serious screenwriter" that she had "been married to for six years." The writer explained why this odd, if loyal, 50s housewife spent so much time with "aspiring actors and actresses, budding playwrights and producers" at Hollywood hotspots like Googie's restaurant: "Her husband often works at home in their tiny apartment, she spends a lot of time with 'the gang' to avoid distracting him." In this way, the magazine sought to explain, and explain away, Maila Nurmi's association with the infamous "night watch," that crew of aspiring actors, failed poets, and West Coast Beats who hung about at one of the only late-night joints in the city.

An industry magazine like *People in TV* had every reason to try to contain the bad girl image Nurmi assiduously cultivated. She borrowed knowingly from images of frighteningly powerful women that had been circulating in American culture since the beginning of the century. She forged these images into a single figure, a sexual and gender outlaw who defiantly asserted herself against the anxious placidity of the times. Vampira became, in Maila Nurmi's own words, "Pola Negri, Marie Antoinette, Marilyn Monroe, Norma Desmond, and Tallulah Bankhead rolled into one."

The image of the "bad girl" had resonated through American culture and moral rhetoric since the late 19th century. It's an image that has served as a register for anxieties over the second industrial revolution, immigration, and the revolutionary growth of cities. In its earliest context, the bad girl appeared most often as the "girl gone bad," a notion that has played a role in the representation of young American women from the 1830s anxiety over the Lowell Mill girls to contemporary moral panics over rainbow parties.

In the cultural myth of the girl gone bad, the draw of work in the city becomes the story of rural innocence falling into corruption.

The "fallen woman" became a recognizable trope in American literature and moral advice. Theodore Dreiser used her as a metonym for the corruptions of the Gilded Age in *Sister Carrie*. Stephen Crane, best known for his Civil War novel *The Red Badge of Courage*, wrote numerous gritty street stories at the turn of the century that featured down-on-their-luck prostitutes, sympathetic and trapped by the system but also emblematic of its corruptions.

Anxiety about these fallen women resulted in the "white slavery" panic of the early 20th century. Tales of the forced prostitution of young white women, almost always occasioned by insidious foreigners, became a cause célèbre during the Progressive era and an obsession of organizations as diverse as the Women's Christian Temperance Union and the Ku Klux Klan. Early films such as *Traffic in Souls* dramatized this allegedly widespread social problem. Released in November of 1913, *Traffic* told a tale of a young woman named "Sister" whose flirtatiousness and disobedience to her father lead, inexorably in the film's logic, to being forced into prostitution.

At the height of the panic, between about 1905 and 1910, American newspapers circulated tales of women who lost their innocence to predators. Slowly the image of the bad girl began to shift. Increasingly, bad girls were presented as anything but "pure" victims. As a sensationalist tract called *The White Slave Hell* put it, "many young females fall victim to their own conduct" including "Sunday walks with merry companions, attending theatres and singing-saloons, keeping late hours, and neglecting home duties." In other words, the woman fallen into the brothel had been a little bit fallen to begin with . . . a bad girl.

Theda Bara and Clara Bow helped shape the concept of the "vamp," the female seducer with no hint of guilt over her crimes. Bara once described the "vamp" or "vampire" as a kind of revenge narrative for women, "the vengeance of my sex on its exploiters." In a 1915 interview for the *Peoria Journal*, Bara described vamps in archetypal terms as "dark women, though some have blood-red hair and green snake-like eyes" who had a "strange, witchlike power over men." Sexually voracious, scheming, and now very powerful, the bad girl appeared everywhere in American culture by the 1920s.

Bad girls were not fallen anymore. They were just hardwired with wickedness and men happily risked their own destruction to dally with them. Film historian Janet Staiger suggests that the proliferation of the vamp image led to the creation of a "fallen man" genre in American film. In a bit of masculine panic over the power that women had begun to assert in American society, film narratives portrayed women who could destroy a man's livelihood, wreck his fortunes, and even take his life.

The changing experience of women in American society generated these images of anxiety and panic over masculine loss of control. By the 1910s, a growing number of young, white, middle-class women entered the workforce, joining working-class and African American women who had long worked in various industrial and domestic settings. Largely employed as clerks and typists, this new class of female worker moved away from home and family right at the time that the automobile shaped a new sociability of privacy between the sexes.

A new set of attitudes emerged about sexuality, influenced by Freud's sudden popularity in America and an economy that pulled young people further away from home. By World War II, the entrance of women into factory and war work often conjoined a new awareness of sexuality to images of female independence. Nicknames like "victory girls," "good time Charlottes," and "khaki wackies" came into common use to describe a new type of "loose" woman. Kay Hearn, a college student in the 1940s, remembered that "all of a sudden you were just a play girl . . . we'd party as much as we could."

These changes in America's sexual culture produced tremendous anxiety for the men returning home from World War II. The bad girl became a central figure in one of America's most popular film genres. Film noir imagined an immoral temptress, usually hiding behind a nimbus of innocence until time to strike. These bad girls had evil as their native climate, sexuality that represented a weapon and a commodity to be traded. Jane Greer played one such archetypal femme fatale in the 1947 film *Out of the Past*. She's a drop-dead gorgeous deadly combination of consumerist greed and sexual potency who destroys Robert Mitchum, not once, but twice. But, making her different from the vamps of the silent era, she's also the pawn of powerful men rather than a force to be reckoned with on her own.

Film noir femme fatales embodied some of the conflicting images of femininity presented to women in the postwar era. Barbara Stanwyk's hotter-than-hot temptress in *Double Indemnity* (1944) knows how to ruin the life of Fred MacMurray. But, paradoxically, she did so out of a position of helplessness. We meet her first as a flawed housewife, the unhappy homemaker, who sees murder and deceit as the only means of escape. Film noir undercut the bad girl's dynamism. The vamp had channeled an almost supernatural power of seduction and deceit. Noir reduced them to schemers wanting to steal insurance money, ruining the men around them in hopes of getting a piece of the postwar economic pie.

Film noir brooded over the impossible demands made on women who tried to conform to the complex social codes of the postwar period. Historian Alan Nadel describes what he calls the "tortured nature" of female sexuality in 50s containment culture, a sexuality that "had to signify abstinence and promise gratification" all at the same time. The 1950s ideal, unlike earlier Victorian notions, did not expect married women to renounce sexuality, only to contain it firmly within the bounds of patriarchal marriage and consecrate it to the service of breeding children. The noir bad girl ran away from these things, trying to secure her economic independence through crime, a funhouse image of the 50s housewife who found economic security through sex and marriage and motherhood.

By the 1950s, misogyny had robbed the bad girl of much of her mythic power. Rather than an image of a diabolically powerful womanhood, the vamp gave way to the bad girl as degenerate, weakened by lust and avarice. The stories being told about bad girls in the 40s and 50s are allowed to exist in noir as a narrative of sexual danger or in psychiatric and sociological texts as an out-of-control body in need of restraint. They are not the supernatural or nearly mythic forces of social and sexual vengeance that Theda Bara and Clara Bow created. They are inevitably punished for their crimes, often brutally.

Maila Nurmi's screams in the night sought to reawaken the darker energies of dangerous women, intertwining social and sexual power. Her background and biography, a strange and shadowy tale that took her through the underground of midcentury America, introduced her to all the tropes she would need to stockpile an arsenal of transgression and deviance. Even her early years prepared her for a lifetime of being a cultural outlaw. They also taught her the power of reinventing the past, creating new identities that allowed her to experience the world as a less harsh and unforgiving place.

*****

Maila Nurmi, like Vampira, was made, not born. And Vampira was not the only character she created.

Elizabeth Maila Syrjäniemi was born in Gloucester, Massachusetts, in 1922. Nurmi later claimed, in practically every interview she ever gave, to have been born in Petsamo, Finland. She named Petsamo as her hometown to strengthen her claim of being related to a famous Finnish Olympic diver from the same city named Paavo Nurmi. Her origins are actually more pedestrian and more interesting.

Her father, Onni, immigrated to North America from Finland

by 1910. He became one of the tens of thousands of Finnish immigrants that entered the United States in the late 19th century. The country's struggle with Tsarist Russia, its traditional enemy and sometime overlord, had intensified over the previous half century. During this same period, the concentration of small farming units into larger latifundia forced many Finns into the cities. Between 1850 and 1900, the tiny country's urban population grew by 200 percent. Rapid industrial growth could not keep up with the landless poor flooding the cities, and Finns began looking elsewhere for work and opportunity, including the United States.

Onni Syrjaniemi, like many of his compatriots, caught *Amerikan Tauti* (American fever) in the first decades of the 20th century. A floodtide of what many Finns called "the children of the poor" began coming to America in about 1864. The period between 1900 and 1915 represented the peak years of Finnish immigration, and by 1920 about 150,000 expatriate Finns lived in the United States. Over the next decade, legislation limiting the number of immigrants who could come from a single country sent Finns elsewhere, but by then a thriving community of Finns had created enclaves of their culture in New England, the upper Midwest, and the Pacific Northwest.

After she became a cult figure in the 1990s, uncertainties about Maila Nurmi's background helped launch insupportable theories about her childhood. A fan account of Nurmi's life, for example, suggests that the entire Syrjaniemi family came to the United States because of the Winter War with the Soviet Union in 1939.

The rather romantic notion of the family fleeing the ravages of war has no basis in reality. If the Syrjaniemis came to the States as late as 1939, she would have been only a teenager when the first episode of *Dig Me Later, Vampira* premiered in 1954. By her own account, she was at least 31. Moreover, there are simply no records for a Syrjaniemi surname (or related names that appear elsewhere in Ellis Island records such as Syranieni and Syrjanene) entering Ellis

Island in 1939–1940. Finnish immigration had slowed to a trickle by the 30s and had essentially come to a full stop by 1939.

Onni appears to have immigrated to America alone. The records of the Ellis Island Foundation indicate that an "Ina Sryjanieni" arrived from Finland in 1910. Given the tendency of port officials to mangle the spelling of "foreign" names, it's very likely that this is a record of Onni entering America. Listed as coming from Haapajarvi (spelled Hapaejarvi by Ellis Island officials), Finland, Onni moved first to the fishing community of Gloucester, Massachusetts, one of the largest concentrations of his fellow countrymen in New England. His brother Nestor had already moved to the Essex County township. He apparently briefly considered moving back to Finland in 1917 during conscription for the First World War. However, he was not drafted and remained in Massachusetts, perhaps because by 1920 he met and married an American woman named Sophia, six years his junior.

Maila Niermi (Onni had shortened his surname for a time) was born to the couple in 1922. They had one previous child, Robert, born soon after their marriage. They also adopted Onni's nephew and namesake, apparently after Nestor's death. At the time of Maila's birth, Onni had begun work as editor of a small Finnish newspaper out of Fitchburg, Massachusetts, that called itself the *Amerikan Suomalainen*, or the *American Finn.*

Over the next two decades, the family moved across the upper tier of the United States, not settling into farming or mining, as did many of their fellow Finns. Onni belonged to the "Temperance Finn" segment of the Scandinavian community and made part of his living as a peripatetic lecturer, traveling from one town temperance hall to another describing the evils of strong drink.

Her mother, according to an interview Maila Nurmi later gave to the *Finn Times,* worked as a part-time journalist and a translator. This seems to have been an extrapolation by Nurmi from her mother's work with her father in the early years. The 1930 census lists

A very young Maila Nurmi on the Gloucester shore with her brother Robert. Mid-1920s. Courtesy of the Clatsop County Historical Society

Sophia as "a bookkeeper," probably for one of Onni's newspapers. It is very likely, however, that the bilingual Sophia made extra money for the family by doing translation work for neighbors.

Onni's work as an editor occasioned the family's numerous moves. Maila Elizabeth was eight when the family moved to Ashtabula, Ohio, for Onni to edit a Finnish newspaper in Cleveland, one that would fail just two years later. In the heart of the Depression, it was several years before Onni could find newspaper work again, this time in the thriving Finnish community of Astoria, Oregon. At 15, Maila found herself uprooted again.

Nurmi showed later in life a profound lack of interest in describing her childhood or her background in Finnish immigrant communities. The scant reference she made to her youth emphasized a restless, activist family whose travels took them through all the American regions that sheltered large Finnish communities.

Rather than describing the places she had lived and the immigrant culture that surrounded her, most of Maila Nurmi's reminiscences of her childhood focus on her troubled inner state, a profound sense of alienation, and the feeling that she didn't belong in the world. She once laughingly said she "never caught the gist" of being alive and that "things outside the womb" would "never cease to be weird and terrifying." Onni and Sophia seem to have been distant parents, often unable to understand their withdrawn and dreamy daughter. Her need to create new characters through which she could interact with the world, to change her skin, likely came from these early, frightening experiences of the world around her.

The gloomy, the grotesque, and the strangely beautiful blends in one of the few stories she ever told of her early childhood. Playing alone on the rocky sand dunes of Gloucester, she recalled a kindly older fisherman that stopped and talked with her. Frequently feeling ignored by her busy parents, she warmed to the grandfatherly old man and perhaps thought she had found a friend to visit her. That day, he went out to sea and drowned in a sudden storm. Seven decades later, she stilled mused about how she had been "the last person to see him alive. I still remember that fine man."

When Nurmi later spoke at all about the details of her young life, she invariably described it in the harshest of terms. This reflected both her sense of marginalization and the family's often uncertain economic situation. There is certainly evidence that the Syrjaniemi family struggled during the Depression. Onni likely collected only small fees on the lecture circuit, and the demand for his work as a newspaperman fluctuated. When the family moved to Astoria in the 30s, he began work as an editor for the *Lannen Sumetar*, a paper that would remain a Finnish-language biweekly until 1946.

This work made Onni Syrjaniemi a well-known if not especially prosperous member of the community. In 1939, he was selected by Finnish community leaders to represent them at San Francisco's Treasure Island World's Fair for "Finnish Day." The family rented a small apartment on Franklin Avenue. Maila herself complained that she went to school in an "ill-fitting assortment" of "rags" that seemed to suggest she was on "[her] way to the poorhouse."

Although the Syrjaniemi family may have struggled with the economics of the Depression, cultural life in the Finnish community had been far richer than Nurmi remembered, or at least related. What we know of this experience, especially in the early part of the 20th century, suggests that the Finns created worlds for themselves that, while somewhat parochial, featured a high degree of sociability and a more open attitude toward religious faith than often appears in immigrant enclaves. Given the trajectory young Elizabeth's life took, it is especially notable that the immigrant Finns also displayed a passion for political radicalism, for publicly challenging the social and economic ethos of their new homeland. She may have learned to raise a lot of hell during her formative years.

Finnish communities centered on both the rhythms of work and efforts to transfer elements of their traditional social life to their new home in the States. In the New England communities where the Syrjaniemis first lived, many of the Finns worked in the fishing industry or in agriculture, including raising blueberries, as they had in rural Finland. Communities remained tight-knit, leading to the frequent accusation of "clannishness." Nurmi later claimed that the family had lived in a log cabin in Finland. This may have been reconstructed from the memory of the family living in a log house in New England built in a *talkoo*, a gathering of neighbors/picnic/home construction done in a "barn raising" fashion. Though sometimes fairly large, communities always subdivided these homes. This was done less for family privacy and more so that new emigrants would have a place to sleep when they arrived.

Tulkaa meille saunomaan, or "come to our house for a sauna," may have been an invitation a young Nurmi heard a great deal. One of the basic social institutions that Finns brought with them to the States, the sauna tradition survived in the cold rural environments many of the immigrant communities favored. A community often built them, borrowing materials from forgotten New England stone walls. Commercial steam baths also flourished near Finnish communities. Building a private sauna for one's home was not uncommon. Evening gatherings always included time in the baths combined with enormous amounts of coffee and *pulla*, a pastry spiced with cardamom.

Not all folk practices and ancestral institutions fared so well in the cross-Atlantic passage. The Lutheran state church faced numerous challenges, never quite gaining traction among the expatriate faithful. The Finns' alienation from their religious background correlated to the attachment of many Finns to the politics of the left.

Radicalism must have taken root quickly among the Finns, given how much their religious leaders worried over its influence. Reino Hannula, a young Finnish immigrant close to Elizabeth's age, remembered pastors in his boyhood railing against socialism and its alleged tendency to lead the devout astray. A temperance tract written by Finnish Lutheran pastor John I. Kolehmainen called "the monster of socialism" a "more dangerous enemy" than alcohol.

Despite such dire warnings, socialist politics disenchanted churchgoers with the traditional faith by giving them a basis to analyze their social conditions and understand their church's frequent collaboration with the powerful. Hannula recalls his own introduction to this idea at age 15 when a friend, a member of the Young Communist League, pointed out to him that Lutheran churches received subsidies from the copper and iron mining companies in Minnesota and Michigan. How could the pastors not be held in thrall to the bosses?

Young Elizabeth did have a significant exposure to the Lutheran faith of the Finns. Her father edited church newspapers as part of his temperance work, and she sang in a Lutheran choir, one of her earliest experiences of performance. Although the combination of church attendance and dedication to the temperance cause seemingly marks the Syrjaniemis as deeply conservative, it is important to note that many within the temperance movement held progressive views even as they attempted to keep up appearances by attending the Lutheran church. Hannula, for example, recalls a number of communist families who attended his seemingly conservative Lutheran parish.

Certainly some of Maila's more mystical inclinations and her later talk of desiring to become a preacher and an evangelist stemmed in part from her experiences in church. However, despite her later claims of wanting to pursue a career as a traveling revivalist, she never attended church regularly as an adult or spoke about religion in either institutional or doctrinal terms. What little religious language she ever used remained highly abstract and, in her mind, always related to psychic, inner experiences. The message she later claimed to want to share with America bore zero relationship to the generally fundamentalist religion propounded by most of America's traveling preachers.

Elizabeth Syrjaniemi experienced more than just conservative Lutheranism, despite her father's predilections. The Finnish Lutheran church leader's anxiety about the triumph of socialism, even among their own congregants, reflected the reality of massive support for the left among the émigrés. Finnish immigrant communities became a mainstay for socialist and other left-leaning parties, contributing time and money to associations and parties that ran the gamut of 1920s and 30s radical politics. Historian Peter Kivisto has noted that Finns represented the "largest foreign-language federation of the Socialist party between 1906 and 1918." During the 1910s, Kivisto notes, Finns "converted in droves" to industrial unionism and then turned in large numbers to the Communist Party in the 1920s. Estimates of membership in the networks of left-leaning groups range from 25 to 40 percent of the close to half a million Finns in the United States during the first half of the century.

The Finns committed themselves to a new vision of America just at a moment of intense struggle over the direction of the country. The history of Finnish immigration to America parallels the rise of intense, violent clashes between the working class and the bosses. The Knights of Labor had been the first American organization to attempt to build "the One Big Union," but its energy had largely dissipated in the face of the government's support for capital and the public relations disaster of the 1886 Haymarket "bombing." But, by 1905, the Industrial Workers of the World (IWW, "the Wobblies") had taken up the banner of a class-consciousness and deeply militant labor unionism. Other left movements proliferated, including the Socialist Party of America and the Young Communist League. Finnish men would be drawn to the United Mine Workers (many settled in mining country) and to the radicalism of the Wobblies.

Finnish women played as significant a role as men in shaping their community's radicalism, and Nurmi likely knew many politically active women, including her mother. Their politics owed something to Finnish traditions of neighborly helpfulness adjusted for the conditions of immigrant life. In San Francisco, female domestic workers established the Finnish Women's Cooperative Home in 1910. These workers pooled their small salaries to rent apartments for common use, a social experiment that proved enormously successful. By 1920, 400 shareholders participated in the home and it became a center of sociability, intellectual activity, and creativity with "music and lectures . . . a sewing club . . . [and] an employment bureau, which is kept busy by housewives in search of domestic workers."

Finnish women also played an integral role in the popularity of the IWW, which made significant inroads into the Finnish community. The Wobblies sponsored at least one women's newspaper that framed its anarchic socialism in maternal terms. "We think of our children's fate," read one editorial. "Capitalism crushes even young lives and uses the best youths of the land like cattle in their bloody sports."

Growing up around Wobblie women, radical farmers, miners, and Lutherans with secret communist sympathies means young Maila must have received an introduction to the politics of marginalization. Nurmi developed a deep and abiding sympathy for challenges to the American consensus. She always understood herself as a freak, as weird, as problematic in relation to the wider culture. Her frequent disparaging references in interviews to "the middle class," and even to "the bourgeoisie," seems one of the more specific influences she received from the kind of political radicalism that surrounded her.

Although she never exhibited any detailed sense of economic radicalism, she may have been thinking of the labor organizers of her youth when she mentioned "the Great Depression" (along with Beat poetry) as one of her many influences. In the 1950s, she had tenuous links to Communist Party members like Harry Hay, links that probably never troubled her given the politics of her fellow

Finns. And, although she likely never read a word of *Das Kapital,* she absorbed her community's sense of something corrupt in American society and the need to struggle against it. This helps explain why she believed forcing a truth on the American public constituted part of her role as a performance artist.

The political language that surrounded her probably did not have as much influence on her as her own sense of personal alienation. In some of her final interviews before her death in 2008, Nurmi described herself as a child primarily in pejorative physical terms, an awkward girl "with hair like wet spaghetti . . . crooked teeth . . . . I was ashamed of myself. I thought I was just a useless slob." She spoke of her sense of having a diminished, unattractive self in relation to her sense of life as "weird and terrifying" and her need to find a means of escape.

Astoria High School seems to have been a special trial to her. She described pulling her "ugly carcass" through the "crowded corridors" between classes. Remembering her high school days for a piece she wrote in 1964, she showed a combination of real authorial skill and an ability to highlight what she saw as her extreme physical limitations:

> Scrawny, knock-kneed, pigeon-toed, flat-chested, and yellow, with what looks like rancid spaghetti for hair, you are clearly no prospect for the "yellleader tryouts!" Your face sports hairless eyes . . . a pig's snout, a mouth perpetually ajar, gasping for breath and revealing a broken picket fence of teeth. The icing on the cake, the ultimate embellishment the countenance wears . . . is a hollow expression, as of a visitor from another planet.

This sense of inadequacy helped to generate a strong attachment to fantasy. She understood her image of herself as "a useless slob" as "sort of the beginning of Vampira." What she called "the world of the vampire" offered a place to find escape, and not just from her interior terrors. The world of dark fantasy, she remembered, later gave her adult self a way to feel she had slipped away from "Big Brother" and "Uncle Sam," radically detached herself from the conservative ethos of her time. And even as a young child, making art became an outlet for her. By the 1930s, her adolescent attention increasingly turned to reading, and then attempting to draw, comic books.

Comics became an escape for many Americans in the 1930s. The hardship of the Great Depression meant more than economic difficulty. Financial failure militated against American conceptions of the "self-made man" and frontier myths about hard work and individualism, neither of which counted for much amid the decade's scarcities. The immense popularity of both films and comic strips in Roosevelt's America speaks to the need to find new myths and to live in fantasy worlds that offered some relief from the grinding poverty and limited horizons that many, including Elizabeth Syrjaniemi, felt during the decade.

Maila, like millions of other American children and adults, found cartoonist Milton Caniff's *Terry and the Pirates* an especially compelling fantasy. First appearing in October 1934, Caniff's work blended elements of science fiction and the 19th-century adventure tale in the escapades of a young American boy in China. The narratives turned on treasure hunts and struggles with caricatured and racially stereotyped villains (the titular "pirates"). By the late 30s, the strip increasingly borrowed political themes, including the Japanese invasion of Manchuria.

Nurmi remembers a special attachment to the character of "the Dragon Lady," a Chinese pirate queen that became both a returning villain and, eventually, a somewhat complex antihero. She appeared in the series' very first strip in 1934, dark, evil, and seductive. But Caniff also eventually portrayed her as a resistance fighter against the Japanese invaders and shaped the rivalry between the Dragon

Lady and Terry as an affectionate one. For example, in an episode of the strip much loved by fans, the Dragon Lady teaches young Terry how to dance.

Nurmi later remembered a deep identification with this character and with the alternate world of adventure the strip produced. Her attraction to the strip seems especially notable given that *Terry and the Pirates* offered transgressive visions of women and sexuality. By 1940, Caniff introduced a villainess named Sanjak, named after an island near the Greek island of Lesbos. Caniff portrayed Sanjak as a French woman who cross-dressed by wearing a men's uniform and had a monocle that gave her the power to hypnotize her prey. She attempted to use the latter against Terry's girlfriend, April Kane, for whom, the strip obliquely suggested, Sanjak had sexual feelings.

Nurmi's love for fantasy worlds led her to create as well as consume them. She remembered lying for hours on her stomach in the family room, drawing and dreaming and trying to create a world less terrifying, a world that she described as "living by its own standards." Neither of the elder Nurmis seems to have known what to make of a dreamy child who saw the world around her as threatening.

Her fascination with comic books certainly made her feel estranged from her parents' active engagement with the world. Nurmi remembers once being deeply bored and asking her mother what she should do with herself. "You could shut up," snapped Sophia, perhaps deep in her translation work or, more likely, worrying over the accounts of one of Onni's struggling newspapers.

Nurmi's relationship with Sophia remained troubled through her childhood. Years later, a teenaged Nurmi literally leaped out of the bathtub to tell Sophia that the voice of Orson Welles on the radio was not only entrancing, it was speaking directly to her. Unwilling to allow her strange daughter a bit of whimsy, Sophia again told her to shut up. "You are just Elizabeth Syrjaniemi and you work at the fish cannery," she reminded her.

Elizabeth undoubtedly retreated further into her comic strips and alternate realities. And she perhaps began to dream of finding a stage where she could speak, act, maybe even scream, and no one would tell her to shut up, ever again. The political traditions of the communities she lived in placed a premium on oratory and public performance, and she remembered having speaking parts in local radio dramas as early as age nine, though the context and contents of these remain unknown.

In high school, she participated in the Rhythm Club, a girl's auxiliary of the Finnish brotherhood "comprised of thirty–forty young women" who "presented numerous and varied programs to the Lodge as well as for their community." And, despite her contention that she was utterly alienated from high school social life, she did at least take part in several theatrical productions. A photograph from her high school yearbook shows her as part of the cast of a musical comedy called *Lauluja Laineilla* (*Song of the Waves*). In the image, she appears in drag as a Chaplinesque-looking sailor.

The example of her father, editing newspapers or on the road, speaking to crowds and sharing a message, must have impressed the young woman who so often sank deep into her own silences and felt threatened by the outside world. What if she could command that world, make it her own? She dreamed of swaying crowds and telling her story, a story she would blend with some evangel, some greater meaning and message. Her strange dream of being an American revivalist became one way she imagined a path to her own public platform.

She wasn't going to find it in Astoria. Asked in the 1960s to write a piece for a "back to school" issue of *LA Weekly*, Maila wrote as if she were speaking to her 18-year-old self: "Nobody knows that you're sexy." She recalled boys at Astoria High greeting her with "Here comes the Bride of Frankenfurter." No one appreciated her sense of humor. A young boy she had a crush on told the future Vampira, "You're not funny, it's the way your mother dresses you."

Maila's memories of alienation and bullying didn't exactly make for the kind of sentimental memories of school days piece that *LA Weekly* wanted. She ended with some hint of her motivations for leaving Oregon right after her graduation in 1940. In doing so, she referenced *Terry and the Pirates*: "You decided you'd show them!" she wrote. "You'd grow up to be the Dragon Lady. They'd see. They'd be sorry."

Maila Elizabeth Syrjaniemi took her first steps toward becoming the Dragon Lady in 1940. While being a "visitor from another planet" in high school urged her toward this decision, so did an apparently troubled relationship with her family. She later spoke darkly of her parents "giving her away." This does not seem to have happened in any literal sense, though it's a frequent metaphor used by those who find themselves deeply at odds with the values of their upbringing. Rock and blues goddess Janis Joplin, for example, told a number of interviewers that her parents had "thrown her out of the house" at the age of 14 when, in fact, they had done no such thing.

Elizabeth Syrjaniemi, (fourth from the right) cross-dressing as a Chaplin-esque figure in a school production, late 1930s. Courtesy of the Clatsop County Historical Society.

Like Joplin, Nurmi explained rather than described her experience of life at home. She may have been alluding to a schism with her straight-laced father or her inattentive mother. She seems to have remained estranged from her father until his death in 1962. She never spoke of him (except to give an interviewer his name) and seldom mentioned her brother, Robert, who continued to live in Astoria until his death in 1977.

Whatever the precipitant conflict, leaving home meant that she followed tens of thousands of other Depression-era teenagers who took to road and rail. It's difficult to tell what leaving home looked like for her since she talked about it most frequently when a certain romance adhered to the hobo life. The folk music revival of the 50s created a public interest in traditional blues, folk, and hillbilly singers whose authenticity received some confirmation from their time traveling America aboard train cars and living on the edge of starvation. Nurmi channeled Woody Guthrie in the 1955 interview with *People Today* when she said simply, "I was a bum. I used to work just enough to buy my meals."

Nurmi had to add some of her own stylish sense of narrative to this simple story of a runaway. She insisted that though forced to sell *The Hobo News* when she arrived in New York, "a wealthy friend" allowed her to borrow his "armored car" so that she could go from street corner to street corner in style. She added that the chauffeur "wore a monocle and a derby and was a Russian count." Including the monocle in her fantasy of life on the street means she never forgot about her long and lonely but wondrous afternoons reading about Sanjak and *Terry and the Pirates*.

Nurmi's fanciful tale hid the harsh realities of life on the road during the Depression. About a quarter million other homeless teenagers, many of whom had fled families broken by the struggles of the decade, also wandered the roads and rode the rails. Teenage boys made up the overwhelming majority of those who took up the wandering life. Girls frequently sought freedom and new prospects as well, some disguising themselves as boys in order to improve their job prospects and to escape sexual assault. This would not have prevented rape or offers of food and protection in return for sex. A 1937 investigation into the experience of indigent teens found that almost every train had its so-called wolves or jockers who forced themselves on younger, often hungry and demoralized, fellow travelers.

The poverty and indigence of the actual life on the road in the 30s included much the same horrors as homelessness today. Maila, if she was "on the road" for even a short time, absolutely encountered varieties of random violence, police brutality, and the mental and physical trials of hunger and malnourishment.

We do know from her that she briefly went to L.A., under very shadowy circumstances, to do one of her first modeling shoots. How she made it from there to Greenwich Village unfortunately remains a mystery. However she made the trip, these experiences became transformative. Elizabeth Maila Syrjaniemi disappeared. By the time the young woman made it to New York City, she had become Maila Nurmi.

*****

Her choice of a new name, Maila Nurmi, signaled her new independence. It implied mystery, a clash of soft vowels and hard consonants that sounds sexy and aggressive on the tongue. She later laughed her name off with an interviewer. "'Nurmi,' she pointed out when her career as Vampira began, "rhymes with 'wormy.'" But in the 1940s it simply gave off an exotic flavor, hard edges and a velvet center.

The shapeshifting went beyond a name change. Maila's creature of the night started to emerge out of several personal and cultural phenomena that Nurmi explored and experimented in. No longer the gawky girl, Nurmi found some quick cash as a cheesecake model. At age 18, she appeared on the cover of the magazine *Glamorous Models*, later to feature a famous Marilyn Monroe cover, possibly the shoot she had done in L.A. She would soon combine this income with reading monologues for radio and some modeling for advertising while working on and off as a cigarette girl in a variety of New York clubs.

Nurmi, who as little Elizabeth Maila had been ashamed of her body, was now getting paid for putting her body on display. But she wanted more. This was not the stage she hoped for. It did, however, become something of a mad scientist's laboratory where she began to construct early versions of her monster.

Understanding the history of American culture's fascination with the female form at midcentury helps explain something about the kind of roles that Nurmi wanted, and didn't want, to perform, why modeling never became the public performance she craved. She described the character she eventually created as "[getting] people's attention by giving them what they wanted, breasts, net stockings, phallic symbols. Once I had gotten their attention, I could preach to them." She wanted a stage so she could deliver a message.

It's doubtful that American men wanted phallic symbols in the 40s and 50s. They certainly didn't want a woman delivering a message. They did want breasts and asses and thighs and a cartoonish representation of available female sexuality. Midcentury America's most famous sexing up of the female form began in 1953 with the first issue of *Playboy*. Hugh Hefner blended fantasies of a bachelorhood surrounded by expensive cars and sound equipment with willing, nude women as trophies.

Unlike Hefner's dream world of girls and gadgets, the American pin-up of the 30s and 40s focused on fantasies closer at hand, girls next door caught in revealing poses and often looking gullible, innocent, caught in the act, sexually innocent, and yet profligate. The origins of "glamour photography" date to the early 20th century and the public's obsession with collecting images of the female cinema stars. The introduction of the Motion Picture Production Code in 1933 tamped down the throbbing sensuality of the film star, creating a market for fantasy female forms. *Esquire* magazine, which had its premiere issue in 1933, offered a middlebrow version of this aesthetic, filling its pages with short stories by John Dos Passos and F. Scott Fitzgerald that competed for reader's attention with the George Petty drawings of "the Petty girls." White, obviously middle class, generally portrayed as naïve about their own effulgent sexuality, the Petty girls (or "cuties," as readers nicknamed them) became the centerfold feature of *Esquire* in 1939.

By the 1940s, *Esquire* had hired Alberto Vargas to create what became the iconic "Vargas girls" of the World War II era. These heartbreakingly attractive women glowed with an almost industrially perfect sheen, legs that went on forever, impossibly balanced

Elizabeth Syrjaniemi begins to transform into a glamour goddess. She's about 16 here, posing in front of a social club for Lutheran young people. Courtesy of the Clatsop County Historical Society.

breasts, and eyes, lips, and hair that seemed out of an alternative universe of aesthetic perfection. Rather than posed in either a domestic or exotic setting, they floated in an abstract void, eyes looking at the viewer with an almost aggressive gaze. You might be staring at the female body, but she was staring back.

Not everyone liked the Vargas girl and her refusal to subordinate herself to the male viewer. Unhappiness with the drawings appeared early in the *Esquire* letters column, a 1940 letter arguing that "women's beauty is—and should be—judged from the standpoint of that which would make her most desirable to men." The letter writer compared the Vargas girls' wantonness and aggressive stance unfavorably to Petty's cuties. The Vargas girl might be "desirable in her own sort of way but . . . is not likely to be taken out in public."

Men wanted a fantasy that they could control, a fantasy that would prove pliable to their demands. Increasingly, 40s pin-ups offered them women who could "be taken out in public," shaped around the idea of submissiveness in response to the male gaze. At a time when actual women went to work in factories in large numbers and, after 1941, joined the military as WAVES and WACS, fantasy women increasingly became childlike and empty-eyed.

The bad girl who was not a vamp and an eternal virgin who put out became the ideal. Feminist scholar Maria Elena Buszek argues that a woman became "desirable either for her asexuality and domestic potential or for her naïve, yet overt, sexuality." In truth, men wanted a combination of both. As a symbol of the times, the Vargas girl disappeared in *Esquire,* to be replaced by giggly, shapely coeds. Albert Vargas himself went to work for Hugh Hefner in the 1950s, drawing the new Vargas girl as nude, submissive, and now with gag lines that made her sound not very bright.

The late 1930s and 1940s represent the golden age of the pin-up magazine. The wave of pin-up mags that swept America owes much of its energy to Robert Harrison. In 1941, Harrison worked for famed entertainment gossip king Martin Quigley, the publisher of the enormously popular *Motion Picture Daily* and *Motion Picture Herald*. Harrison had the idea of translating some of the conceits of the burlesque show into magazine form, creating a sensual, private experience for readers that offered more than just a hint of flesh.

Harrison believed that this new style of pin-up would encapsulate the pleasures of the burlesque show and tame what some men saw as its less desirable aspects. Pin-up girls could be possessed in a way that the women of the Burly-Q could never be. Burlesque had always traded in the idea that the women who presented themselves to you were ultimately unavailable. Indeed, the idea of the "blow-off," the refusal to take part in and ally with male fantasy, formed an essential element in the burlesque. It always promised more than it gave, inciting and frustrating desire all at once.

The pin-up, on the other hand, removed the performer's assertion of self, her ability to lay claim to their privacy and subjectivity. Between the pages of magazines, held in sweaty hands across the country and by soldiers on foreign shores, the bodies of women became collectible artifacts, conduits of the pleasure of possession. The pin-up represented a mass-produced cult of erotic ownership, women's bodies as symbolic capital to be hoarded. She could never refuse you.

Staying hours after work each day, Harrison pasted and patched together his first effort at a "girlie magazine," which he christened with the modest moniker *Beauty Parade*. When his employer discovered his extracurricular work, Harrison received an immediate pink slip (on Christmas Eve, according to one version of the story). Harrison stuck with his idea and, along with artist Earl Moran, continued to try to find ways to tap into the American male's horny dreams.

A mash-up of sexuality and nervous humor, Harrison included jokey tales about women wrestling, bad wives getting spanked, or women attempting and failing to do "men's work." Wanting to close the icy distance between the viewer and the Vargas girl, Harrison found success by placing photographs and drawings into a narrative structure. An early issue of *Beauty Parade,* for example, featured a young woman inexplicably dressed in bra, panties, and high heels while she works, unsuccessfully and incompetently, to assemble a deck chair. Unable to complete her simple task, she takes an axe and chops the chair into firewood.

Control over women's bodies often became something more than subtext and symbolism. In the early years of the Harrison magazines, women submit demurely to the often-violent desires of men. The camera photographed model "Agnes Dane" as a slave chained on an auction block with "abject misery and suffering . . . etched on her delicate features." Another feature called "Links of Love" included a photograph of a underwear-clad Nora Brendt on the floor, her wrists chained and wearing an ankle bracelet that appears to be some kind of manacle. Accompanying text refers to the picture as "a slave study of a pathetic pretty." The viewer is assured she likes it since she has discovered that her chains are "wrought of pure love."

Unlike the early Vargas girls, you didn't have to worry about the object of your desire looking back at you. In an overwhelming number of Harrison images, the pin-up girl's gaze refuses to meet the eye of the male viewer. They are frequently looking away from the viewer or, most commonly, glance in the viewer's direction with looks of sly embarrassment, as if their bodies are being revealed against their will. They have been caught coming out of washtubs, losing their pajama bottoms, or, as was the case of one cover, having a dog steal their bath towel from them.

These fantasies of female weakness are allied with an increasing number of images of women in mainstream advertising that placed the white, middle-class housewife in various poses of submission that promised erotic pleasure and pain. A Chase and Sanborn coffee ad that ran in the early 50s warned that a wife had better "fresh test" her husband's coffee or end up over his knee. The ad showed her with a look of terror, and delight, as her husband spanks her.

Even advertising that did not include the threat of violence showed women cleaning, getting ready to clean, or despairing that they cannot clean adequately. Other ads combined the image of female incompetence with the promise of sexual subservience. An ad for Del Monte ketchup, proffering its new "easy open lid," showed a woman flashing a look of seductive surprise that, combined with holding the phallic bottle close to her face, suggested oral sex. "You mean a woman can open it?" the caption wonders with a wink.

Cultural efforts to domesticate the problematic women of the 20s and 30s extend beyond ad copy and pin-up magazines. Maria Elena Buszek uses the example of Joan Crawford, who during the Depression and the Second World War portrayed a variety of "tough, working-class characters." The decline of Crawford's popularity led to her efforts to "instigate a comeback as a happy homemaker." In 1946, an MGM promotional still photo showed her happily mopping a kitchen floor.

These representations of women suggest that the men of the "greatest generation" needed continual assurance of their own masculinity. And yet, the floodtide of images of submissive and willing women did little to salve their anxieties. Articles and essays in pin-up mags like *Flirt* and *Wink* increasingly turned to the problem of male priapic disasters. At times, they seemed to offer gentle advice for male readers, as in an article that proffered "hints for bashful bachelors." One such issue promised to explain to readers "How to Become a Playboy." An article in *Titter* magazine provided a list for male lonely hearts called "Seven Ways to Get a Babe."

Later Harrison endeavors, especially *Wink* and *Whisper*, seemed to unconsciously attack their own readership. In both mags, male characters are often included in the photographic layouts, suggesting the possibility that pin-ups, unlike the Vargas girl, could be a part of real life experience. Most of these men are shown bumbling over themselves in awe over the perfect bodies with which they have come in contact. Photographers portrayed them wearing mismatched suits in loud checkerboard patterns, with slightly old-fashioned accouterments. Almost all the hapless male models sported the then-out-of-fashion mustache (that would, ironically, become a mainstay of the male porn star by the 1970s).

This undercurrent of disdain for the reader also erupted in the kinds of ads that appeared in all of the Harrison publications. Advertisements in *Beauty Parade* promised "renewed virility" that would help clients "to live married life to its fullest." The Jowett Courses also marketed themselves in its pages, promising a program of physical culture to turn "physical wrecks" into "an ALL Around He-Man." The successful student could learn to "master any situation" after following Jowett's regimen. Another article in *Whisper* promised to explain how to find "over the counter virility." These magazines featured more ads for products to prevent male impotence than today's Fox News Channel.

The cheesecake tradition contained much that Maila Nurmi could use to make her monster and more than a few elements that she rejected. There's no question that cheesecake modeling shaped certain elements of her creature's style, especially in relation to Vampira's exaggerated sexuality. But this was far from the stage she wanted and not even close to the kind of performance art she hoped to give America.

The shock value of Vampira came from her refusal to submit to the male gaze. She wanted to attack it instead. The world of airbrushed misogyny helped Nurmi to know what to distinguish herself from, the kinds of images that sold because they offered easy orgasms that held little of enduring value beyond the masturbatory moment.

Vampira represented both homage and satire of the pin-up tradition. Cheesecake came with a heavy dose of gothic morbidity and transformed the sexual politics and imagery of midcentury America into a sandbox she could play in.

Modeling for glamour mags certainly was not her reason for running away from home. When she left Astoria, she hoped to find freaks like herself, to escape the confines of her provincial if well-traveled background. "I knew there were others," she said, and she rightly thought of Greenwich Village as the best place to go looking for them.

"The Village" had been a destination for politically and culturally radical women since the early 20th century. Called "Bohemian Girls," "New Women," and "Rebel Girls," women like Edna St. Vincent Millay, Emma Goldman, and Margaret Sanger made Greenwich Village into an enclave of outsiders. Producing small press magazines, becoming fiery advocates for sex education and liberalized divorce laws, or turning their apartments into salons for artists and writers, numerous women made the trek to New York and transformed the Greenwich blocks into a definable "scene."

Nurmi arrived in the Village at a time when mid-20th-century hipsters increasingly defined what they were up to as the "Beat movement." The Beats came together as a self-conscious group in the 1940s, at first as less a literary movement and more a loose network of people who shared a fascination with drugs, alternative sexuality, and finding bizarre ways of expressing themselves in their art and lifestyle. The 1950s would see Beat writers create the classics that came to define them, including Allen Ginsberg's *Howl* (1954) Jack Kerouac's *On the Road* (1957), and Burroughs's *Naked Lunch* (1959).

"Beat" represented a sensibility as much as a group. Nurmi frequently referenced the Beats in her descriptions of herself and was delighted to have even a bit part in a 1959 crime drama called *The Beat Generation.* She loved their style, their rejection of conventionality, and their desire to turn midcentury America upside down. When Allen Ginsberg's friend Carl Solomon hurled potato salad at a college lecturer delivering an address on surrealism, he perhaps defined the Beat notions of authenticity that Nurmi found so enticing and wanted to imitate. Here were freaks who had found their stage, and she wanted to join them.

Male writers like Kerouac, Ginsberg, and Burroughs remain the representative figures among the Beat Generation even today. This hides the experience of the hundreds of "rebel girls" who, like Maila Nurmi, flocked to the Village in the 40s. Some, like Diane di Prima and Ruth Weiss, did become important poets, though their work did not receive its due for decades.

Other women seemingly disappeared, at least in the minds of their male counterparts. Poet Greg Corso, part of the Ginsberg inner circle, described women in the scene as if they were mysterious figures that society carted away. "There were women, they were there . . . their families put them in institutions, they were given electric shock." Corso suggested, rightly, that the 50s male could become a rebel but that women could find themselves "locked up." He also described them as if they floated in and out of the scene, filmy and insubstantial, rather than being a central part of it.

Corso seems to suggest that traditional American society, the same one that male Beats saw as corrupt, should be held responsible for what happened to women associated with the movement. This conveniently ignores the role that the Beats themselves played in shipwrecking the lives of their female comrades. A strongly masculine ethos guided the men in the movement, leading them to view women as opportunities to break sexual mores or as means of financial support. Anne Waldman, a young poet who associated with the Beats in the final years of the movement, remembered "interesting, creative women who became junkies for their boyfriends, who stole for their boyfriends, who concealed their poetry. . . . " Many of them went to work as hatcheck girls, cigarette girls, waitresses, and sometimes sex workers. Cultural historian John Leland puts it best when he writes that "Beat women were saddled with feeding downwardly mobile men whose rebellion meant shedding any return obligations."

Nurmi had a different experience. She did not have a man to support in the 40s and almost immediately found work that might make her famous. No longer a gawky kid with bad hair, her blonde

Scandinavian looks offered her the possibility of life on the stage. She supported herself by using these looks throughout the war years. But she also never gave up on her artistic aspirations and sold some of her work on the street, work that gained some limited interest if never making her very much money.

Much of her art at this time apparently took the form of bizarre comic strips, mixing and matching the sci-fi and fantasy characters that enchanted her. They also focused on sex, and while, in an interview late in life, she claimed her own morals had been "pristine" in those days, she also claimed she knew "how to be pornographic with her own pen." This comment seems to suggest that it was in the mid-40s that she became interested in New York's emerging sexual underground, a rejection of moral conventionality inspired by the Beats and finding some expression in John Willie's *Bizarre* magazine that directly influenced the creation of Vampira.

She took the stage when she could find one. In 1944, Nurmi received a small role in a New York–based "spook show" that undoubtedly proved determinative for her macabre interests. The spook shows had become one of the more popular traveling vaudeville acts in the 1930s, borrowing content from both magic shows and Universal Studios' popular monster films.

Dr. Silkini's Spook Show (1933) became one of the earliest and most popular. Writing in the 1940s, a reviewer for *Tops* magazine remembered the Silkini show beginning with "a routine magic show opening" followed by a "Make a Monster" skit that borrowed directly from *Frankenstein*. The Monster rose and strangled a hunchbacked assistant, leading, the reviewer wrote, to "the screaming of teenage girls" in the audience reaching "a crescendo." The show typically closed with the scariest sequence, "the black out," the lights suddenly dropping and hurling a frightened audience into total darkness. Silkini ended the show by putting on some more magical illusions and introducing the audience to his players.

In 1944, producer Mike Todd decided to create a New

York–based spook show of his own. Todd would achieve enormous success in 1956 as the producer of *Around the World in 80 Days* and as Elizabeth Taylor's third husband. In 1944, he was a struggling impresario at the beginning of his career. He picked Maila Nurmi to play a small part in the production. Some accounts suggest she worked only once for the show. It remains unclear whether she actually appeared onstage at all or simply acted as a kind of living lobby art. In 1954, Nurmi told a reporter that she "wore a lavender shroud and lay in a coffin in the lobby."

But she had something to show the world, and her first time in a coffin opened up the possibilities of stardom. Howard Hawks, one of the most powerful figures in 1940s Hollywood, happened to catch her act and developed at least some degree of fascination with her. Most of what we know of his relationship to Nurmi comes from her own account, so the depth of his interest remains unclear. It is true that Hawks, like many of the era's producers, saw himself as a patron who could turn starlets into stars, as he believed he had done for Lauren Bacall.

Hawks put Nurmi under contract for a role in a planned film of the Russian novel *Dreadful Hollow* with a screenplay written by none other than William Faulkner. The story centered on a vampire countess and included such gruesome conceits as a corpse being sewn up inside a taxidermied wolf.

She thought she had found her stage. Nurmi moved to Los Angeles in 1945. Unfortunately for her, the development of the film seems to have been doomed from the start. Hawks's first attempt to have the film made (he was still trying as late as 1951) faltered because of the studio's lack of interest in the overlong and, the studio insisted, derivative screenplay. Nurmi's own account blames Hawks for not moving more quickly with the film and claims that she herself broke the contract with him because of delays. "I thought he was stupid, so I tore up my contract," she later claimed. "I told him to kindly find a place for it in one of his numerous wastebaskets."

Elizabeth's 1940 graduation picture. The girl they called "The Bride of Frankenfurter" becomes Maila Nurmi, the very image of Hollywood glamour in a promo shot for Howard Hawks, 1946. Graduation picture Courtesy of the Clatsop County Historical Society.

Although insulting the powerful Hawks may seem an unlikely tale, it actually has the ring of truth. Nurmi showed this kind of defiance, this sense that her own dignity represented a commodity to be bought dear, throughout her life. While seemingly unbelievable that she would reject any future opportunity that Hawks might bring her, burning her bridges with one of America's most important producer/directors with a scathing rant seems entirely in character with what we know of the rest of her life. Nurmi sought to be an outlaw, not just play one in the movies. She always paid a high price for her dignity.

When Nurmi arrived in 1945, Los Angeles combined an urban glamour with frontier rawness that makes the film noir genre a snapshot of an era. Under the glow of the city's bright lights thrived a hidden history more seedy than even this period's scandal rags could imagine. So did hopes for human liberation that give the lie to notions of L.A.'s inherent vacuity, the stereotype of the city of suntans and failed hopes.

Nurmi would spend most of her life seeking stardom in L.A. Like tens of thousands of others, she never succeeded. But unlike most, she came deliciously and heartbreakingly close. Contrary to the city's antimyths, not everyone found themselves chewed up and spit out by the city. In Vampira's case, the boulevard of broken dreams never digested her, and she set up shop in the beast's belly for almost six decades.

Los Angeles had been a boomtown since the 20s, swelling in a decade from a dusty outpost in 1910 to a city of 600,000 in 1922. Traffic snarls were a reality here before anywhere else in the country while developers threw skyscrapers in the air along Spring Street ("the Wall Street of the West") in a riot of urban hubris.

It was also a city with the mob intertwined around its vitals. Bingo and bookmaking rackets had been a part of life there since the 1910s, and brothels, as in much of the woman-starved immigrant West, thrived. Forty years later, around the time of Nurmi's arrival, the city's rawness remained much the same. In fact, organized crime had become even better organized. In the early 1950s, former small-time crook turned crime boss Mickey Cohen divided up the city's graft, prostitution, and gambling assets among his associates in an L.A. County hotel suite as though he were carving up the duck two ways at the Brown Derby.

The L.A. mob thrived in part because of its links to the silver screen. In 1958, Cohen did some work on behalf of Columbia Pictures boss Harry Cohn. Kim Novak, who had recently smoldered in *Vertigo*, had been linked romantically in the papers with black actor and singer Sammy Davis Jr. Rather than knocking off Davis, as Cohn apparently hinted that he wanted to, Cohen visited the star in Las Vegas to warn him that continuing to date the white star could prove a health risk. Davis not only broke off the relationship with Novak, he apparently felt indebted to Cohen. He testified on the mob boss's behalf following an April 4, 1958, incident in which Cohen beat up a waiter at the Villa Capri, a Las Vegas restaurant owned by Frank Sinatra and Peter Lawford.

Even before the mob set up shop, Hollywood had a shadowy past. The film industry itself helped create the city's outlaw tradition. In the 1910s, filmmakers increasingly found New York City a dangerous place to work. The Edison Company, developer of some of the first motion pictures in America, used strong-arm tactics to create a near monopoly over visual entertainment. A private army of lawyers and detectives hired by the company ferreted out attempts by filmmakers to use cameras based on the Edison design . . . and almost every camera in use owed something to the Edison original.

Hoping to escape the Edison Company's long reach, a minstrel show impresario who called himself Colonel William Selig discovered Hollywood while shooting a western in Arizona. Three thousand miles away from NYC, less than a hundred miles from Mexico should legal troubles present themselves, Los Angeles promised a wealth of environments for filming that included desert and ocean-front as well as a growing urban center.

Soon, the muscular growth of American motion pictures made the stars come out to shine over the freshwater-starved little valley. As early as the 1920s, the cranny hillside that overlooked Hollywood Boulevard had become Whitley Heights, a celebrity neighborhood that became home to silver screen idols like Judy Garland, Barbara Stanwyck, Rudolph Valentino, and W. C. Fields.

Such a critical mass of star power virtually ensured that the motion picture industry would transform the town into the dream factory it became. But the movies were not the only entertainment game in town during Nurmi's early years in the city. The year after she followed Howard Hawks to the city, L.A.'s KLTA became the first commercial television station west of the Mississippi River. In the same year, one of the first fictional TV series, *Public Prosecutor*, was filmed in Hollywood. In 1952, CBS built a major studio at Fairfax Avenue and Beverley Boulevard. KABC, home to *The Vampira Show*, started out as KECA in 1947, based east of Hollywood in Los Feliz.

Los Angeles also produced dreams that had little to do with film fame or seedy criminal empires. Like many frontier communities, it had a utopian tradition. Born from outlawry, more than a few dreamers had come to try to create a new kind of society. Nurmi, although never explicitly political in any traditional sense, had links with some of the most radical elements of midcentury Los Angeles life.

L.A. had a radical tradition going back to the 1890s, when a severe economic depression inspired marches by the unemployed demanding that the tiny town initiate public works programs that would provide full employment. By the 1920s, with the population of the city exploding, the class-oriented IWW movement had come to the L.A. docks only to be crushed by an alliance between employers and the LAPD's so-called Red Squad.

In the 1940s, despite extraordinary harassment from conservative mayor Fletcher Bowron, the left flourished in Tinseltown and its environs. Rodger Young, a WWII veteran who lived in a public housing project near Griffith Park, published an influential communist newspaper called *The People's World*. In 1946, a popular front organization that included communists as well as New Deal liberals formed the Progressive Citizens of America. Charlotta Bass, editor of the popular African American newspaper *The California Eagle*, took part in this movement that threw their support behind Henry Wallace's left-wing challenge to Truman in the 1948 presidential election.

L.A.'s class struggles in the 30s and 40s also forged warriors for sexual liberation. Harry Hay, who once described himself "missing [out on] the forties" because he had "been married and a member of the Communist Party," became a leading figure in the emerging politicization of the gay community.

In 1950, Hay founded the Mattachine Society after an unsuccessful effort to start a "Bachelors for Wallace" movement two years previously. Hay borrowed the name "Mattachine" from peasant organizations in medieval France who donned masks during the vernal equinox and performed public dramas mocking the aristocracy and the church. In Hay's view, the secrecy of his organization mirrored the need of medieval workers to perform a "masque" in order to challenge the reigning order.

The organization emerged from a document simply entitled "The Call," which insisted on full equality for gay and lesbian relationships. Hay and friends set up an organizational structure for their work modeled on the cell-based organization of the Communist Party that Hay knew well.

Based in Silver Lake, a neighborhood southeast of Los Feliz clustered around the Silver Lake reservoir, Hay, along with ally Dale Jennings, published *ONE*, the first gay rights newspaper with a significant public presence in the United States. Over the next decade, Hay and other original founders would find themselves ejected from their own organization, their left-wing pasts viewed as an added burden on a movement that already seemed on the verge of being persecuted out of existence.

Rudi Gernreich was the cofounder and primary financial support of the Mattachine Society, as well as the great love of Harry Hay's life. He later became one of the links between Nurmi and L.A.'s gay and lesbian community.

In 1946, Maila Nurmi found herself adrift in a city that seemed both eternally young and old before its time. Needing to make her way, her hopes of becoming a Hollywood star on hold, Nurmi found ways to use her "blonde bombshell" character to get by. The so-called leg shows offered Nurmi the best chance at a steady income.

The infamous Earl Carroll had opened a "vanities" theater on Sunset Boulevard in 1938. Carroll had achieved enormous notoriety on the East Coast after the first incarnation of his *Vanities* appeared on Broadway in 1924. Promising to show more skin than any of the other leg shows in the city made Carroll a target for censors. Beleaguered by legal troubles and scandal, hoping for a new start in California, he had built his own theater and brought his vision of upscale burlesque to the City of Angels. Nurmi may have worked for Carroll as early as 1946.

It's likely as one of Carroll's dancing vanities that Nurmi met her future husband, Dean Riesner. Riesner had been a child star, once appearing in a film with Chaplin. Now a hopeful screenwriter, he eventually achieved fame as the scribe for *Dirty Harry.* They began living together as common-law man and wife in 1949, and possibly at Riesner's request, Nurmi quit dancing. She then became a part-time hatcheck girl and a full-time housewife while continuing to do a bit of modeling when she could. They lived in a small apartment in the Hollywood Hills, soon to become a tony neighborhood bounded by Mulholland Drive and Griffith Park to the north and Melrose Avenue to the south. Nurmi had begun her long association with North and West Hollywood, the latter to become funky WeHo during her time there.

The relationship between Riesner and Nurmi seems never to have been an especially happy one. Nurmi later described this as a period in which she was "stuck in a marriage" and "failing at being a housewife." Moreover, Riesner's need to find inspiration with frequent trips to the movies became a burden to Maila. She remembered their having a regular Saturday night date that involved a trip to the movie theater, almost always to see the westerns that fascinated Riesner and much of America in this period. "Cowboys were big in those days," she remembered. "How I hated it." She often excused herself to go to the ladies' room and, instead of returning to the film, sat in the lobby and watched the people "dressing a certain way and buying popcorn." Why people felt they needed to buy popcorn proved more interesting to her than Hollywood's latest shoot-'em-up.

She began to find opportunities for more sophisticated modeling work than she had ever done for the cheesecake mags. Working with Rudi Gernreich (and, she later claimed, Man Ray and Alberto Vargas), Nurmi further developed her increasingly idiosyncratic style.

Gernreich deserves credit as one of the most significant influences on Nurmi and the creation of the character of Vampira. Born in Vienna in 1922, Gernreich fled Austria following Hitler's rise and Germany's annexation of Austria. By the end of the Second World War, he worked as an instructor for the Lester Horton dance company. He soon became an important element in the cutting-edge (and most controversial) movements in fashion design, associating himself with both William Claxton and Peggy Moffitt. His ideas for the monokini (essentially a topless bikini) and the pubkini (which was just what it sounds like), not surprisingly, never caught on. One of his creations, the infamous thong, has enjoyed on-again/off-again popularity. Classic sci-fi TV aficionados have seen his designs in the "Moonbase Alpha" uniforms on *Space: 1999.*

Gernreich almost certainly snagged Nurmi her invitation to Lester Horton's Bal Caribe Halloween extravaganza in 1953. The Bal

Caribe represented the most outré gathering in 1950s Hollywood that brought together the city's gay elite, political radicals, and a hefty portion of campy glamour. Horton had long been part of Hollywood's gay scene, and his work outside of film frequently sought to challenge conservative American mores. In 1946, he and his longtime partner William Bowne joined with the avant-garde dancer Bella Rebecca Lewitzky to form an experimental troupe called simply Dance Theater. The company produced choreographed interpretations based on themes critical of American religious intolerance and anti-Semitism. Moreover, Horton and Lewitzky worked to make the dance company biracial as a direct criticism of the continuing power of Jim Crow in America.

Gernreich getting Nurmi into the Bal Caribe offered her entree to both the worlds of Hollywood glamour and political radicalism. The annual event featured Hollywood's most important and most outrageous characters, and the costumes included variations on the theme of drag and camp. The costume that Nurmi put together was extraordinarily simple, indeed simpler than the character she later crafted for television. She donned a tattered black gown, wore high heels, and applied heavy pancake makeup, much more than she would employ in her show. This gave her complexion the pall of death. An exuberant display of cleavage seems to have been part of the original costume as well.

But she wasn't Vampira. Not yet. Nurmi frequently told interviewers that, at this stage, her character was little more than a "female vampire." She was not yet the subversive parody of American womanhood she made for TV. Still, it's a testament to the cultural jouissance of the "female vampire" character Nurmi invented that her creation won the prize for best costume out of a bevy of flamboyant, campy creations. It's also true that the dice may have been loaded: Her pal Gernreich served as one of the judges.

Hunt Stromberg Jr., son of the legendary film producer, remembered her winning the prize. The world of Vampira fans know Stromberg today as the man who gave her a big break. But it was actually after his short association with her that he made his best-known marks on American television history. In the 1960s, he moved to the top echelons at CBS where he played a significant role in the production of TV standards like *The Beverly Hillbillies*, *Hogan's Heroes*, and *Green Acres*. Ironically, given the role he played in introducing the world to Vampira, he later became a producer of unmemorable horror films like *Frankenstein: The True Story* (1973) and *Curse of King Tut's Tomb* (1980).

Nurmi's brief brushes with fame had certainly not made her a well-known quantity in Hollywood. Stromberg apparently gave her little thought at first, and it took him, even according to Nurmi, "several months" to locate her. Gernreich, in fact, provided him with Nurmi's phone number. During this time period, they may have been near neighbors, as Gernreich also lived in Hollywood Hills.

Nurmi continued to shape the persona of Vampira as she prepared for her first show. She later admitted that her ex-husband came up with the name, though she rightly emphasized her own work in creating the character. She stitched together her monster out of the horrors of American family life, the limitations of which she knew so well.

One slow night, while checking hats and coats at a Sunset Strip club, she began thinking about the growing popularity of family serials, shows like *I Love Lucy* and *Leave It to Beaver* that imagined nearly perfect familial bliss. Writers and producers premised the comedy of these shows on the idea that nothing truly catastrophic could befall any of the characters, that the gentle humor took place in a safe and orderly world where no one, ultimately, got hurt. Nurmi saw this as something to be satirized. Maybe she could bring the macabre home.

Vampira emerged from Nurmi's sense of cultural rebellion rather than a simple desire to entertain. Her own experience as a failed housewife in a failing marriage encouraged her to mold a character that took the assumptions about married love, gender roles, and family life then on display in popular "soap operas" and turn them upside down. She described the increasingly staid cultural landscape of television as "warping people's minds" and hoped she could "take improbable people and make them do all these bourgeois things." In this way, she could ridicule the image of the submissive housewife and the sexy doxy all at once. Long before it became the motto of second-wave feminism, Nurmi made the personal political.

Always happy to build her legend of the macabre, Nurmi claimed that her first walk through the gates of KABC's East Hollywood studios to see Stromberg received a gothic approbation. The skies darkened and a dramatic clap of thunder seemingly announced her arrival, "an erotic young woman whose nature matched well the weather." Her black "coat-cape" swirled around her in the strong breeze. As she looked for Stromberg's office in Bungalow 13, scriptwriters, clerical workers, set designers, and physical plant workmen looked out of their office or away from their work. Vampira remembered one remarking, "Oh, that's Hunt's Vampire."

"Hunt's Vampire" informed him at their first meeting that she wanted to re-create New Yorker cartoonist Charles Addams's cockeyed vision of family life. She hoped to use domestic horrors to challenge American conformity, to follow Addams so closely that her character would take the name "Mrs. Addams." Stromberg immediately refused because of copyright issues and potential costs. He did give her the green light to borrow liberally from Addams's "female ghoul" character, the unnamed wife of the Addams family cartoons, later to be called "Morticia" in the 1964–1966 television series.

Nurmi's interest in Addams's work provides important clues for the message she wanted to give America. Addams had become a household name by 1954, a name that signified both an eccentric personal and aesthetic style. Novelist John O'Hara described him as having "millions of admiring, fascinated, sometimes mystified,

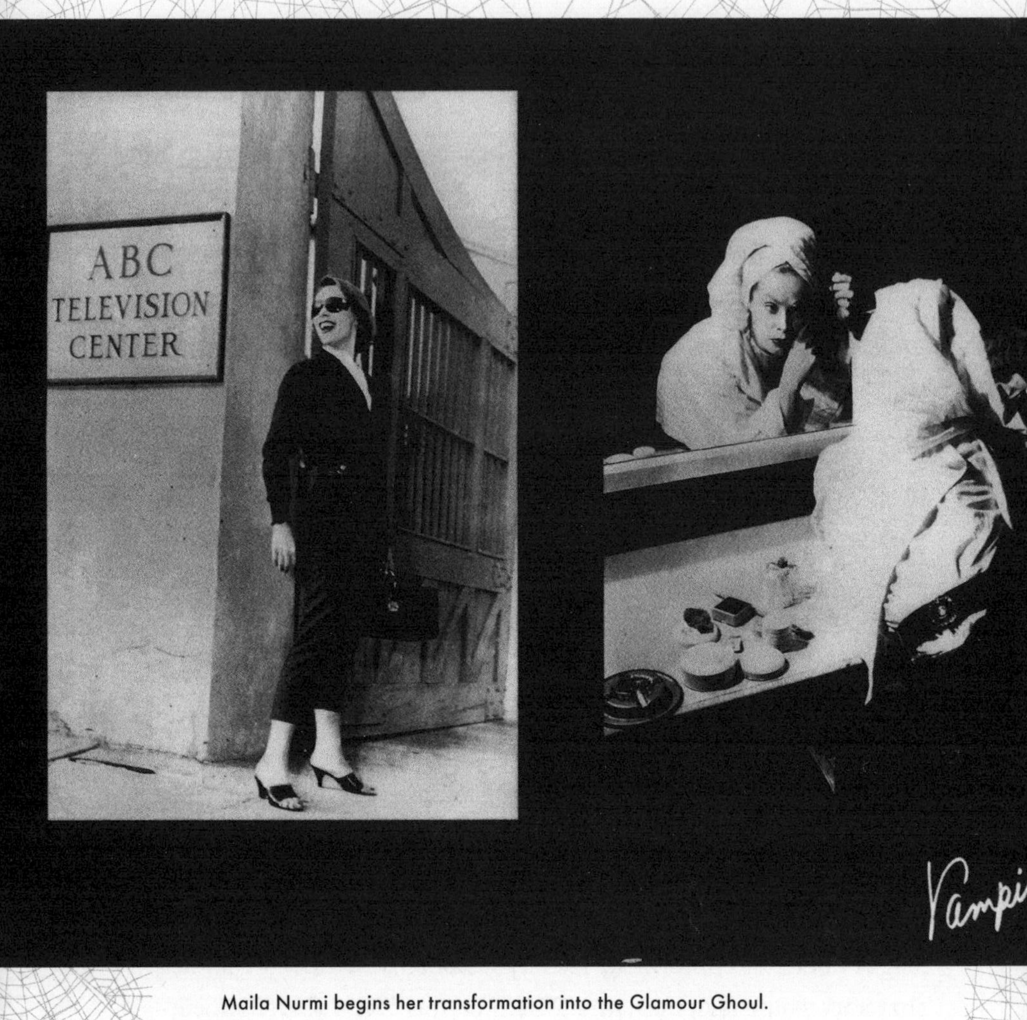

Maila Nurmi begins her transformation into the Glamour Ghoul.

often frightened" fans. His work for *The New Yorker*, mordant, bleak, macabre, and hilarious, had become a running commentary on the American dream. His vision constituted a twisted mirror image of *Father Knows Best* and *Leave It to Beaver* that spun horror and humor out of the postwar obsession with creating and maintaining the traditional family.

Addams dropped out of school in the 30s to take a job retouching homicide photographs for *True Detective* magazine. Beginning in 1936, he became a regular staff contributor to *The New Yorker* and by the 40s had created a body of work that perfectly captured the anxiety produced by the supposed desiderata of married life in the suburbs. Addams used his extraordinary humor to skewer middle-class American marriage and gender roles. Some of his most popular work focused on a family that simply became known as "the Homebodies."

Addams made "the Homebodies" a family of misfits, the parents taking pride in the destructive aptitude of the two children. In an age that worried over juvenile delinquency, these parents admired their kids' violent high jinks that included guillotined dolls and preparing poison arrows at the bathroom sink. Although the inspiration for *The Addams Family*, these early drawings gave none of the characters any names.

Addams also used his talent to burst the bubble of family bliss and the consumer revolution. In a 1950 collection of his cartoons called *Monster Rally*, a wife sits in a chair eating from a box of chocolates while her husband comes up behind her. "Now don't come back asking me to forgive you," she snips. What she doesn't see is that her husband holds a hatchet in one hand and a bag for her body parts in the other. In another of his most infamous images, Addams commented on the relationship between consumerism and the allegedly ideal American family. A "happy" housewife explains to police investigators how she killed her husband:

> I disconnected the booster from the Electro-Snuggie blanket and put him in the deep freeze. In the morning I defrosted him and ran him through the Handi Home Slicer and the Jiffy Burger grind and after that I fed him down the Dispose-All. Then I washed my clothes in the Bendix, tidied up the kitchen, and went to a movie.

Addams suggested that the façade of the 50s housewife and the perfect suburban existence hid wishes for savage violence, a way to tear down the walls of containment in an apocalypse of rage. Vampira's ability to satire what she called "the bourgeois world" had the same violent edge and displayed at least as much macabre energy.

Nurmi borrowed heavily from Addams's mordant and shocking humor. She owed a great deal of her inspiration to his mockery of bourgeois notions of family and respectability. She did not borrow from him the look of her "glamour ghoul." Though Nurmi obviously wrapped herself in the tattered gown of Addams's macabre matriarch from the Homebodies, the cartoonist had given his "female ghoul" almost no hint of sexuality. A character that scorched the air around her with sex and death in Vampira appeared in the Addams cartoons as willowy and shapeless.

The vernacular art form of late-night TV in the early 50s shaped Nurmi's vision as much as the influence of Addams. In 1954, television still represented a new entertainment frontier. A TV transmitter had actually been installed in the Empire State Building in the early 1930s, but the Great Depression and the Second World War significantly slowed the expansion of the new technology. In 1944, CBS and NBC put on something like a regular fall season, though the programming covered only a few hours a week and mainly involved the broadcast of live sports events, particularly boxing matches. In the late 40s, most televisions in existence could be found in bars rather than in private homes.

A relatively small audience in comparison with radio combined with no official censorship allowed for some incredibly interesting experiments and creative opportunities. In the late 40s, variety shows featuring Jack Benny, Fred Allan, Milton Berle, and Red Skelton had a steely edge, whip smart and eager to offend. Influenced by the vaudeville tradition, these efforts melded ethnic humor with slightly risqué material, all ring-mastered by what TV historian Lynn Spigel calls the "abrasive personalities of numerous variety clowns." The "abrasive" nature of this humor, even in the earliest years of television, caused some in the audience more than a little discomfort. A respondent to a survey conducted by the National Council of Catholic Women described Berle as "loud . . . vulgar . . . even insane."

This is not meant to imply that early television became a truly wild frontier. The cultural politics of sex and race policed certain boundaries without the aid of censorship codes and legislated enforcement. Early television still poked holes in those boundaries whenever possible. Lynn Spigel points out that, in a period when Jim Crow laws segregated public life, *The Milton Berle Show*'s integrated audiences constituted a limited, but very real, political statement. Spigel notes that, rather obviously, Berle's "habit of cross-dressing" (he once kissed singer Tony Martin while in drag) did nothing to endear him to traditionalists who made his show one of their prime targets when a wave of legislative censorship of the new medium began in 1951–52.

Censorship came with TV's increased popularity and the medium's growing reach. By 1951, television reached only about one-quarter of the nation's households. But by 1956, Americans purchased 20,000 televisions a day. By the end up the decade, 60 million American homes had rearranged their living rooms to accommodate the new family member. This rapid extension of the medium's reach meant that the early creative period of TV gave way to the demands of a mass audience and to the voracious nature of a fuller broadcasting schedule that demanded content.

Maila becomes Vampira, surrounded by her morbid props and her comedy about death.

Larger audiences mainstreamed the medium. Berle's ethnic humor, for example, irritated the sensibilities and prejudices of rural audiences. The television sitcom, having proven its popularity after the appearance of *I Love Lucy* in 1951, offered studios an easier format to maintain than the variety show. Their situational humor borrowed increasingly from the immediately recognizable and mostly banal conflicts of domestic life.

Moral censorship further undercut television's early burst of creativity. As early as 1951, Archbishop Richard Cushing warned of the "perverted sense of humor" that allegedly appeared daily on America's small screen. In this same year, the National Association of Radio and Television Broadcasters created an elaborate code of censorship that restricted displays of sexuality and sexual humor.

Vampira would still have her day, or at least her night. Early efforts at censorship ignored much of what happened after 10 PM. Late-night television seemed too marginal for most censors to care about even in this period. In these late-night slots, oddities continued to flourish, especially on the West Coast.

The show that Maila Nurmi put together ignored many of the precepts of the national code. It also had something of a folk art quality about it. *Dig Me Later, Vampira* (the somewhat unofficial title of the program) had a total crew of about seven, including a cameraman who had apprenticed under a photographer that had used old-fashioned flash powder and significant amounts of high, harsh Victorian lighting. The first two episodes featured no script. During the third week, an aspiring writer named Peter Robinson sent in a script through the mail. It proved funny enough for Stromberg to hire him to rough out each episode, though much of the banter remained impromptu.

Dig Me Later, Vampira first aired on April 30, 1954. A list of the first 14 episodes, through July 1954, shows that Vampira introduced late-night audiences to eclectic fare, ranging from crime thrillers like *The Charge Is Murder* to B-movie horror like *Revenge of the Zombies* to more classic monster fare like Bela Lugosi's *White Zombie.* Lugosi and aspiring director Ed Wood watched the latter episode in Lugosi's L.A. home, Lugosi remarking that he would like to work with Vampira at some point. They would appear together in June 1954 as guests on the enormously popular *Red Skelton Show* along with Lon Chaney Jr. and Peter Lorre.

"Once we had the opening show," Nurmi later recalled, it was "like a bomb went off." Nurmi's memory of the show's "immediate success" appears not to have been exaggerated. Forrest Ackerman, who a few years later created the enormously successful magazine *Famous Monsters of Filmland*, describes an audience that "couldn't wait for Saturday night." Moreover, Nurmi soon found herself attending everything from telethons to grocery store ribbon cuttings. She quickly became more than a local celebrity. A *Life* magazine shoot in the summer of 1954 came soon after a photographer had spotted her at a film opening she attended with Hollywood royalty Edward G. Robinson.

The *Life* shoot, done by an 18-year-old photographer named Dennis Stock, who himself seems to have been a Vampira fan, triggered both a larger audience for the show and the first hints that Vampira would have an enduring cultural meaning. Fan clubs began to form across the United States, clubs that captured some of her spirit of sexy subversion. Nurmi remembered a group of teenage girls who came up to her after a show to say they had formed one such club giggling about "the terrible things we have to do to get into the club."

People couldn't stop looking at the vampire she had created. Her form startled and obsessed. Nurmi surely exaggerated when she claimed that in her first year on television she became "the most photographed person, besides the president, in America." But she seems to have been right, however, about the surprising number of images photographers took of her and held on to. The bevy of images that have appeared of her online since her death support her belief. It's all the more surprising given how briefly she appeared on a local network that didn't even bother to save any of the footage of her show.

The fame and fascination that came with the *Life* photographs put her on George Gobel's hugely popular comedy variety show on NBC. Gobel, though mostly forgotten today, became one of the most well-known comedians of the 1950s. James Dean mimics him briefly in *Rebel Without a Cause.* All of America, not just L.A., would get to see something of *The Vampira Show.*

The skit she appears in with Gobel is still hilarious today. A mock-terrified Gobel enters Vampira's house and jumps as she screams, "Don't step on the cat's tail!" "I don't see a cat!" he yelps. "Well," she says in her best aristocratic camp voice, "I don't have a cat. Just a cat's tail."

R. H. Greene, the filmmaker who discovered this footage in 2001, notes that this appearance is not Maila Nurmi playing Vampira; it's Vampira playing a character simply called "Mrs. Jones." Here she plays up subversion of suburban housewives to the hilt, telling straight man Gobel at one point that she's "just plain Mrs. Jones . . . the next-door neighbor you might meet anywhere in any neighborhood in America."

It's a measure of how well-known she has become that Gobel doesn't even introduce her. In their skit, he quips to "Mrs. Jones" that she looks a little like Vampira. He doesn't have to explain to his appreciative live audience who this is. At the end of the night, Gobel asks her if that's really her waist or if she comes in two segments. "Two pieces, I'm kind of a do-it-yourself kit . . . bye," she says as she strolls off the stage.

Nurmi's one-year contract with KABC required her to make these public appearances to support the show. In fact, even before the debut of *Dig Me Later, Vampira*, the studio had a driver take Nurmi to busy Pershing Square "crowded with people walking to and from lunch." Nurmi, in full Vampira rig, would get out of the hearse-like rental car and leave flowers in the square as if she were "leaving flowers for someone long dead."

Her public performance art continued after the show premiered and, in fact, Vampira's June *Life* magazine spread included a number of images of Vampira riding around L.A. in the back of her car, an umbrella protecting her deathly pallor from the sun while onlookers gaped in consternation and delight.

In another promotional gig, she held a public ballot for her election as "night mayor of Hollywood." She took pictures with the L.A. City Council at the start of a "Safe Driving Economy Race" and showed more than a little leg to the camera as she pretended to pop a car tire with one of her long, elegantly macabre claws. "I was everywhere," Nurmi later remembered, "like horseshit at the turn of the century."

Death had never been so funny or so sexy. Maila Nurmi's public appearances conjoined with the macabre humor of the show to create a celebrity unlike anything that ever appeared in American popular culture. Previous bad girls of stage and screen had dripped eroticism but none had combined the sex appeal with mortality. As horror and Hollywood historian David J. Skal points out, her overt sensuality allied the bedroom and the grave. Her use of humor gelled perfectly with these themes. Vampira became an elaborate form of macabre slapstick, an intertwining of the decidedly lowbrow "come hither" humor of the Burly-Q with the sophisticated ironies of Charles Addams.

Sexier than the cheesecake pin-ups she had once posed for, she turned sex appeal into a graveyard ramble at midnight. Her show became an elaborate joke about death, gallows humor that traded on the darker ponderings of the Beats.

In one advertisement for the show, Vampira appears draped on top of a coffin. "VAMPIRA," the tagline reads, "YOUR PIN DOWN GIRL."

Death became her answer to media portrayals of the glazed-eyed 50s housewife. She created sight gags like a tombstone coffee

Performance art shaped the character of Vampira, transforming her into much more than late-night TV show. She became Maila's living, and undead, creation.

table, posed with skulls and engaged in a direct send-up of the optimistic façade of 50s life. "Don't you love it?" she purred when holding up one of her boiling concoctions from her witch's kitchen. "Well," she growled, "it HATES YOU!"

Vampira's homemaker shtick makes sense only at a moment when ads for toothpaste and cigarettes promised male viewers demure women, all who appeared to be pin-ups who had taken to housewifery. Nurmi never missed an opportunity to play with conceptions of gendered labor in the household, centering tales of terror around the allegedly sedate housewife in much the same way Charles Addams had done.

Vampira brutally slashed the idea of the household with images of chaos and murder. In the May 13, 1955, issue of *Housekeeping Monthly*, readers had been encouraged to "greet him [the husband] with a warm smile" since the home must be "a haven of rest and order." The final bit of advice reminded readers that a wife's job was, ultimately, "to please her husband."

But in Vampira's attic, there brewed a stew that involved pouring a skull-and-crossbones-inscribed bottle that read ACID. All the while her pet "spider" Rollo sits on her shoulder (an idea later borrowed for *The Addams Family* and the name of Wednesday's pet spider). "Tomb Sweet Tomb," rather than the popular postwar phrase "Home Sweet Home," became one of the show's prominent taglines.

Vampira mimicked the image of the housewife waiting for her husband to come home from work, martini in hand. Wearing an apron over her ragged graveyard gear, she mixed a drink called "the zombie cocktail" that promised any man walking through the door a quick death rather than a submissive welcome. Making it out of "one jigger formaldehyde, two jiggers vulture blood, garnish with a glass eye," she composed a chant for her and the camera crew that satirized a popular Pepsi jingle. No man in a gray flannel suit wanted to be greeted with this bit of boneyard doggerel:

Here's to zombies, the living dead
May you find one beneath your bed
They live on blood and you should too;
Hemoglobin is a drink for you!
Trickle, trickle, trickle . . . .

Of course, no man ever walked through the door. Lucille Ball and Dinah Shore have often received credit for being some of the first TV women who had shows built around them. *The Vampira Show* problematizes this idea. Both Ball and Shore subverted their ownership of their time slots by creating a kabuki theater of submissiveness, ritual reminders that the men in their lives held the real cultural power.

On *The Vampira Show*, Nurmi made it clear that she held the ultimate, indeed the supernatural, power. She saw herself as hypnotizing her audience, drawing them into her web. Her direct stare into the camera, often surrounded by a gothic void of dry ice, made her an undead Vargas girl, demanding rather than offering.

Vampira went beyond satirizing middle-class mores about marriage. She proffered an alternative sexuality, lurid and strange, that defied every convention of the era. Her plunging neckline alone inspired a rash of complaints to the FCC and various moral watchdog organizations. As the show was a live performance, she sometimes let out a line or too of truly bizarre Freudian patter. She once told *Fangoria* magazine that her first FCC complaint came because she made an impromptu joke about her sister being "lynched for raping a snake."

She exuded laughter and sexy play with a "Saturday night bath" skit that featured her sitting, apparently nude, in a steaming cauldron and brushing her back with the help of Rollo the spider. She shared the tub with a phallic electric eel and Igor, a scuba diver. The audience never saw the latter, only hearing "Vampi's responses to his below-decks behavior." While she chatted with her two bath-time companions "she sometimes softly sang *rub a dub dub three geeks in a tub.*"

In March of 1955, Maila Nurmi received an Emmy nomination for "Best Outstanding New Female Personality." Although she didn't win, it is extraordinary that what remained a local program received a nomination for an award won by Lucille Ball for the *I Love Lucy* show. She was famous enough to appear on the national comedy/game show *Place That Face*, in which she had to identify someone from her past (only a few moments of footage exist).

The living dead girl image Nurmi created had become recognizable enough to the American public that in January 1955 *The Red Skelton Show* parodied its former guest in a special episode featuring Peter Lorre. A parody of the popular sitcom *The Honeymooners* featured a Vampira look-alike, jealous of Lorre's character who "gets to drive a hearse" at work. The parody is flat and the unnamed actress who portrays Vampira captured none of her mannerisms—though enough of her look that even some Vampira fans today claim that it's Maila Nurmi herself. But it is just a spoof of Nurmi's spoof of the American housewife, the first indication that American popular culture would be borrowing, and stealing, her image for the next half century.

Her shocking and titillating image placed her on the verge of major stardom. Unfortunately, she wasn't getting rich off of her growing popularity. Nurmi took home about $58 a week for the work on her show and her intensive promotional obligations. Meanwhile, she was actually buying some of her own makeup and even paying for cab fare to and from the studio. But she believed in the stage she had found. Her popularity suggested she could renegotiate her contract in 1955. But she would never get that chance.

*****

By 1955, Nurmi had lived much of her life in an interstice that escaped the cultural claims of the 1950s. Her escape from her immigrant parents and their community signifies her early willingness to abandon expectation. Her fascination with the Beats and the adoption of elements of their style reveals her desire to militate against dominant cultural ideals. She had rebelled against the insistence that women bear children (Nurmi never would) and offer themselves, in almost every public representation, as instruments for household labor and male desire.

America's long fascination with the bad girl got a new, palpably exciting twist with Vampira. She was not the fallen woman; her character had not been ruined by bad company. She had no interest in vamping men and seducing them out of their money. Her character's bizarre humor laughed out loud at the narratives of female evil followed by female punishment so beloved in American entertainment.

Instead, she was a dead girl, long past the need for material gain. The dark sexual energy she exuded proved so intoxicating that it didn't need to tempt. It could simply overwhelm and destroy without ever desiring anything from you in return.

Nurmi fashioned characters that interlinked worlds of horror, fantasy, and sexual appeal. She brought together Dracula, Flash Gordon, and the pin-up. She sculptured her body into an object of desire that resisted objectification. Given the opportunity to construct a public persona, to say her own lines, and to create a character, she borrowed from comic books, subversive images of American domesticity, and the hidden world of bondage aficionados. You couldn't pin her up and you could never, despite the ad copy, truly pin her down

KABC couldn't contain her image, though it certainly tried. Attempting to explain her highly nontraditional marriage in traditional terms failed. The breakdown of an already unconventional marriage and rumors of affairs might be fine for starlets and stars, but a woman who dabbled in macabre and deviant imagery could little risk it. Vampira's scream demolished the boundaries of containment to such a degree that she had to be disappeared.

Part II

BONDAGE

"Taste the whip, now plead for me"
—The Velvet Underground, "Venus in Furs"

Now that she finally found her stage, she held an audience under her thrall. She didn't want to steal their hearts. She wanted their souls. In one of the final interviews Maila gave to *Rue Morgue Magazine* before her death in 2008, she described how she was "hypnotizing the camera" in all of the 56 episodes she put together for KABC. "I was hypnotizing them and they didn't know it," she insisted, "and I guess it was working."

Vampira violently seized the exuberant fantasy life of Los Angeles in 1954. Adolescents stayed up late, with or without their parents' permission, to see her cleavage, her humor, her strange style. Kids from a children's hospital wrote her to say they hoped to learn how to make her "zombie cocktail." Adults watched too. Saturday night Vampira parties and even fan clubs started to pop up. Women, some of them describing themselves as housewives, began calling in to KABC asking for tips about dressing themselves as Vampira. Perhaps their husbands wanted Vampira in the bedroom. Maybe these women wanted her there too. They knew what she was doing.

Vampira offered something that much of America didn't know it wanted, brought to it dark treasures that only a few had been willing to search after. She joined together several elements that had never mingled in exactly this way. In her, the erotic met the sinister as it had so often done. But usually it had been male monsters like Bela Lugosi who pulled off this sexy morbidity.

There had been powerful, deadly women before. They'd seldom had a sense of humor or a heady dose of cultural criticism to deliver. Bundling together sex and laughter, her combination of sex and death, the gothic and the campy, became irresistible.

There's no other way to explain her appeal. She was sexy, but L.A. had an embarrassment of riches when it came to sexy, then as now. During Vampira's run, KABC featured another late-night TV hostess, Voluptua, who conformed to the period's cheesecake ideal more closely than did Nurmi. A living pin-up, Voluptua flitted about her boudoir introducing romantic films and pretending that she was making herself up "for *YOU*." And of course, beyond late-night TV, L.A. had Monroe and Novak and literally hundreds of imitators sizzling the silver screen—or dreaming of how they someday would.

Nurmi brought something more. Women could be sexy in the 50s; indeed, the culture demanded it of them. But sexy didn't mean sexual. Objects couldn't desire, only receive desire. The scream that Nurmi used to open every show, followed by a low growl of release and satisfaction, signaled her freedom from these constraints. She told filmmaker R. H. Greene that her scream replicated "an orgasm . . . or at least that's what I thought and what I wanted to imply . . . in a ladylike manner."

She was ladylike, but like a lady of darkness. She always followed up her macabre scream with the words "screaming relaxes me so," a double entendre that even adolescent audiences, maybe especially adolescent audiences, could not misunderstand. "That turned them on I guess," an elderly Nurmi later reflected.

Her monster has been built to reflect the sexual outlawry that hid just beneath the surface of 40s and 50s America. She wore a cinch belt, a fashion accessory that did double duty in the early 50s. Used to restrict the waist to create an hourglass shape, it went with the poodle skirt. But it also had become an essential part of the uniform of bondage fetish, especially when coupled with the high heels and mesh hose Vampira favored. Nurmi herself described what she had created as "a Victorian, matronly dominatrix."

She had become a dark matron without children, an homage to de Sade by way of Betty Crocker. Her shtick demolished the shibboleths surrounding the 50s housewife, remaking the comfortable image into something deliciously terrifying. Vampira created a June Cleaver in black mesh hose and high heels, the night mother who joked that she loved children because "they're delicious." Her aesthetic placed normalcy on trial, demanded that it give an account of itself, and then laughed at it. She borrowed from older dark dreams, new leather-clad fantasies, updating all of America's nightmares for the space age, the Cold War, and the variety of sexual panics that seized postwar America.

It's not supposition or overheated imagination that Maila's monster was a bondage goddess. Nurmi always owned the fact that she borrowed the most subversive elements in her performance art "from the world of bondage." John Willie's underground magazine *Bizarre*, first published in 1946, molded the erotic elements of Vampira's style. When Nurmi suited up in "mesh hose, high heels, a black patent leather belt, a waist cincher, and long phallic nails," she offered a detailed homage to Willie's work.

Nurmi apparently came across *Bizarre* magazine sometime in the mid-40s and remembered that it "did bondage beautifully . . . a lot of phallic symbols . . . There were daggers, cinching, spiked shoes, spiked collars." Vampira included all of these fashion fetishes as she became an incarnation of sexual fetish.

She even acted out dominatrix fantasies on her show. Although the footage does not survive (only a promo KABC made for the show actually does), Nurmi once had her friend James Dean appear with her on television, in disguise. They created a tableau in which she played a schoolteacher, though a schoolteacher dressed as a lady of darkness and bondage goddess. He played an errant schoolboy. "He was a bad boy," Nurmi remembered. "He got his knuckles rapped."

Nurmi's willingness to link terror, desire, and a parody of bondage and restraint are not simply the products of her own creative genius, fertile as that genius might have been. The experiments she carried out with *The Vampira Show* are the whitecap of a particularly powerful wave building across the placidity of postwar America. Amid dreams of abundance and promises of serenity, a yearning underside of American culture clawed its way to the surface.

After a period of very real experimentation with sexual experience in the 20s and 30s, postwar America claimed to have gone into erotic lockdown. Joyce Johnson's memoir of teenage life in the 1950s describes sex as "the great forbidden castle" of the decade. In contrast to the roaring 20s and the Freud-fascinated 30s, the refusal to discuss sexuality in public, the repression of any hint of sexual "deviance," and constant warnings about premarital sex as the great destroyer of the 50s dream of conjugal bliss all became important elements of postwar cultural life.

And yet, the sex no one was having appeared everywhere. The pin-up had reached the height of its popularity in World War II, soon to be superseded by the even more elaborate bachelor fantasies of Hugh Hefner and his *Playboy* empire. Female Hollywood stars became known primarily for their verdant sensuality and bulging breasts. Teenage dating culture made the backseats of cars into erotic playrooms since, as Barbara Norfleet remembers of her 50s youth, "with the ultimate sex act forbidden, we did everything but." The baby boom itself reminds us that Ricky and Lucy didn't always sleep chastely in their single beds.

"Everything but" suggests a wide range of speculation. The infamous Kinsey reports went off like a bomb when they first appeared in 1948. Alfred Kinsey's research suggested that sex outside of marriage, same-sex experiences, and sexual experimentation was as American as baseball and apple pie. His conclusions became part of whispered kitchen conversation in every suburb in the country. Sex was referenced and cross-referenced in the themes of films even as film magazines started to focus on the private lives, usually the sex lives, of celebrities instead of the entertainment they produced.

Sex sold magazines, no big surprise there. Robert Harrison, whose pin-up empire began to collapse after 1950, found a way to make a second fortune with the publication of scandal rags. *Confidential*, simultaneously the most popular and the most hated of the genre, exercised enormous influence over an America eager to ferret out bedroom secrets.

Confidential began publication in December 1952 and unleashed a torrent of stories about Hollywood's "gay pajama parties," avuncular Bing Crosby as a domestic abuser, and heiresses having torrid affairs with their black chauffeurs. Everyone in America complained about how awful it all was and worried about what the magazine's popularity might mean for the future of morality. Meanwhile, the magazine broke all records for sales, exceeding 4 million newsstand issues.

Confidential peddled much more than celebrity gossip. Behind all the lurid stories of morally bankrupt Hollywood lurked an effort to police the boundaries of the American Cold War consensus. *Confidential*'s editor, Howard Rushmore, was a right-wing fanatic who once accused Roosevelt of being a secret Trotskyite whose real name was Rosenfeld. Rushmore's magazine became an especially lethal mouthpiece for the Lavender Scare. The July 1953 issue warned of the "Lavender Skeletons in TV's Closet." The magazine used innuendo to suggest the homosexuality of a number of screen stars (including Rock Hudson) and seldom missed a chance to draw connections between the "swishes" and "the commies."

Confidential, with its reactionary politics and lurid tone, incarnated all it feared. The impossible efforts to contain a growing sexual revolution in American life resulted in a very real sexual panic in straight, middle-class, patriarchal culture. Had women become more sexually aware while the boys were on the beaches of Normandy and Iwo Jima? Golly, it sure seemed like it. And what did manhood mean now that the war was over, especially for those whose bodies had been traumatized by combat? Sex is power, and America was about to begin a massive struggle for power, decades of conflict over whether or not the white men, guided by experts, would rule their streets, their lunch counters, their households, and their bedrooms.

Vampira tapped into the underground 50s. She's a reminder that the era belonged to the forces of subversion as much as to the forces of order and control. Mass culture, the state, and the needs of the middle class may have wanted a culture in bondage, but the whole structure had started to rot and collapse from within. Vampira's renegade persona drew its strength from this subversive impulse. Her popularity, and her downfall, owed itself to the anxieties it created.

*****

Midcentury America's cauldron of change proved especially terrifying for white men. Men returning home from World War II found girlfriends in trousers, many still working industrial jobs. They talked more loudly than the vets remembered and told stories about how "the other girls" had fought against sexual harassment on the shop floor and had girls' nights out after long days at the factory. Some of the men's fiancées, imagined as little more than children in 1941, filled the ears of their returning men with titillating and disturbing stories of "friends" that practiced some of the new sexual freedom that became a part of life in port cities and near military bases, casual liaisons produced by a period of national mobilization. Returning vets had a hard time shaking the fear that these "other girls" and "friends" were the very women they had come home to marry and impregnate.

Servicemen came home, GI Bill in hand, to find all kinds of cracks appearing in the edifice of order. Sometimes they created these cracks themselves. Black World War II vets, such as Medgar Evers of Mississippi, became some of the most important leaders in the freedom struggle. A newly active NAACP won numerous legal victories in the late 40s and early 50s. The 1944 Supreme Court decision *Smith v. Allwright* opened the door to the eventual expansion of voting rights in the Southern states. In 1954, *Brown v. Board of Education* laid the groundwork for the integration of American public schools, though it would be close to two decades before anything resembling implementation of the ruling began.

African American women had also become politically active in a variety of local and national struggles for justice, some of them continuing work they had been doing for decades. Rosa Parks did not suddenly decide to sit in the white section of a Birmingham bus in 1955. She had long worked as an activist in community and state struggles for justice. In Mississippi, segregated America's heart of darkness, Ella Baker had been struggling to bring Jim Crow to its knees since the 1930s, training everyone from Bob Moses to Stokely Carmichael to carry on the fight.

Most disturbing to white men who wanted to bind themselves, and everyone around them, into clear gender roles, was the emergence of a public gay and lesbian community despite massive and targeted persecution. The war itself had made gay and lesbian life more widely known and self-conscious. Wartime mobilization had, for the first time, introduced many gay soldiers, sailors, marines, and airmen from rural America to the fact that other men had same-sex desires, that they did not carry some sort of special burden or exhibit an idiosyncratic kink. Meanwhile, older gay communities, especially in port cities, flourished.

Lesbians, bisexuals, and transgendered people also received some benefit from access to new urban settings. The first known lesbian newspaper in the United States began distribution in 1947. In the decade after the Second World War, the Daughters of Bilitis, one of the first lesbian rights organizations, appeared. In 1950, the Mattachine Society, organized primarily by gay men but open to lesbians, began its work in Vampira's L.A.

A culture of hypermasculinity found itself terrified by even these relatively minor acts of assertion by sexual minorities. Manliness as a mass cultural obsession led, tragically, to an especially intensive suppression of America's emerging queer culture. Gay and lesbian life reached a nadir in the late 1940s. Quincy Troupe, a confidante of James Baldwin, said of the period that "you weren't just in the closet, you were in the basement. Under the basement floor."

Even New Deal liberals got in on the act, tying their sexual panic to their fears of communist subversion. Arthur Schlesinger Jr.'s enormously influential *The Vital Center* (1949) provides a sense of the form this backlash took. Schlesinger, a progressive who later served as an advisor to the Kennedy administration, was also a virulent anticommunist. In *The Vital Center*, Schlesinger compared the conspiratorial meeting of subversive communists "to the way in which homosexuals identified one another when looking for sex." Historian Robert J. Corber uses this passage to show that even New Deal liberals sought to slow, or to prevent, any efforts at social change in the interest of creating a Cold War consensus. The defense of Cold War America demanded a supercharged masculine identity.

The authoritative, overwhelmingly male voices that sought to craft this Cold War consensus saw gender confusion as a threat to national security. The home must be a factory for the replication of proper gender roles to prevent gender chaos that could, in turn, become a national security issue. At a 1950 conference on parenting held at the White House, über-expert Benjamin Spock described the job of parenting boys as making them aware of "their destiny to become manly." Parents should strive to ensure that properly gendered home activities, such as playing at "driving cars, shooting guns, going to work, and building skyscrapers" guided biologically male children into following "the pattern of their fathers." Meanwhile, the biologically female child followed proper patterns, indeed proved her devotion to her mother, by "turning more and more to doll care and other feminine fascinations."

American manliness needed women who fulfilled Dr. Spock's ideal of blithe creatures obsessed with "feminine fascinations." Women who performed this role became symbols of the abundance of American capitalism, ideological weapons in the Cold War. The American press consistently constructed Eastern bloc and Soviet women as "doughty" and contrasted them with the "glamour" of American women. Fashion historian Jane Pavitt notes that the 1959 American Exhibition in Moscow, the context for Nixon and Khrushchev's "kitchen debate," showcased American fashions and even featured a hairdressing exhibition called "Coiffures Americana."

Only real men could defeat the Soviet threat. The "destiny to become manly" had special meaning in a country freezing itself into a Cold War. The appearance of John Wayne's 1949 film *Sands of Iwo Jima* signaled a new kind of war movie, one that steered clear of gritty portrayals of combat and instead extolled bravery, sacrifice, and masculinity as necessary precursors to an inevitable American victory.

The celebration of manly men with a mission also appeared in the popularity of the 50s western, the genre Nurmi so hated that she'd prefer to sit in the lobby and watch the concession stand. Nevertheless, cowboy schlock, both on television and the big screen, saturated the popular imagination. Cowboy heroes patrolled, and contained, the savagery of the frontier.

The men at the center of these narratives are honed down to their sharp edges, forged as warriors by the gunplay of the West much like male fans of cowboy tales believed they had been transformed by World War II and made ready for new global struggle. Meanwhile, the United States government created an arsenal of terrifying weapons in preparation for that struggle, the Pentagon's budget exploding from $10.9 billion in 1948 to $49.6 billion in 1953.

War-readiness meant that no fifth column of sexual kink could be allowed. "Deviant sexuality" threatened to unleash desires that could weaken America. Psychiatric texts from the era, such as James Melvin Reinhardt's 1957 *Sex Perversions and Sex Crimes,* viewed alternative sexual practices as a danger to capitalism and democracy. Reinhardt imagined sadomasochism (S&M) only in terms of violence, indeed violence in its most extreme forms. Creating the broadest possible definition of bondage, discipline, and sadomasochism (BDSM) practices, Reinhardt describes S&M as everything from "normal coitus achieved with the aid of some punching, slapping, or biting" to "a fiendish lust craving . . . the murder and mutilation of the victim."

S&M, according to Reinhardt, encouraged violence between bedroom partners. It also had political implications. Indeed, the sexual tendencies of the sadomasochist threatened to destroy the bountiful world of postwar America with a bang and not a whimper. Reinhardt suggested that S&M, and indeed alternative sexual practices of all varieties, found their perfect expression in pyromania and the attendant destruction of property. Deviant practices, in his view, embodied an unqualified yearning for sexual release, a violent outlet for extreme existential tensions. He defined pyromania in the same terms and suggested a firm psychological link between "unnatural" varieties of sexual release and the desire to start fires, a link between buggery and the firebug.

Sex did not have to come in the form of leather and blindfolds to suggest social danger. Psychiatry and sociology frequently suggested the idea that uncontained sexuality, even "straight" practices, threatened America's order and stability. Winston Ehrmann, in a 1959 study called *Premarital Dating Behavior*, claimed that adolescent girls slept with men for the thrill of rebellion rather than out of desire. Ehrmann here managed to both deny the reality of female sexual desire and warn his readers of the dangers of delinquent young women. In the same year, a writer for *The Atlantic Monthly* suggested that women who chose nonmonogamous sex over "going steady" did so with full knowledge that they challenged normative ideals. Don't worry, these texts claimed, that women might have the same compelling sexual desires as men . . . they just don't.

Psychiatrists of the era who, like Reinhardt, wrote about the dangers of sexual perversion revealed the confusion and anxiety of the times. They insisted that America had become sex-obsessed, that "deviants" consumed by unbridled lusts roamed the streets of America. At the same time, they shook their heads over a supposed crisis of manliness, the fear that the greatest generation had been too traumatized by the war to fuck like men. Thus, while Reinhardt claimed that excessive and "unnatural desire" might literally set the world on fire, psychologist Iago Galdston worried about an epidemic of "*ejaculation praecox* and . . . the precipitous and periodic loss of virility."

A war to control the culture had begun. Vampira once described her relationship to James Dean as one in which they recognized each other as "the same kind of soldiers." She always believed that they marched together at the vanguard of cultural change, a struggle to be free from containment culture, to challenge all the efforts by elites and experts and Mom and Dad to limit sexuality, constrain identity, and place a new generation in the bonds of respectability. The struggle for power in America would be a struggle against bondage that used literal bondage to camp it up. Laughter and leather, playing around with the imagery of bondage, suddenly became popular and public.

Magazines that focused on BDSM flourished in the years following the Second World War. The secretive (and in most places unlawful) distribution of these magazines ensured that they would have a low circulation. Nurmi's inspiration, *Bizarre*, had a circulation of only 5,000 at its height. But the magazine's imagery and interests influenced sexual imagery far beyond its underground constituency.

The girl next door had a whip and was not afraid to use it. *Bizarre* not only inspired Vampira, but also helped to create Bettie Page, one of the most subversive icons of the 1950s. The New York–based brother-and-sister photography team of Paula and Irving Klaw made Page famous, her ironic BDSM posing and winking at the camera combining the fantasy of the vamp, the bad girl, and the virtuous cutie next door all at once. Page even caught the eye of Hugh Hefner, who featured her in a centerfold for *Playboy.* Her appearance in the gigantically popular magazine broke Hefner's stated rule of using only "newcomers" and, perhaps more importantly, of never showing what he called the "mysterious, difficult woman, femme fatales." But suddenly BDSM had conquered the bourgeois wet dreams of the *Playboy* set.

The growing popularity of bondage also influenced the cheesecake mags that had previously focused on fairly conventional sexual practices. Page even turned up in Harrison publications such as *Eyeful* and *Titter* in their struggle to compete with the *Playboy* juggernaut. These photographic narratives included female-on-female wrestling and scenes of domination. In many of them, Page smiles and giggles and camps up her supposed terror at being bound and gagged. She openly mocks the camera and, by extension, the men who held the magazine in sweaty hands. She perfectly illustrated historian of sexuality Anne McClintock's claim that S&M shows up social power as nothing more than a performance, an act, theater, a kabuki play. This subverts the social order by making fun of it, showing that society's norms are "sanctioned neither by fate or by social convention and tradition, and thus as open to historical change."

Both magazines, it should be noted, continued to represent women caught in compromised positions, feeding male fantasy about the alleged link between female sexuality and ineffectuality. A *Titter* cover from this era shows a woman catching a fishing line in her bikini bottom while another cover features a barely dressed blonde falling off her bicycle, her face clouded with pouty rage. But Page's popularity reveals an incitement to new kinds of desires, as do the advertisements in *Flirt* for "Fighting Girl Photos" taken by Irving Klaw, as well as "New Fighting Girl Movies!" by the same.

The Harrison magazines' forays into BDSM are pallid imitations of what *Bizarre* gave its male and female readership. John "Willie" Coutts, generally known simply as John Willie, photographed and illustrated women in positions of sexual dominance, mixing and matching imagery from the cheesecake tradition with the female dominatrix.

Although Nurmi never appeared in a credited photograph for *Bizarre*, it's possible that she may have worked as a model for one of Willie's drawings. Willie made use of a number of unnamed models, usually chosen from among women who showed some interest in his work and thus an openness to alternative sexual practices. Nurmi certainly had a profound fascination for *Bizarre,* mentioning it in every single interview in which she answered a question about her inspiration for creating Vampira.

She probably loved *Bizarre* for its revolutionary aspects as well as its sinister and appealing aesthetic. How we imagine sex in different eras tells us about social change rather than simply changes in "moral values" or "standards." *Bizarre* frequently referenced the changing role of women and changing representation of gender outside the world of BDSM. A Willie sketch from *Volume I* (1954) shows women working in factories, drinking beer and smoking cigars, wearing a man's fedora, trousers, and, the punch line, bare-breasted in men's bathing trunks.

Bizarre reimagined the dynamics of power, a change the world of the 50s found both threatening and titillating. Cheesecake pin-ups focused on women losing control of their appearance, some accidental wardrobe malfunction that revealed cleavage and ass. Male photographers caught cheesecake models off guard, caught them in the act. The female dominatrix gave women the power and pleasure and felt as good as an adolescent's first orgasm to a culture pretty well contained by its terrors, its uncrossable boundaries, and, worst of all, what William Burroughs once called "the inner policeman" that comes to inhabit the psychology of a repressed world.

Bizarre often reveled in the preparations of fetish, the intensive efforts of women to re-create themselves. At least part of the sexual excitement generated by the images had to do with a new kind of display of ingenuity, prowess, and even the toughness it required to endure some pain in pursuit of pleasure. Even the corset, often viewed as an instrument of Victorian repression reborn in the Dior style, became a tool for the women of BDSM to restructure their bodies in ways that cut against the grain of most 40s and 50s representations of female sexuality. In one 1954 image from *Bizarre*, a woman corsets her waist to ghastly proportions with the help of a female domestic worker. "You must make it meet," she pleads with the help, who raises a knee into her lady's buttocks to pull the corset tight, revealing that she herself wears mesh stockings.

The bondage dungeon offered a new kind of imaginative space, sex play with no patriarch present to supervise. The fantasy world of bondage involved the creation of characters that could live out the extremities of human desire, allowing both participants and viewers some distance from the implied violence of the fantasies. *Bizarre* always traded in fantastic scenarios and models always took false names to emphasize their creation of a character.

Images of men are essentially absent from *Bizarre*, and when they do appear, they are little more than abstracted body parts placed in submission to female dominance and desire. In one example, a male hand with fingers twisted in pain lays on a wooden board. A high heel pins it down at the wrist, preventing the viewer from even seeing if the hand comes with a body attached. The caption simply reads "Enough of this!"

Women do appear as submissives in *Bizarre*, but only to other women. Bettie Page provides a perfect example of how they pose their submissiveness with a combination of comedy and erotic delight. She and other BDSM models put on a travesty of patriarchal power. Stone-cold sexy images that suggested female power outside the bedroom/dungeon expanded the basically political message. In one set piece that combined Willie illustrations with photographs, a woman in the Dior cut of the 40s with a longish skirt works on a car. As she competently bends over the engine (and in one illustration curses just as a male mechanic might as she crawls underneath with a wrench), we get a full view of her mesh stockings and stiletto heels.

The collaborative nature of putting together *Bizarre* magazine reveals even more of the subversive potential of BDSM. Willie would leave stacks of his magazine in both bars and drugstores in Greenwich Village, take a seat, and wait for women to come in who showed an interest in the photographs. Willie approached them about becoming a subject. Many of the pictures that appear in the magazine are of Willie's wife, Holly Baram, herself a bondage enthusiast. At least some of the models came from the ranks of the 50s bohemia that had made the Village their home, eager to explore the sexual adventurousness that Burroughs, Ginsberg, and Kerouac preached.

Nurmi once said that she knew that daytime soaps had become one of the most popular kinds of shows on daytime TV. But they featured "wholesome people" and, she once told R. H. Greene, "I don't do wholesome people." Instead, she wanted "to satirize them." Her adoption of the complicated shadow play of the BDSM magazine shows her own whip-smart awareness of the demands being placed on women by the culture of the 1950s. She would militate against the boundaries of sexual control, the efforts to retrofit the feminine form for life as daytime housewife, nighttime playmate, and full-time mother.

Vampira became something of the antihousewife, and not simply through the adoption of bondage wear. A performance artist with a message, Nurmi crafted a character meant to deliver a body blow to American notions of normal. She would show some of the same ingenuity implied in the bondage wear of the *Bizarre* models. "I made up at home," Nurmi remembered of her preparations for the first installments of *The Vampira Show.* Creating her "girl ghoul" took about four hours. Soon she learned a few shortcuts and, based on photographic evidence, she began getting ready at KABC. After a certain point, she could arrive at around 10:30 and be ready to go on at midnight.

"I squeezed and stretched and dieted," she later remembered, her efforts to become the girl ghoul an imitation as well as a parody of what many women believed they had to do to please husbands and steadies. Hours of work on makeup, hair, dress, and nails accounted for only part of the preparations. She fasted herself down to the bone, doing what she called "some body sculpting."

Forrest Ackerman, a close friend of Nurmi's at the time, claimed that she sometimes "fasted for three days" and made herself so slim that a pair of enthusiastic and doubtlessly admiring male hands could "encompass her entire waist." Rumors circulated that she either had a rib removed or purposefully broke her own ribs to achieve her impossible shape, a charge she later denied.

She did, however, engage in some rather dangerous behavior that may have affected her health in later years. Beginning her fasts on Friday, she went to the steam baths to soak on Friday night. Still unable to achieve the ghastly look that she wanted to project, she explored other methods of murdering her flesh. Learning that papaya powder was the ingredient in meat tenderizer that absorbed fat, she slathered her stomach with it and wrapped an inner tube around her waist before she went to bed. Her stomach, she claimed, was "digesting itself," as if she had become a literal horror host to some inner grotesquerie, her body eating itself from the inside so that Maila Nurmi could shapeshift into Vampira at midnight.

Like so many women in the 1950s, Nurmi rearranged her body to match an ideal. But it was an ideal she had made, a monster from her inner laboratory. The creature she crafted owed something to the glamour dolls imagined by Dior and other fashion tsars, but only in the way a funhouse image resembles its subject. Her body became a living critique of the conventions of feminine beauty in postwar America. This, perhaps more than any other element of her presentation, simultaneously explains her appeal, her shock value, and her eventual failure as a 50s icon.

*****

Nurmi's outrageous body sculpting into Vampira stood at odds with what had become an American middle-class love affair with the normal. The word "normal" had been around a while, first coming into common use in the 19th century. But, as cultural theorist Anna G. Creadick points out, the term "normalcy" first became a regular entry in the *Reader's Guide to Periodical Literature* in 1945. By the mid-50s, Creadick argues, Americans anxiously talked about what normal might mean and, in the context of family structures, sexuality, and gender roles, wanted to make sure that, whatever normal was, they were it.

"Norma" and "Norman," two model sculptures acquired by the Cleveland Health Museum in the summer of 1945, best illustrates this obsession. Dr. Robert L. Dickinson designed the plaster models as paradigms of the ideal male and female body, their measurements, morphology, and facial structure drawn from what Dickinson described as the results of "a lifetime of research." This "lifetime of research" focused entirely on young, middle-class white bodies, what one of Dickinson's fellow researchers described as "special studies of old American stock." He took samplings from the Chicago World's Fair and "college men and women from various parts of the country."

Norman and Norma might seem like oddities from the racist origins of American anthropological study. Clearly this racialized conception of normalcy assumed the typicality of white, northern European bodies, indeed suggested that these bodies represented "true Americanness."

But what's especially interesting is how Cleveland, Ohio, responded to its museum's new inhabitants. *The Cleveland Plain Dealer* created a contest for young Ohio women, a search for "Norma." The winner would be a young woman who most closely approximated the normal, essentially the most normal girl in Ohio. She would receive $100 in war bonds.

The 1950s American body had become a melting pot that absorbed difference. To be truly normal meant to be truly American. A few months before Vampira made her first appearance on TV, the syndicated CBS program *Adventure* rather grossly illustrated the links between normalcy and nationalism. Featuring "Norma" as a special guest, the show purported to give a history of American women's fashions, ending with this message that the "exaggerations" of the Gibson girl and "the flapper" should be disdained for the conventionality of Norma. The show ended with an interplay of animated silhouettes in which the viewer sees outlines of immigrant women hobbling onto what appears to be Ellis Island disappearing into the larger silhouette of Norma, transformed into the true American shape. The host concluded the show by revealing Norma's measurements (33-29-39) and encouraging women at home to "get a measuring tape" and see how closely they resembled the American ideal.

Vampira's restructured body challenged Norma and the true American shape. Her gruesome ministrations shrunk her waist more than 10 inches smaller than Norma's. R. H. Greene points out that the radical restriction of her waistline suggested that she had no womb, that she could not become the bearer of children that the generous hips of most cheesecake models implied they could become. If American culture expected her to become a housewife, she would be the "failed housewife." If American culture wanted her to breed children, she would make gruesome jokes about eating them. If it wanted her to be sexy, she would be sexually voracious instead. And if it wanted normal, she would give it great heaping spoonfuls of weird.

Nurmi's ability to "body sculpt" a form that offered, and then denied, the pleasures of her body to the male viewer represents one of her most important contributions to the art of cultural subversion. The impossible shape she created with the cinch belt and her rigorous regimen travestied those parts of the female body most closely connected with reproduction. The 50s fascination with fertility and abundance, images with the clean sheen of cheesecake, met their demise in the cold figure of death she created.

Some of her critics called her a cartoon, and in some sense, that's exactly what she became. The joke, however, was not on her. America wanted a conversation about normalcy, the limits of sexual experience, and gender identity. Vampira's evocation of monsters on late-night TV rudely interrupted the conversation, made fun of it. The dank and the dark, rather than simply being threatening, became a source of both humor and satire. The constraints of normalcy fell victim to gothic excess, and it was the funniest thing anyone had seen in a long time.

Nurmi's emergence out of dry ice, her peculiar body shape

Vampira celebrates Halloween, 1955.

breaking the darkness and preparing viewers to hear her scream, ran contrariwise to almost every representation of women then current in mainstream American culture. *The Saturday Evening Post*, for example, ran an ad in the spring of 1948 that juxtaposed the new Magic Chef oven with a svelte blonde, glamorous in a black house dress and dripping with jewelry as she talks on the phone and gestures toward her gleaming white fetish. "It's Brand New!" shouts the masthead over an arrangement that encloses the housewife and the appliance. It's "the range you dreamed about . . . automatic, more beautiful, easier to cook on, easier to clean." Like the woman who shares commercial space with it, the Magic Chef services and aesthetically pleases; it's a source of pride and production.

While Nurmi showed how a woman could reshape her body according to her own desires, technology increasingly provided metaphors for women's bodies in both private and public imagination. Women became identified as appliances directed toward the production of children and servicing the needs of home, husband, and country. Advertising for home appliances insistently connected the display of new stoves and refrigerators with the display of the young, middle-class, white, and married female body.

The cultural leaders of Maila Nurmi's world wanted to see women laboring in the home and fucking and not much else. Lovell Thompson, an influential publisher at Houghton Mifflin, suggested that women in the 1950s had evolved beyond the vamps of the 20s into something healthier, more prosperous, and literally more productive. The 50s woman was no longer "the honeypot of the Oldsmobile." She had become, in the new age of prosperity, "strapping and strapless . . . the girl in the station wagon with safety belts" that was "built for a stern purpose." Women were like new cars, their bodies part of the built environment of a new America, constructed for the "stern purpose" of motherhood in an era full of both delights and dangers.

When not comparing women to a car or an appliance, men wrote about the 1950s female body as a kind of architecture. This idea germinated in the world of high fashion and the creation of what cultural critic Roland Barthes referred to as the "fashion system"—a new, complex postwar relationship between designers, magazines, department stores, and the consumer public that emerged after World War II. Christian Dior's designs, which created the "New Look" revolution of the 1940s, emphasized elegance and tradition in constraining the female body. Indeed, as fashion historian Nicholas de Monchaux points out, the "New Look" actually "reconfigured the feminine silhouette" by using numerous heavy layers of foundation garments and clothing. Sometimes employing 60 pounds of cloth for a single dress, the "New Look" understood the female body as a combination monument and skyscraper.

In his 1957 autobiography, Dior described his style as informed by a "love of architecture and clear cut design." Employing structural metaphors to explain his style whenever the opportunity presented itself, Dior emphasized the importance of layers of underwear to shape the female form. "Without foundations," he quipped, "there can be no fashion." Binding and layering the female body created a structure that, according to Dior, "emphasized the width of the hips and gave the bust its true prominence."

The bust certainly took over postwar America. Indeed, breasts seemed to be taking over the world. The brassiere, or bra, became (along with the corset) the most discussed item of women's clothing in the 1940s and 50s. The new style manufactured sexual desire centered on the size, proportion, fertility, and abundance. Dior was far from alone in believing that the female breast needed to be given "its true prominence." The so-called sweater girl bra became extremely popular, with its goal, according to fashion writer Pearl Binder, of creating "two spiked cones . . . related only to the female form in African sculpture."

Boobs became as popular in postwar America as westerns and

hood ornaments. European observers of American popular culture noted the country's sexual fascination with the size of breasts and compared it to their own culture's relative lack of interest in mammary proportions. American film stars from Lauren Bacall to Marilyn Monroe offered dark canyons of cleavage or impossibly conical hillocks pointing outward from under angora sweaters. Americans purchased 4.5 million "falsies" in 1948 alone to replicate this aesthetic of overabundance. Positioning and structuring the breasts had become an American obsession. The bra became central signifier of sexual appeal and an object of both fascination and humor. In Alfred Hitchcock's *Vertigo,* Scottie's friend Midge makes a joke about a new brassiere that provides "revolutionary uplift." Working "on the principle of the cantilevered bridge" it had been designed "by an aeronautical engineer."

Architectural metaphors didn't remain metaphors. Young women found themselves barraged with the idea that they had to transform their bodies into palaces of male pleasure. Caryl Rivers, in her memoir of the 50s, describes how she attempted the look of the women of film and magazines. Rivers writes that "I pumiced and brushed and I sprayed and I bleached and I rinsed and I polished and I trimmed and I squirted and I slathered and I rubbed." Mixing and matching metaphors of industrial production and erotic allure, Rivers's description perfectly captures the social purposing of the feminine form.

Vampira participated in this sense of the woman's body as construction site. She was, after all, building a monster. Rivers's description of what she did to herself for her Saturday night dates doesn't sound terribly different from how Nurmi prepared herself for her Saturday nights with Los Angeles.

But like the cinch belt that belonged both to the world of straights and to the world of *Bizarre*, Nurmi put her sculpted body to a more subversive purpose than pleasing men. Her explosive sexuality prevented her from becoming simply an object of desire.

Her body's impossible proportions challenged any easy equation between her sensuality and the conventional objects of heterosexual desire. But she played with those desires nevertheless, tweaking them to suit her purposes.

Vampira turned her body into a running joke about death. She seized control of it, made sure her admirers knew it belonged to her. Her breasts entranced viewers but also directed their eyes downward into that cinched waist that suggested death rather than life, a skeleton that also had cleavage to compete with Monroe. It's not going too far to suggest that America's postwar breast fever had something to do with its baby fever, making a sexual fetish out of a symbol of motherhood. Vampira, the dark mother, draped her breasts in black and took America to a funeral rather than the nursery.

She reimagined body horror and made it funny. The frights and fears of the Cold War combined with some of the forgotten legacies of World War II made jokes about the body's destruction delicious for some and horrifying for others. Body horror appeared everywhere in the 50s and was supposed to be no laughing matter. Wounded soldiers, many of them horribly mutilated by modern warfare, had been a part of the iconography of the Second World War.

World War II produced a lot of mangled bodies. The War Department sought to carefully control these images and transform them into symbols of Allied triumph. Cultural historian David Serlin describes these representations of the wounded veteran as "unduly cheery narratives of tolerance in the face of adversity" that linked patriotism and the willingness to endure extreme physical trauma. Such images became integral to creating a new narrative of struggle for the Cold War era.

The greatest generation already thought they were the greatest back in Vampira's time. American culture celebrated the GIs coming home. But more than half a million did not come back, and hundreds of thousands returned with catastrophic mental and physical wounds.

The American public dealt with this mountain of human suffering by making individual cases of wounded veterans into cause célèbre. Quadruple amputee Jimmy Wilson provides one example. A survivor of a plane crash in the Pacific, Wilson became the beneficiary of a campaign that raised more than $100,000 on his behalf. He, like other wounded vets and their symbolic images, came to represent perseverance and masculinity.

But the culture could not escape the unavoidable fact, seen on the streets and occasionally portrayed in film, of tens of thousands of disabled bodies, bodies that did not conform to the heroic pattern of manhood. In a period that celebrated hyperheterosexuality, the "wounded warrior" became an uncomfortable specter, the corpse at the reproductive banquet. A physical therapy manual from 1957 wondered aloud whether or not an amputee would "be acceptable to his wife or sweetheart? Can he live a normal sex life? . . . Must he give up having fun?" According to Serlin, postwar culture dealt with these questions, in part, by placing the wounded veteran in settings that stressed patriotic pride, emphasizing the "warrior" aspect of their identities over their status as wounded.

The effort to restore the disabled manhood of veterans found expression in both popular culture and in more official propaganda efforts. Bix the war amputee became a regular fixture in the newspaper comic strip *Gasoline Alley.* Bix, unlike many of the walking wounded, finds employment. He's even described as being able to go dancing on his prosthetic legs because "modern medicine and surgery have been doing wonders for our war causalities." In fact, all of the strips' narratives about Bix are essentially stories about his ability to prove his normalcy, particularly his masculine normalcy, to the skeptical. "He wants to show he's a good as anybody," comments one character, "that makes him better."

Politicized versions of disabled 50s manhood achieving potency became stock political rhetoric. In 1944, amputee Thomas Sorento posed in front of the Lincoln Memorial for a War

Department recruitment ad, one hand raised in a salute, the other sleeve dangling empty with the subscript "Freedom shall not perish from the earth." Infamous Redhunter Joseph McCarthy used the story of veteran amputee Bob Smith to lash out at Secretary of State Dean Acheson (whom McCarthy believed to be "Red"). McCarthy told the Senate floor that as soon as Smith received "his artificial limbs" he should go to Acheson and "the rest of the lace handkerchief crowd" and tell them to go work for their "real masters in the Soviet Union." McCarthy's absurd outburst managed to take the shadow of impotence away from the gored bodies of vets and instead suggest the effeminacy and traitorous nature of moderate liberalism.

The women of the 50s were not only being urged to accept this torn and dismembered image of manhood meets nationalism; they were being ordered to fuck it and to fuck it hard. Posing wounded vets with flags and monuments juxtaposed their maimed bodies with the idea of sacrifice to the cause, eliminating questions about the meaning of their act.

Photographs presented the wounded as guardians of the icons of American patriotism. They insisted that the viewer accept their manhood and see them as models for the kinds of sacrifices needed to win the Cold War. Perhaps even more significantly, they promised a sexual vitality that American women were told they must not ignore. Bix could compete on the dance floor with the best of them, his experience as a warrior carried over into his postwar identity as a disabled vet so that he became 'better" than other men.

Postwar manliness brooked no challenges. Or so it seemed. At least part of Vampira's subversive appeal came from her ability to upend cultural expectations, her refusal to staunch the wounds of postwar manhood. She opened up fresh ones instead by raunchily rejecting mass culture's attempt to turn women's bodies into baby factories and link them to domesticity. Maila Nurmi's "glamour ghoul" represented a literal graveyard for the most common image of women in the 1950s, the visual narrative of woman as "glamour doll," represented as a technology for the production of children.

Vampira told an extended joke about death and sex that reminded America of these anxieties, made fun of them, and raised possibilities that few wanted to ponder and even fewer wanted to try out. What if, Vampira asked, sexual pleasure could occur in absolute freedom, making bondage into a game played by willing partners rather than a cultural ideal? What if the corpse and the shattered body didn't need to go into hiding? What if it could be a sex symbol free of the nationalistic and patriarchal baggage?

Vampira's body art and bondage aesthetic raised all these questions. But something more swam in the zombie cocktail, excited viewers when she lit her cigarette with her skull-and-bones candelabra or when she minced her way down the aisle of dry ice and bragged about her orgasm. She had a new kind of style, one that seemed both unknown and instantly recognizable. In truth, viewers saw something new based on something very old. Vampira the "matronly dominatrix" embodied a new version of the gothic villain and a new style of gothic that eventually became American goth.

*****

As fresh and hot as Vampira seemed, the roots of her character went even deeper than the influences she claimed, back into the world of gothic literature. Gothic has traditionally been understood as a literary form that emerged in the late 18th century, romanticism's twisted sister. Gothic writers imagined ruined castles, innocent female victims, and male villains who mixed savagery and sexual appeal.

Horace Walpole's 1764 *The Castle of Otranto* usually gets the nod as the first gothic novel. Ann Radcliffe's *Mysteries of Udolpho* appears next in the canon. Simply noting such well-known works hides the fact that the 18th and early 19th century produced literally hundreds of highly formulaic novels that followed the genre's conventions. Wicked aristocrats hid secrets in crumbling castles. Young female innocents found themselves trapped in these terrible places. Although these innocents generally escaped, writers like Anthony "Monk" Lewis gave readers the thrill of seeing innocence stripped and degraded, naïveté discovering the macabre in hidden passageways of terrible places and terrible selves.

It's not really surprising that the age of revolution, inaugurated by the British monarchy getting a bloody nose in North America and the French guillotining centuries of royal rule, produced a literature about evil concentrated in the aristocratic class. The Marquis de Sade once suggested that the age of revolution had turned everything upside down and that only a celebration of the bizarre and disturbing could match the violence of daily life.

What is surprising is how pliable the genre proved. It lived long after the age of waistcoasts, muskets, tricornered hats, and crumbling ruins. For more than two centuries, gothic has exhibited a dark energy that allows it to leap energetically out of the crypt at least once a generation. The gothic strains of 18th-century literature made Lord Byron, Percy Shelley, and Mary Godwin Shelley want to tell ghost stories on their Swiss summer holiday in 1816. Mary Shelley's *Frankenstein* resulted from these romantics trying to spook one another, and the tale of dismembered corpses come to life began its haunting of Western culture. In the 1890s, the lengthening shadows cast by the gothic ruin became Castle Dracula in the imagination of Bram Stoker. Both creatures found renewed life in the oddities and excesses of the 20th-century horror movie, thrilling audiences with terrors.

A hundred years later, 1990s America would still be telling gothic tales . . . and not just in its horror films. The popularity of daytime talk shows grew from the need to hear stories of rapacious evils, ancestral ghosts in the guise of abusive parents, or Poe-esque tales of incest and madness. Always some shadowy evil loomed over the innocent, the heroic victims barely making it out alive.

These themes remained central in American culture into the 21st century, incarnated in the exploration of family secrets in our fascination with therapy. The violent and grotesque side of the gothic has exploded into the open in the films of the Coen brothers and Quentin Tarantino. Urban legends recycle gothic excess. Lurid tales of teenage rainbow parties and bath-salt cannibals bloom like midnight flowers out of our cultural compost.

The 1950s seem like a time period when the gothic could find little purchase. A time in which the "greatest generation" had "won" the Second World War, moved to the suburbs, created ideal domestic enclosures, and raised their children to be optimists about American capitalism and culture seems far removed from our dark obsessions.

Europe may have been the ruined castle in the postwar era, but America had become the gleaming city on a hill, part factory and part garden spot suburb. The outrages that modern warfare visited on the bodies of American servicemen had been ignored and even sexualized, made manly again. Sexy bodies that made babies generated most of the interest. Backyard barbeques in the bright sunshine and liking Ike left no time for the gothic.

Could the gothic castle live in Levittown? In the years immediately after World War II, the danse macabre of Universal Studios' classic monsters had gone out of fashion. Hard-luck audiences in the 1930s thrilled to the horrors of Frankenstein and his Bride, Dracula, the Invisible Man, and a dank dungeon full of mad scientists and maniacs. As late as 1941, Lon Chaney Jr. created a new monster in *The Wolf Man.*

After the beginning of World War II, the Universal Studios monsters seemed dated, at best. In a world at war, the drama of things back from the grave, creatures wandering through the dry-ice fog of faux European fairylands, had become a joke. In fact, the classic monsters out of the shadowy darkness became figures of fun, appearing in a series of slaphappy comedies starting in 1943 with Abbot and Costello in *Abbott and Costello Meet Frankenstein.*

The threat of an invasion from other worlds replaced the gothic horrors of crypts and secrets for moviegoers. Science fiction became, other than the western, the most popular film genre after 1945. At the height of the sci-fi obsession, studios released no fewer than 40 alien invasion films in a single year. The plots almost always involved an attack by advanced alien races, warded off by an alliance of the American military and the scientific establishment. A subgenre of the alien invasion film, the "creature feature," preyed on other 50s fears. "Radiation" or "atomic rays" created giant lizards, giant bugs, and even 50-foot women that military and scientific authorities quickly defeated. Usually a love story, often between a male and female scientist, reached its denouement at the end, promising future domestic bliss now that the atomic age threats had been dispelled by American bravery and know-how.

Taken together, the new style of horror tapped into American fears of the threat from beyond, forces that broke the walls of containment to destroy and corrupt. The best of these films are particularly intense cultural nightmares, transmogrifications of geopolitical fears into cinematic terror. All stressed the possibility of an invading force threatening to destroy the safety and security of American life. Some, such as *Invasion of the Body Snatchers* and *Invaders from Mars,* pose threats to the body itself, the possibility of the loss of control. Even after evoking such fears, most promised that American life remained secure and stable, that military machismo and scientific skill defeated the threat in the end.

This environment would seem an especially unfriendly one to Vampira and her gothic nightmare. But the coming of the flying saucers did not completely replace the crumbling old castle. The gothic darkness nipped around the edges of American culture in the 50s, salivating like the wolf over the little girl in the red hood. Things from the sky did not simply replace things from the crypt. Little green men may have eclipsed chthonic monsters of the dark, but the terrors of the night only waited, brooding, for the opportunity to reawaken.

The popularity of Charles Addams offered proof of this gothic return. Addams's hilarious and ghastly daydreams turned the domestic home into an incipient slaughterhouse. Vampira drew directly on Addams's ability to uncover the horrors of bed and board.

You didn't need to read *The New Yorker* to find gothic reimaginings of the American family. Adolescents and young adults thrilled to the macabre tales of Entertaining Comics (known simply as E.C.), whose titles included the *Tales from the Vault*, *Tales from the Crypt*, and *Crime Suspensestories.* Featuring corpses back from the grave, love triangles turned murderous, and even the occasional vampire and werewolf, E.C. used gothic humor to reveal the shadows on white America's sunny optimism.

In one comic titled "A Neat Job," a typical 50s housewife faces incessant browbeating by her husband about her cleaning abilities. Unable to bear him anymore, she hacks him up and then cans and preserves his body parts, showing the police that she did "a neat job." In story after story, E.C. artists turned the American dream into a nightmare. In the E.C. universe, murder and mayhem present a twisted version of Norman Rockwell's idylls of innocence. In one infamous E.C. tale, even the all-American game of baseball became a bizarre death match played with body parts.

By the late 50s, the macabre became a way to put American culture under the interrogation light. Rod Serling's *The Twilight Zone,* along with much of the fiction of Ray Bradbury and Richard Matheson, blended gothic themes with social and political satire. Even the creatures of the Universal Studios monster cycle of tales returned. In 1958, Nurmi's friend Forrest Ackerman published the first issue of *Famous Monsters of Filmland* and introduced the children of the atom to the children of the night.

Maila Nurmi drank deep from the blood of subversion. Vampira's appearance on live television gave viewers the unscripted macabre and a sense of things being more or less out of control. This allowed her to shape her character in startling ways, including the explicitly sexual that conjoined the macabre and the erotic. Her threateningly sexual persona reintroduced the darkest shadings of the gothic, the kind of decadence that de Sade had understood to be at the roots of the form. Except she could make you laugh at it all. Like Bettie Page, she knew how to turn sex into a joke without making her own powerful sexuality one bit funny. She was the new de Sade . . . minus the pretension.

R. H. Greene, in his documentary *Vampira and Me,* makes a comparison between Maila Nurmi and Bettie Page that seems based on his many conversations with Maila about her role in American culture. He suggests that, unlike Page, who "brought the dungeon out of the basement," Maila placed the "dungeon in the household." While Greene probably goes too far in calling Maila "the antithesis of Bettie Page" (that was probably Betty Crocker), he captured perfectly why Vampira's style—gothic aristocrat meets happy homemaker—drove the 50s wild, made it mad, made it horny.

Maila Nurmi later said she would change nothing about her creation, "her child," as she called Vampira. In describing how she'd given birth to her monstrous progeny, she never claimed sole responsibility for the character. "It was not all my creation," she said just before her death. "Like when a chef makes a famous dish . . . there is inventing and things he knows from history. Everything comes into creation, my inspirations were manifold."

Vampira used ostentation and a faux-aristocratic demeanor to skewer middle-class mores. Vampira always called her viewers "darlings," lengthening out the last consonant until it became a patronizing *z*. She smoked from a dinner-length cigarette holder that she lit on a skull-and-crossbones candelabrum, sometimes blowing out the light just as the film of the night started. She was paying homage to Sanjak and the Dragon Lady, but also to Gloria Swanson's unforgettable performance in *Sunset Boulevard* and Joan Crawford's recent 1953 *Torch Song*. Blending these identities together enabled her to become a new female version of the gothic villain, the evil dark lord vamping sweet little American culture until it begged her for more.

Her gothic villainy fused together several cultural influences to create her "Victorian dominatrix." She may or may not have known about the history of the dominatrix, but it's interesting that she chose the adjective "Victorian" to describe what she was up to, since that era had contributed its fair share to the allurements of bondage and discipline. In 1870, Austrian author Leopold von Sacher-Masoch published his novel *Venus in Furs*. The basis for the Velvet Underground's 1967 song of the same name, it tells the story of a German aristocrat whose fascination with a woman leads him to ask that she enslave and degrade him.

Venus in Furs was perhaps the first effort to turn the alluring, hypnotic villains of gothic literature into a female character of almost supernatural power. But the reality had become a fixture in European popular culture already. Eighteenth-century London had become fascinated with a new kind of prostitute, the "female flagellants." The most famous of these, Theresa Berkeley, operated a brothel on Charlotte Street in central London. Calling herself "the Governess," she used birches and canes on her clients but also created a paddling machine that worked off the winch and pulley system.

Although shimmering in the alluring faces of Theda Bara and Greta Garbo, the dominatrix remained largely a suppressed figure in American culture. It's likely that the class system of Victorian England made the dominatrix an appealing figure, a perversion and satire of power. In 1931, Bela Lugosi's *Dracula* combined sinister sexual appeal with the theatricality of aristocracy. But he was the master of women, the dominant in charge of his submissive vampire wives. In the American films of the 30s and 40s, it was almost always male monsters that threatened female victims.

One notable exception provided some possible inspiration for Maila Nurmi. In 1936, Gloria Holden played the titular monster in *Dracula's Daughter*. Her female vampire had all the elements of the silent era's vamp, as well as the hint of domination fantasies. In one especially memorable scene, she uses her hypnotic power to seduce a young blonde model named Lili. Holden plied her supernatural charm in a sequence so scorched with desire that film historian Steve Simels calls it "a lesbian seduction scene so hot it's impossible to imagine how it ever got past '30s censors."

The dominatrix always borrows images of power from dungeons, aristocracies, and empires, and Vampira was no exception. She built her characters from older images. Nurmi never mentioned Holden's performance as a possible influence, though it is highly unlikely that she didn't know of it. Her friendship with *Famous Monsters* founder "Forry" Ackerman probably introduced her to most of the Universal Studios horror films, at least by reputation. And she certainly seemed to be channeling what Simels calls Holden's "patrician eroticism."

Like Charlie Chaplin ransacking the props department at Keystone to create "the little tramp," Maila Nurmi ransacked the cultural imagery of sinister, powerful female villains to create Vampira's signature style. But the ostentation of Garbo, the supernatural power of Holden, and the bondage aesthetic of *Bizarre* needed something more. Maila added the poetry of her humor to her gothic goddess.

In the middle of Nurmi's popularity, KABC released a list of "Vampira's Witty Slayings" to the magazine *TV Revue.* Her show, the promotional ad claimed, had "started a fad of macabre anecdotes" that borrowed Charles Addams's style of mordant camp to mock America's love affair with the normal. Complete with a drawing of Vampira smiling while placing one very desirable leg through a guillotine, the promotion perfectly defined her "come hither so I can kill you" style.

Nurmi's "witty slayings" took on almost every aspect of 1950s life. In answer to the middle-class male's fascination with the suburban workshop, "the slayings" asserted that Vampira had built "a home suicide kit." The "happy Hollywood ending" of an increasing number of Tinseltown productions received her scorn. "When movies end happily," the slayings noted, Vampira pointed out "how unhappy those lovers will be as they live out their miserable lives together." She mocked the home beauty craze by describing how she "uses lye in place of soap, preferring steel wool to sponges." Adding acid to her bathwater, she puts on "banishing cream."

Vampira's humor became part of her message, part of her mission. She was satirizing respectability with her patter that expressed enormous disdain for the conventional. Vampira consistently laughed at middle-class expectation. Why didn't her "attic" have electricity?" Oh, darlingzzzzz, she giggled, everyone knows that electricity is for chairs! What should a prospective suitor bring her? Well, darlingzzzzz, of course "a necklace of teeth and chapeaux worn by the most fashionable axe murderers." Did American culture romanticize the home, turn it into a paradise on earth? "Well, remember darlingzzzzz, be it ever so crumbling, there's no place like the tomb."

Invoking tombs and electric chairs in the context of a joke may have been her true comic stroke of genius. Vampira became the skeleton at the feast during a cultural moment when the realities of death had been made plain to an entire generation in the Second World War and when the atomic age threatened incineration of every nicely kept lawn and every dream of prosperity and abundance. By coupling sex and death, she found the funny bone in the boneyard of American anxieties about both.

Her humor balanced the scarier elements of her character, particularly the musical chairs Vampira played with gender conventions. She became a woman crossed-dressed as a woman. Her throaty voice and commanding manner nodded to the male gothic villain in the crumbling old castle. And yet by exaggerating the characteristics of her own body and turning it into a paradox of male desire, she threatened and welcomed male viewers all at once, subverted both expectation and sexual codes of conduct. And Nurmi had not been the first to do it. In fact, it's likely learned from the best.

Nurmi's sense of humor about her own female identity marks her as a "female female impersonator," a term first used in the 1930s to describe actress and playwright Mae West. In 1944, Maila Nurmi had made a short and apparently controversial appearance in a play that West had written for Broadway, a comedic historical send-up called *Catherine Was Great*. Nurmi had been fired from the production under uncertain circumstances and she seems to have blamed West herself. Nevertheless, she always admired West and always spoke with pride of her association with her.

It's easy to understand why. Long before Broadway's *Catherine Was Great*, West's film career created her instantly recognizable persona, a powerful, sexual woman who made no apology for her desires and refused to play out the moral cautionary tales in which even the most transgressive screen vamps seemed perpetually trapped. In films like 1932's *Night After Night*, West's character sizzles the celluloid, making leading man George Raft look like a bit player. Writing about West's early film roles, French author Colette argues that its impossible to compare West to "the dull catalogue of heroines" that appeared in most Hollywood productions. In describing West's roles in contrast to the other sexy women of early Hollywood, Colette writes,

> She alone . . . does not get married at the end of the film, does not die, does not take the road to exile, does not gaze sadly at her declining youth in a silver-framed mirror . . . this impudent woman is, in her style, as solitary as Chaplin used to be.

American film had allowed women to be the bad girl, but only if the narrative punished them. West created an enormously powerful female presence that refused the punishment that a male-dominated society wanted to mete out to women who stepped out of line.

Reviewers frequently compared West favorably to other powerful women of the screen like Greta Garbo and Marlene Dietrich. In the 1930s, a writer for *Photoplay* described West as satirizing and "making our old fashioned vampires, those mysterious pallid, emaciated, smokey eyed females, appear as futile as they usually are in real life." The influential magazine *Motion Picture* called West "the first real Waterloo of the Garbo and Dietrich schools of sultry."

Nurmi borrowed Mae West's style to create something even more alluring. Unlike West, Vampira was certainly "mysterious, pallid, emaciated" and embodied some of Garbo and Dietrich's sinister ostentation and overwhelming sense of dignity. And yet, she mixed this with sexy, quirky humor, laughter at the expectations of middle-class mores that enabled her to make even death a big joke. She was Dietrich with a pet spider, Garbo popping hilariously out of a coffin, and yet also Mae West as Lord and Lady of Darkness, campy and sexy as hell.

*****

Maila Nurmi revealed that something rotted in the contained coffin of American culture. Perhaps more than its most avid practitioners, Nurmi understood that bondage replicated the structures of power in postwar America. The bound and blindfolded female body correlated to the female body harnessed to the appliance, confined in the home and forbidden to understand and make use of her own desires. But the woman who bound herself or who became a dominatrix laid claim to her own body and her own sexuality. Men held political, social, and domestic power in the 1950s, and they wielded that power like petty tyrants. Bondage play reversed the order of power, reimagined society and how society could work. And Vampira's laughter in the dark gave straight society the willies.

Vampira brought bondage into the open. She wanted to "frighten audiences out of their complacency," and her ability to play the dark mother, to draw the links between sex and death, proved a potent weapon. It was never simply about entertainment or about the desire to become a star. Maila Nurmi wanted to start a crusade and fuck everything up.

The most prominent example of the display of bondage wear in the 1950s planned to become "an evangelist." In numerous interviews over more than half a century after her brief stardom, Nurmi insisted that her goal in going into television had been to raise enough money become an unlikely preacher of a message about nonconformity and "peace."

Nurmi's inspiration for this idea likely came from two sources. The most immediate would have been her father, the traveling temperance lecturer. Although she found him prudish and almost certainly decided to leave home after conflict with both her parents, something about his peripatetic lifestyle and public performance must have appealed to her. It's easy to imagine the quiet, dreamy child looking up to her father the orator and fantasizing about seizing the stage herself someday.

Pentecostal evangelist Aimee Semple McPherson may have been a very immediate role model. Nurmi arrived in Los Angeles two years after McPherson had died of a drug overdose while conducting a series of revivals in Oakland. But the evangelist still cast a long shadow over California, and indeed over American life.

McPherson had her start as a traveling evangelist in the 1910s. Preaching a conservative Pentecostal message, she nevertheless garnered more than a few male critics who saw her rise to prominence as a kind of religious flapperism. Numerous financial and sex scandals dogged her, the most well-known being an incident in which she apparently faked her own kidnapping in order to cover up an extramarital dalliance.

It's easy to see why Nurmi would have looked to McPherson

as a role model. While she shared none of her conservative beliefs, she was probably drawn to the image of a woman who had created a media empire around her own personality. McPherson had used show business techniques (while preaching against the evils of Hollywood) and became the second woman in American history to hold a broadcaster's license. She made use of both radio and print media to great effect, creating her own denominational church that would have millions of followers. Maila saw "Sister Saint Francis" as a way to do much the same. Like Vampira, Sister Saint Francis would have been yet another character that would deliver uncomfortable messages.

Cracking the façade of 50s America would be no small task. The mind-numbing placidity that government, business, and media proffered had its appeal. In an interview done almost 50 years after her premiere on KABC, Nurmi said she believed she could "get people's attention by giving them what they wanted: breasts, net stockings, and phallic symbols. Once I had gotten their attention, I could preach to them."

But, she added, "I never got to that point."

She never did. Her wild ride didn't last. Maybe it couldn't. Maybe she had found her stage a few years too early. Although *The Vampira Show* remained enormously popular, KABC did not renew Nurmi's contract for the fall 1955 season. It suddenly canceled the show in March, 1955, taking it off the schedule the day it was supposed to air.

Admirers expressed immediate shock that Vampira had disappeared. Walter Ames, in the March 29 edition of the *Los Angeles Times*, complained that local TV stations seemed to think "that they can hold an audience even though they cancel out the star." He complained that he, "along with thousands of viewers" of the same mind, sat themselves down for Vampira only to find local personality Bill Stewart putting on a decidedly different show. Ames knew his readership would want some explanation, and so he contacted KABC the following day only to be "informed Vampira was canceled out late Friday." Ames quipped that one of these "flacks" mentioned to him that they had been ordered "not to say anything about it."

Hunt Stromberg Jr. may have had little to do with the decision. Nurmi always spoke highly of the young producer, especially his willingness to be, as she described him, "fanatical"—he would try, or let her try, anything. But executives at the network had reservations about the show from the start. Its very late nighttime slot, later to become standard among horror hosts, had been assigned to her with the idea that it didn't matter much what she got up to at midnight. Nobody would be watching anyway.

Vampira made America stay up late. *The Vampira Show* exploded and Maila's simple "work for hire" contract couldn't protect her. Although she claimed to own the character she had created, ABC management had the idea of turning Vampira into a franchise rather than a national TV show. Each region could have its own Vampira, and Maila Nurmi would simply be the glamour ghoul for greater L.A.

Maila said no. She had created the character, and she always insisted she had "51 percent ownership" to her dark progeny. This was a woman who had told Howard Hawks where to put her contract. She was taking no guff from the suits at a television network.

Contractual disagreements precipitated her firing, but ABC's unhappiness with Nurmi went deeper. The previous summer, hopeful singer Sharon Dexter sued KABC for an incident that occurred during her May 1954 appearance in the studio. The up-and-coming pop thrush had done a series of live songs for the L.A. audience when someone (it is not clear who) had the idea of superimposing an image of Vampira's face over Dexter's, an advertising gimmick for *The Vampira Show*. Dexter's $100,000 suit claimed that this ruined her image, her girl-next-door look covered over by an image meant to "inspire horror, fear, and fright." Though Nurmi had been in no way responsible for this incident, it suggested to some at KABC that their macabre programming had caused a bit too much trouble.

Previous controversy combined with contractual disputes and salary probably still does not explain Nurmi's firing. Her failure to balance her macabre act with a conventional daily life shoulders most of the responsibility for ABC's unhappiness. Over the year of Nurmi's popularity, her marriage to Dean Riesner fell apart and they had separated. Although separation and divorce were certainly not uncommon in Hollywood, TV sought to warm itself by America's domestic fires. As the *People in TV* profile showed, KABC hoped to tamp down the possibly controversial aspects of *The Vampira Show* by stressing Nurmi's alleged conventionality beneath the makeup.

Both the breakup with Riesner, and the rumors about her relationship with James Dean, warred with this image. Dean spent a lot of time with the still-married Nurmi in the fall of 1954 at Googie's restaurant, one of the few places in the Hollywood of the early 50s that stayed open past midnight. Dean's friend and sometime-lover William Bast remembered this hangout as the place in town where you met all "the kooky and interesting" people. Dean himself referred to his late-night friends as "the spooks."

Years later, Nurmi sometimes remembered first seeing Dean at a screening of Audrey Hepburn's *Roman Holiday* at the old Paramount Theatre on Hollywood Boulevard. She went during the height of her fame assuming that she was "the golden girl and could have met anybody in town." She wanted to meet "the little boy who came with [actress] Terry Moore." Later that night, she remembered that same uncombed and angry-looking "little boy" roaring up on his motorcycle outside of Googie's. Their meeting, she claimed, had been "karmic." They felt a psychic connection, Nurmi averred, because "we're both from other planets."

Bast himself met the "kooky and interesting" Vampira while seeking out Dean after a screening of avant-garde director Kenneth

Anger's *Inauguration of the Pleasure Dome*. Though Bast claims he found the late-night conviviality of Googie's "seedy and oppressive," it was the place he knew he was certain to locate Dean, at this time just about to pop to stardom in the days before the release of *East of Eden*.

Nurmi, dressed in full Vampira regalia, looked at Bast with what he remembered as "heavy-lidded eyes glazed in intense detachment." Drinking a strawberry milkshake, she produced a rosary she dipped into the shake and then "slowly drew the beads between her lips and lingered on the cross at the end." In a "contralto voice" she said, "Hi Willie." Clearly, Nurmi had come to fully inhabit her character and sought to represent her vision of Sturm und Drang sensibility at every turn.

James Dean's relationship with Nurmi seems to have been far less intense than she (or rumor) suggested. Dean biographer David Dalton describes her as "one of the first women to be romantically linked with Jimmy in Hollywood." But this romantic link seems tenuous at best and maybe mostly one-sided. After a brief association based on a mutual interest in the occult, Dean scathingly attacked her in a conversation with infamous Hollywood gossip columnist Hedda Hopper. "I don't go out with witches," he said, brutally adding, "and I dig dating cartoon characters even less."

Such comments deeply wounded Nurmi, who developed an idée fixe on Dean she kept for much of her life. Decades later, she insisted that "their souls" had always had a special connection and that they had known each other in another life. He probably became, in death, the love of Maila Nurmi's life.

She worried about the young actor's self-destructive tendencies. This probably did not lead to an incident that local L.A. writer Logan Smiley, a mutual friend of Dean and Nurmi's, later claimed knowledge of. Smiley insisted that about seven months before Dean's death in an automobile accident, he helped Nurmi construct an occult altar meant to "stop him [Dean] from killing himself."

Smiley's story seems doubtful, in part because it owes something to the bizarre controversy that surrounded Nurmi after Dean's death.

On September 30, 1955, while driving up the California coast in his brand-new Porsche Spyder, Dean died in a fatal crash at a stop sign. He had been ticketed for speeding earlier in the afternoon. The legend surrounding his death grew from the emerging cult of James Dean, itself growing out of the release of *Rebel Without a Cause* just four days after the fatal crash on October 3. Along with making the switchblade and the automobile race seem like paradigmatic elements in American teen culture, the film helped transform Dean into a brooding symbol of youthful alienation. Fan clubs with names like "The James Dean Memory Ring" met to watch his movies and circulated tales that he had lived through the crash but had been so disfigured by it that the studio had hidden him away in an institution. This was, after all, the age of American institutionalization, and it proved perhaps easier for some to believe that Dean had simply flown over the cuckoo's nest rather than accept he was dead.

Tabloid stories joined in the frenzy. William Bast remembered hearing various macabre tales of "a necrophiliac desecration" of the body the night before the funeral. Bizarre rumors circulated that Dean had been "the ringleader of a satanic cult." Bast's description of the strange tale may have been how Maila Nurmi became entangled in the story of Dean's death, and her alleged implication in his demise provided the last national press she would receive for decades.

Nurmi's own macabre humor prepared the ground for the controversy. During the period of her infatuation with her young friend (and his increasing lack of interest in her), Nurmi sent him a homemade postcard that featured her sitting alone on a folding chair in front of an open grave in a cemetery. The postcard read "Darling, Come and Join Me." The unfortunate timing of the joke led to rumors that she had cursed Dean because of the disparaging

Maila apparently thought any publicity was good publicity. Here she poses with a young actor portraying the urban legend that Dean survived his crash and lived in seclusion, hidden by bandages because of his scars.

comments he made about her in an interview with that dark lord of scandal-mongering, Hedda Hopper. Hollywood wags and the irrationally inclined connected the postcards and stories of Nurmi's practice of "black magic" back to rumors about the interest of the "night watch" in occult practices. In the gossip surrounding Dean's mangled body, Vampira became the queen of darkness who had vamped and killed the golden child.

Nurmi did little to dispel the rumors. She perhaps saw them, wrongly, as a new kind of useful publicity. She had her picture taken while hanging upside down like a bat, surrounded by gothic bric-a-brac that appeared to be the ritual altar where she had cursed the rebel without a cause. Worse still, she crashed a Hollywood party garbed in a version of her Vampira costume that included a witch's hat and a good deal more cleavage than she normally revealed. She came attended by an unidentified escort who appeared, according to one account, "dressed as a resurrected Dean, his face completely covered with bandages." Clearly, she thought all publicity was good publicity.

Nurmi's twisted sense of humor prepared the ground for the inane, if career-wounding, controversy. A very damaging cover story in *Whisper* magazine linked her to Dean's death and took her image and transformed it into the archetypal image of the witch. Hollywood gossipmongers connected the postcards and stories of Nurmi's practice of "black magic" back to earlier rumors about the interest of the "night watch" in occult practices.

In the aftermath of Dean's death and the cancelation of her show, Nurmi sought to bring Vampira back from the dead. She cut a deal with KABC's rival, KHJ Channel 9, to bring back the character in 1956. Discussions of the show's format suggest that KHJ hoped to borrow more directly from the fad for domestic comedies, creating an off-kilter *I Love Lucy.* Highly sympathetic reports in the press suggest that Channel 9 planned to nuance her ghastly image and make it more family-friendly.

ALL THE WORLD KNOWS how brilliant young actor James Dean met death on the evening of September 30, 1955 in a shattering sportscar crash near the small town of Cholane, California. But what the world does *not* know about that tragedy makes one of the most shocking stories ever to come out of Hollywood, U.S.A.

It's a story so chilling, so gruesome and macabre, that more than once in the course of tracking it down this reporter was tempted to drop it cold and run.

After much checking and rechecking of the facts, after many talks with the persons involved, and after several days of taking exclusive on-the-spot photographs, the final decision was that the story should and must be told. . . .

TURN THE PAGE 13

Nurmi's own macabre humor prepared the ground for the controversy . . .

Walter Ames, the *Los Angeles Times* TV critic and a great fan of Nurmi's earlier work, reported that the new program would not feature her as "a prowling creature of the shadowy streets" but instead as "the average friendly neighbor" with a macabre twist. In line with the 50s fascination with young romance, the new Vampira show would include "boy meets ghoul dramas."

It is something of a mystery why KHJ thought Maila Nurmi would rein in her instincts for horror and subversion. Set to return to television on May 18, 1956, Vampira continued to confound her handlers. In the press, she seemed to mock the idea that she would become the demure housewife with horror effects. "I've undergone a grave change," Vampira told Ames in the May 11 edition of the *Los Angeles Times.* "My motto now is Home Sweet Homicide." A publicity photo appearing on the day she returned to the L.A. airwaves looks exactly like her 1954–55 appearances, leg revealed, hands defiantly on hips, neckline plunging, and gazing directly at her viewers with a look that offered a punch in the face rather than submission to male desire.

Her attempt at a comeback failed miserably. The controversy over Dean's death may have doomed Nurmi's hopes of becoming anything more than a cult figure. Rumor of her use of black magic and her public transformation into the vamp that took the vital fluids of young American manhood and then killed it spread beyond the pages of *Whisper* magazine. Within two months of attempting to relaunch her show, a damaging article appeared about her and Dean in the July 27 edition of *The Washington Post.* This piece all but assured her disappearance into B-movies and ultimately into obscurity.

The *Post* article managed to use much the same language as *Whisper* while giving off the aura of big-time journalistic objectivity. Reporting on Dean's death, the article noted that alleged discrepancies in the accident report helped spread "the fantastic rumor that Dean was not killed in the crash, but was so badly burned that his studio and family decided to tell the world that he died while he

The legends that grew up quickly around the death of James Dean may have meant the end of Vampira's brief career.

lives out his days in a sanitarium." This obviously provides a textbook example of benefitting off the lurid and the sensational while distancing oneself from it.

The *Post* mentioned Dean's "romances" with Ursula Andress and Vampira, although the later received the most attention by far. Calling her "Myla" Nurmi, the writer noted, in a remarkably effective use of passive voice, that "Nurmi was believed by her acquaintances to have some knowledge of mysticism." The article went on to describe how fellow partygoers, at an unnamed soiree, had heard Nurmi assert, "James Dean will die soon," and that she knew this because she was a witch. The piece dutifully reported the "Darling, Come and Join Me" postcard story and, of course, the tale of the "weird altar."

Nurmi, and many who have written about her, have claimed that she was "blacklisted" from television after 1956. Blacklisting had more than one meaning in 1950s film and television. The term is largely linked to the House Un-American Activities Committee (HUAC) and McCarthyite Red Scare in which directors, writers, and performers found themselves unable to find work because of their alleged ties with communist or left-wing organizations. There seems to be no sense in which Nurmi found herself out of work because of politics, despite her tenuous connection to radicals like Rudi Gernreich and Harry Hay.

But "blacklisting" also functioned in Hollywood as an informal gentleman's agreement that allowed the industry to deal with troublesome employees. Nurmi does seem to have had her options closed off to her by this practice. It's almost impossible to otherwise explain why someone who garnered so much attention in America's entertainment capital found herself definitively out of the business. She apparently had no long-term contractual agreement with KHJ and was fired after only 13 episodes.

*****

She had lost her stage or it had been taken away from her. She had screamed out her frustrations and desires and had been silenced. She was back to that day her busy mother suggested she just shut the fuck up.

This was what Vampira was for . . . a way to get in trouble with a world she was certain didn't understand her. And to cause trouble for a world that she thought needed shaking up. She had succeeded, though she may not have realized that American culture takes its greatest revenge by making you disappear.

So, what was she going to do now?

Part III

B-MOVIES

"Downy sins of streetlight fancy"
—The Velvet Underground, "Venus in Furs"

Nurmi's firing from KABC became for her the beginning of more than 50 years riding a hard and crooked road.

In the late spring of 1955, Hollywood gossip columnists like Earl Wilson still reported her as dating James Dean, just a few months before his death. She had a deal to do an album of Edgar Allan Poe readings for RCA Victor. And she'd made another valuable connection, Valentino Liberace (formerly Walter Liberace of Milwaukee, Wisconsin).

Like Maila Nurmi, Liberace had his start as a local L.A. television star. He successfully parlayed the 15-minute-long *Liberace Show,* which began in the summer of 1952, into a syndicated series. In April 1956, after Liberace experienced a disappointing start at a film career, Hollywood reporter Aline Mosby wrote in the *Los Angeles Times* that he had "grander plans: a lavish Las Vegas Night Club act." Set to open at the Riviera Theatre on April 24, the show would "feature Vampira, local TV glamour ghoul."

Vampira's role in Liberace's musical revue remains unclear.

Certainly, her patrician style perfectly suited the camp effect that Liberace sought to convey. Her ghoulish humor, however, would seem to strike a dissonant note in Liberace's bubbly extravaganzas. Photographs of the two together do suggest, however, that she may have been integral to the performance, at least for part of the tour. It's even possible that she sang, given that she briefly attempted a kind of bluesy lounge act around the same time of a brief and ill-fated trip back to New York.

When Nurmi arrived in Las Vegas in the spring of 1956, she joined Liberace's entourage in trying to see as many of the other Vegas acts as possible. This had long been something of a tradition for performers on the strip, and so, on the night of April 24, Nurmi joined "Lee" and his band at the famous New Frontier just hours before they were due to go on at the Riviera.

One performance stood out. Nurmi remembered "this one kid" who walked out onstage and launched into a show that most of the over-40 crowd found ear-splitting, objectionable, and just plain weird. Nurmi became fascinated, especially by what she remembered as his "eye shadow" and "hip thrusting." She described herself as "stunned," and he stunned the audience as well, though in a much less admiring fashion. "They didn't know what to make of it," Nurmi remembered, and "finally someone booed. And then everyone started to boo."

Vegas booed Elvis Presley.

Although demolished in 2007 and now the site of a Trump Hotel, the New Frontier already reigned as a grand old dame of the strip in the 1950s. It had been around since the 1930s and always made money for the Detroit Mafiosi who took the lion's share of its earnings. It catered almost entirely to middle-aged patrons who came for the lounge acts and the slightly risqué humor of its stand-up comedians.

Colonel Tom Parker, Elvis's controversial manager, saw two weeks' worth of gigs at the New Frontier as part of a larger strategy to break the young singer out of the honky-tonk tradition of his native South. The hip-swiveling performer had just turned 21, signed a contract with RCA records, and released what would become the chart-busting hit "Heartbreak Hotel." A 24-foot cutout of Elvis went up in front of the New Frontier, although he was actually set to open for only a couple of tried-and-true Vegas lounge acts, Freddy Martin and His Orchestra and the comedian Shecky Greene.

The sensation from Memphis went onstage his first night dressed in an ill-fitting tuxedo to face the dinner-theater crowd, who looked at him stonily and somewhat uncomprehendingly over their elaborate cocktails. Shecky Greene remembered that Elvis seemed "scared to death," and according to *Newsweek,* his set "went down like corn liquor at a champagne party." Only a few of the night's patrons seemed to have enjoyed the show, including Phil Silvers (TV's "Sergeant Bilko") and Tina Louise, later to become "Ginger" on the 60s hit *Gilligan's Island.* And, of course, Maila Nurmi.

Maila Nurmi was finding out in her own career what it was like to have the crowd turn on you, to lose interest, or to be so shocked they decide you're easy to forget about. Nurmi remembers seeking Elvis outside later that night, apparently while he took a break between sets. She found him in despair by the swimming pool of the New Frontier, having exchanged his lounge-singer tux for a "canary yellow jacket." She introduced herself as a performer and tried to console Presley by telling him she "admired his courage" and that the oldsters who booed him were nothing but sheep. "They've never seen anything like you," she told him, "and it frightened them."

Elvis mumbled to her something about praying to God every time he went on stage. He believed then, and for the rest of his life, that the God of the gospel hymns he loved so much helped him put on a good show night after night. What had happened this night? Nurmi remembered him saying that as soon as he "saw all those white heads and all those glasses," he knew he was in trouble.

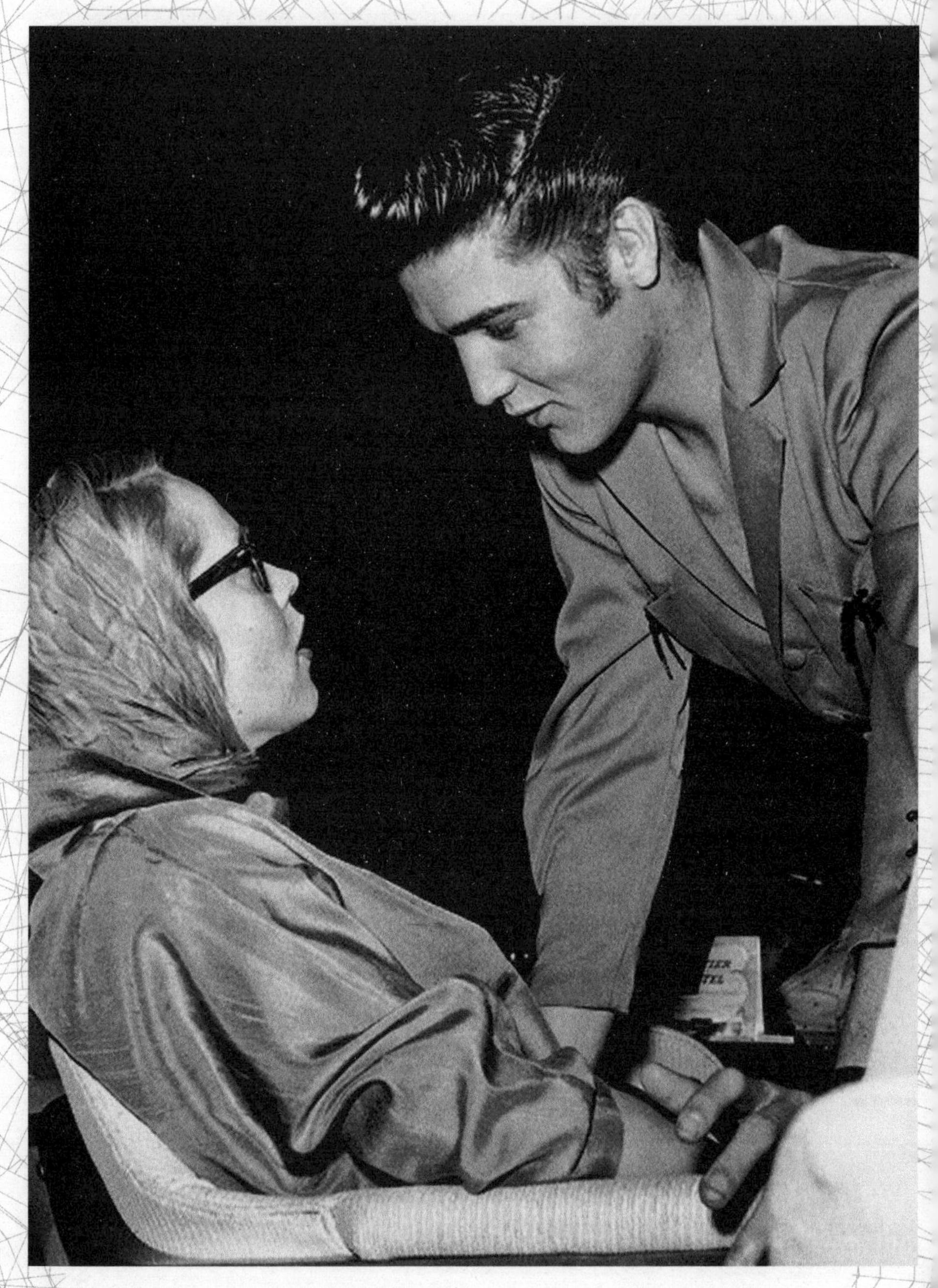

Two 50s rebels playfully embrace, 1956.

Elvis Presley would one day own the Vegas strip, of course. Like an old married couple that can joke about how badly their first date went, Elvis and Vegas became utterly identified with one another after the 1964 film *Viva Las Vegas* and the hit song that went with it. Nurmi claimed she prophesied to Elvis that everyone would soon be "kissing his feet," trying to reassure him as he sat dejectedly by the azure water, face partially lit by the glitzy wattage streaming out of the double doors of the New Frontier casino.

She also remembered that Elvis made her an offer that sounds exactly like what a 21-year-old still discovering what it means to be a star might make. Likely thinking she would be dazzled, Presley told his new 33-year-old friend that he knew she "was getting old and all, but if you'd like to come back after the show, I'd be proud to take you back to my bungalow."

Nurmi, who often showed little interest in having sex even with the men she idolized, found this cockeyed come-on charming rather than insulting. The two became friends and spent a significant amount of time together over the next two weeks, going to see shows at the Sands and the Sahara Lounge, patrons remembering them as sitting right up front at the bar, seemingly having the time of their lives. They were even sighted riding the bumper cars at the New Frontier's Western Village amusement park, Vampira slamming into Presley's car and yelling, "Here I come, Elvis, bang!"

Two very different fates awaited the two friends driving bumper cars in a faux-western frontier town on those warm spring nights. Despite the disappointing two weeks at the New Frontier, 1956 would be the year Elvis Presley passed from mega-stardom into that other transcendent category that makes a performer into a cultural icon. Maila Nurmi would have only limited success back on local L.A. TV and touring with Liberace. And then she would disappear into obscurity for 40 years.

Nurmi's erstwhile successes in 1956 came married to a series of personal disasters. Her career took an even stranger turn, one that buried her in oblivion and would raise her back out of it again. Her appearance in a series of B-movies in the late 50s and early 60s, including the notoriously awful Ed Wood–helmed *Plan 9 from Outer Space*, marked both the definitive collapse of her career and prepared her to become a different kind of iconic celebrity. Vampira was about to become immortal, even as Maila Nurmi faded way into the background.

*****

The young Maila Nurmi's dream of a stage had been born at a time when movie moguls ruled over the studio system like dinosaurs once ruled the earth. Her brief experience with Howard Hawks had been one shared with more than a few hopeful starlets who inhabited the bottom rung of the feudal hierarchy that made up old Hollywood. Contracted out to the system, they waited for the bosses to tell them what to do, how to dress, what to be, and whether or not they would make it. Some of the studio's spirit of supervision and control bled over into television as stars were made, and destroyed, based largely on whether the emerging networks wanted them to shine in the sky or not.

But the meaning of stardom itself had begun to change. A revolution in both technology and society administered a series of shocks to old Hollywood that at first appeared to destroy it and then remade it all over again. Television struck only one of the blows to the old mastodon of a system, a beast that fought back with all of its impressive powers. Hollywood did survive and even thrive, but only after more than two decades of upheaval that definitively transformed both the way that America experienced the movies and the kinds of movies they experienced.

The changes in the world of entertainment symbolized the upheavals and panic that Nurmi experienced in her own life. Nurmi began 1956 with a terrifying experience, one that changed her outlook on the world. She had attempted to jump-start a singing career in the fall of 1955 and moved to New York City, apparently to try out a bluesy lounge act. Dorothy Kilgallen's November 15, 1955, column noted that "Vampira, who caused a brief sensation on the West Coast video tubes," had attempted to start what the journalist called "a blues warbling career in the East." Her divorce from Riesner plus the end of her television career likely propelled her to try something new and return to the place of some of her early, marginal successes. But the move back to New York turned out to be short-lived.

On January 8, Nurmi cracked open the door of her apartment to what she described as "a wiry little man" who forced his way in claiming that "he was looking for a girl named Peggy." The "wiry little man" turned out to be a serial rapist named Ellis Barber, who the NYPD had nicknamed, in a dark irony, "the Vamp." He grabbed Nurmi after bullying his way in and began choking and beating her while trying to tear off her clothes.

Police reports and newspaper articles suggest that Nurmi did nothing to make things easy for Barber. During what became a two-hour ordeal, she fought him, finally escaping wearing nothing but a pair of pants and seeking help from a nearby department store. Police captured Barber an hour later. Nurmi forever after refused to talk about the incident. She returned to L.A. the same month.

Given the circumstances, it was anything but a happy return. And it would get worse. Nurmi spent part of 1956 unsuccessfully suing Gene Shacove, the owner and operator of a Beverly Hills salon, for a dryer accident that allegedly set her hair on fire. She lost most of her beautiful blonde hair in the incident and apparently shaved the rest off and donned a wig. It is possible that this incident generated the rumor that she shaved her head to impress James Dean.

Maila's beauty salon accident became for her an opportunity for more experimentation. A photograph from this period shows Nurmi with her head almost completely shaved, only a few tufts of hair covering her forehead. She's wearing jewelry, including extravagant earrings, influenced by the era's science-fiction comics. Perhaps most striking of all, she's sporting a pair of pointed prosthetic ears that resemble nothing so much as the iconic Vulcan ears of *Star Trek*'s "Dr. Spock," more than a decade before Gene Roddenberry introduced the character. The photograph suggests that Nurmi had continued to model for Gernreich, who displayed an increasing interest in using science fiction imagery in his designs.

Nurmi attempted her failed comeback on TV in midsummer. She clearly had other options, and her time at the Riviera with Liberace became, later in the year, an opportunity to create an international fan base. It was an opportunity that never came to fruition and led to circumstances that ended her professional relationship to Liberace.

Liberace found himself at a turning point in his career in 1956. In the spring, entertainment reporter Aline Mosby wrote that "the pretty tooth pianist" had decided to say good-bye "to his television series that had made him a living room idol." The generally outlandishly and campily garbed performer sat that April at Hollywood's Brown Derby (in "silk suit and a polkadot shirt with matching tie") and discussed his upcoming Las Vegas show, his plans for a concert at the Hollywood Bowl, and "a foreign tour in October."

Liberace's optimism hid the fact that his hopes for a film career had been dashed in late 1955 with the failure of his mawkish comedy *Sincerely Yours*. He did, however, have the promise of a foreign tour, taking him to Cuba, the European continent, and an extended idyll in England. Nurmi apparently joined him for the latter, and the trip had to have been one of the most rewarding of her life.

The tour itself cannot be called a success, despite some large crowds and even an opportunity to perform for the Queen. Worries over domestic terrorism in the wake of the Suez Canal crisis with Egypt led to the cancelation of some performances. Liberace's show

Maila may have created this science fiction version of herself with the aid of Rudi Gernreich after having her hair burned off in a dryer accident in 1956. Rumors falsely suggested she shaved her head to impress James Dean.

appealed to a specific, mostly female demographic in British society, and they showered him with attention. He was, in his way, the first gay boyfriend many women ever had.

Critics, however, lashed out with a vitriol that seems to have shocked the entertainer. "Liberace is no more a concert pianist than I am a Zulu princess," wrote a reviewer in the *London News Chronicle.* Perhaps most humiliating for Maila's friend and patron, he found the British media, unlike their American counterparts, perfectly willing to write about his sexual identity. A British comic named Jimmy Thompson composed a bawdy lyric about the performer that read, in part:

> My fan mail is really tremendous
> It's going so fast my head whirls
> I get more and more
> They propose by the score—
> And at least one or two are from girls

The gay panic that Liberace inspired in some men even emerged during some of his performances. Nurmi remembered hearing someone yell "Liberace is a fag!" from beneath the footlights, and that she had leaned out into the crowd "and spit right into the heckler's face." It is hard to imagine that Liberace appreciated her response, bringing even more attention to incidents that already must have humiliated him. Nurmi remembers that he never mentioned the incident to her at all, though she later claimed she could tell he "appreciated her loyalty."

Nurmi had returned to L.A. by late 1956, and she had come back to stay. Her travels, according to a brief mention in the *Los Angeles Times,* created for her something of an international audience. But, not unlike her experience in America, this had not translated into permanent stardom or, of most concern, a meaningful revenue stream.

This did not mean that she had dropped out of the local spotlight. She remained much in demand for horror events, at this time becoming increasingly popular because of the renaissance of the classic Universal Monsters films and a more general growing interest in horror.

Nurmi, unfortunately, received only slight benefit from the new craze. Local theaters like the Orpheum and the Fox Inglewood, trying desperately to woo audiences away from the small screen and the comfort of their living rooms, attempted to transform film screenings into major public events. In late June and early July, Nurmi made appearances in both theaters to publicize the horror flicks *The Black Sleep* and *The Creeping Unknown.*

Both films nodded to the classic monster shows of the 30s even as they suffered from low production values and poor scripting. *The Black Sleep* featured a flock of actors from the golden era of Universal Pictures, including very, very brief appearances by Bela Lugosi and Lon Chaney. Basil Rathbone had the starring role as a mad scientist attempting to create an army of the undead. *The Creeping Unknown* walked the line between horror and science fiction, an elastic boundary becoming more pliable all the time with the influence of Roger Corman. *The Creeping Unknown* told the tale of a rocket returning to Earth with an alien infection that metastasizes into a blob that consumes the Tower of London.

Nurmi continued to be a kind of horror host, and her role as a local celebrity kept her especially busy, though often with gigs that undoubtedly pained her. Always ready to produce hokum if it maintained an ironic sheen, she undoubtedly wilted in the harsh glare of local boosterism. In June 1956, she became one of the "TV Stars in Person" to make an appearance at the 11th Annual Los Angeles Home Show. Later in the fall she made the bizarre decision, given the nature of Dean's death, to take part in the Junior Chamber of Commerce automobile safety campaign and, according to the advertisements, appeared "in all her gloomy glamour." Ad copy for the campaign claimed that she put "a Double Whammy" on the crowd and took advantage of her reputation for morbid humor by suggesting that the spell she cast urged drivers "to go through every stop signal they encountered."

These local ads kept Nurmi in the public eye. It's very unlikely, however, that after the KABC dust-up and the controversy over her connection to Dean that she commanded particularly high appearance fees. The decisions she made over the next several years suggests someone desperately in need of funds, a career on the rise suddenly floundering.

The death of James Dean and the stories that surrounded it do seem to have played a substantial role in the backlash against her. Maila's persona, the sexy dead girl, offered gossipmongers plenty of lurid images to attach to Dean's death. She may have aided and abetted this process by some of her own actions, though here separating the facts of her life from legendary material becomes especially tricky. Not long after appearing at the automobile safety event, rumors circulated in November of 1956 that Maila had shown up with a "young actor" at a Halloween party. Maila had of course shown up as Vampira, but her unnamed young companion came swathed in bandages. Vampira had more or less reenacted the urban legend of Dean having survived the car wreck, living out in some state so hideously deformed that he had to hide himself behind bandages.

Nurmi herself never described this incident in any official interviews, though that's perhaps not surprising given her unwillingness to say very much to journalists about the scandal surrounding Dean's death. The only written account seems to be Erskine Johnson's Hearst syndicated gossip column that reported in December 1956 that Vampira had attended a Halloween party with "a young actor dressed as the resurrected Dean, his face completely covered in bandages."

It's been impossible to determine whether or not Nurmi actually pulled this stunt. However, a photograph of Nurmi and what appears to be a young actor playing the dead James Dean does survive, though I haven't been able to determine the context. She was never really interested in good taste. If it happened, it's not entirely out of character. Given the strange combination of sweetness and morbidity that seems to have driven Nurmi's own personality, she may well have thought of this as some combination of publicity and a loving tribute to her dead friend. Her whole shtick did, after all, depend on the resurrection of the dead.

Two things are notable about this photograph, other than the macabre invocation of Dean. First, Nurmi's hawking more cleavage than she ever did in her canonical portrayals of her lady vampire. Most interesting of all though, she's added a witch's hat. Maybe that's not so surprising given that it's likely a Halloween party. But it could also be that she's jeering at her critics, the ones who had accused her of practicing a literal black magic on her dead friend. She was not going down without a fight.

Dean's death underscored for the American public the outlaw impulses that Vampira awakened. Stories of her obsession with him and related rumors of her interest in the occult traced out an image of dark female sexuality on the loose, uncontained in an era that demanded all kinds of containment. The postcard she had so unfortunately sent him just before his accident showed her willingness to dance playfully at the borders of life and death. An increasingly religious America that had transformed Billy Graham into a household name would never elevate a woman to stardom who embodied both ancient terrors and the modern threats of the sexual revolution.

*****

A little over a decade earlier, Maila Nurmi had come very close to appearing in a Howard Hawks picture. By early 1957, her prospects had dwindled to near zero. Now in her late 30s at a time when aging actors with star-studded résumés struggled to find worthwhile projects, Nurmi had no hope of becoming the new Lauren Bacall as Hawks had dreamed she might. But the new realities of moviemaking offered her at least some opportunities.

In the 1930s and 1940s, all the major film houses—Paramount, Universal, Warner Bros., United Artists—had produced a tremendous amount of celluloid for movie-hungry audiences using a stable of stars whose contracts they owned. The studios even had proprietary rights over all of the marquee theaters where their films appeared. The major players used the practice of "block booking" to maintain strict control over the distribution of their films. "Block booking" essentially forced theaters to accept all the product that a studio wanted to sell them in return for being given the right to screen a major release.

In 1946, the Supreme Court handed down an antitrust ruling in a case against Paramount that essentially ended the studio system. The practice of block booking now no longer allowed, the studios radically cut back production on smaller pictures, their "B-pictures" that had traditionally been sold to the theaters as part of what was called a "double bill."

Americans still loved the pictures in the 1950s. But the old studio system that had kept the Hollywood dream factory humming for decades had died. B-pictures, however, did not, even if they soon acquired a new definition. Increasingly, the term was used by the film industry, and the public, to refer to films that emanated not from Hollywood but from start-ups that made movies outside the traditional studio pipeline. Genre pictures, cowboys, motorcycle gangs, space aliens, and giant monsters from outer space became the special province of the B-picture, often made cheaply in the hopes of scoring quick returns and reinvesting in the next tale of gods and monsters run amok.

The life's work of producer/director Roger Corman best illustrates the possibilities of the B-movie while explaining why it gained some of the cultural characteristics that now define it. Corman, who for a while had been a messenger boy for 20th Century Fox Studios, managed to get together $12,000 for the production of a 1954 creature feature called *Monster from the Ocean Floor.* Shot in less than a week, the picture made back several times its production costs. Corman went on to make B-movie classics such as *Little Shop of Horrors* and *The Slumber Party Massacre*, as well as a host of now highly regarded films loosely (very loosely) based on the stories of Edgar Allan Poe.

Although often made with schlocky special effects and with scripts too quickly hurled into production to make much sense, Corman's films attracted a mob of talented and creative actors, directors, technicians, and cinematographers who used his guerrilla filmmaking style as a finishing school for their own careers. At one time or another, Corman produced films that included the work of Jack Nicholson, Martin Scorsese, Francis Ford Coppola, and a host of other figures who later became luminaries in acting, directing, screenwriting, cinematography, and special effects.

Corman himself explained the success of his films, and the reemergence of the B-picture, as a result of the major studios' unwillingness to grasp what the coming of television meant. The ease of sitting in your pajamas to be entertained at home forever changed America's relationship with the movies. Corman believed that only by keeping production costs low and churning out product quickly could you truly turn a meaningful profit and go on to make more movies.

Corman happily called his work "exploitation films," not especially liking the term "B-movies" because of its older definition. Corman defined his chosen trade as an effort in which "you made your film about something wild with a great deal of action, a little sex, and possibly some sort of strange gimmick." Corman's work spanned every genre he could link with a high concept and lots of sensationalism, lots of lurid material, and, it must be added, an unwavering love for the fun of making movies and the craft that made them an American obsession.

Edward D. Wood Jr. brought to his exploitation pictures the same verve as Corman. Unfortunately for him, and for many of those who worked with him, he did not have the funding, the luck, or the talent of Roger Corman. Also, unlike Corman, he never successfully gathered the kind of up-and-coming talent that would make up for his own deficiencies. If anything, he went in the opposite direction. Wood created exploitation pictures that literally exploited names and faces recognizable from other entertainment venues (like professional wrestling) or that summoned images of pop-culture past, including Bela Lugosi and, of course, Vampira.

Wood's background informed his films in ways that gave him an eerie resemblance to the much more talented auteur from earlier in the century, Tod Browning, who had worked closely with Lon Chaney and, later, Bela Lugosi in *Dracula*. A former U.S. Marine, Wood had, like Browning, traveled on the carnival circuit. According to one of Wood's friends from the late 1940s, the former marine corporal had portrayed a "half-man, half-woman" character in the sideshow, an appropriate performance for an active and often outspoken transvestite who told of wearing a pink bra and what he called "pink panties" during the brutal Battle of Tarawa.

By the late 1940s, Wood successfully scraped together funds to get into the independent film business. And by 1955 he, again like Tod Browning, would be forever linked with Bela Lugosi, the Hungarian actor who had portrayed Dracula in the eponymous 1931 film classic.

Lugosi first appeared in Ed Wood's *Glen or Glenda?*, an exploitation romp that explored both transvestitism and hermaphroditism. Wood certainly played off his own personal interest in the topic (some of the film was directly autobiographical) but also believed the flick might successfully draw on interest in the recent Christine Jorgensen case. Although dealing with questions of psychiatry and gender identity, Wood framed the film with various genre effects including Lugosi as a godlike narrator, something along the lines of an incarnation of fate. *Glen or Glenda?* mixed even more magical realism into the deeply strange film with the appearance of Wood's agent playing a satanic tempter.

Ed Wood cast Lugosi even more prominently in the utterly bizarre *Bride of the Monster* (also known as *Bride of the Atom*) in 1955. Lugosi plays a mad scientist hiding away from humanity in the depths of an unidentified jungle. Here he builds a Frankenstein-like monster, portrayed by the wrestler Tor Johnson. Known as "the Swedish Angel," Johnson had been a bit actor in films since the early 1930s and appeared in Abbot and Costello films as recently as 1950. Like Nurmi, Johnson had become a kind of West Hollywood local celebrity and made a number of paid public appearances with her at film openings.

Nurmi several times told the story of meeting Ed Wood, thinking him an idiot and later being deeply offended at his audacity in saying that he wanted her to star in one of his films. This would have been sometime in 1955, around the time Nurmi continued to be a minor but rising star in the entertainment firmament and a year after Wood had directed not only *Bride of the Atom* but also a crime drama that sought to lure the emerging grindhouse crowd with the title *Jail Bait.*

In fact, the two would have been aware of one another because they moved in the some of the same circles even at the high tide of Nurmi's career. Nurmi knew Tor Johnson from the local public appearance circuit. She was a friend and admirer of another key member of the Ed Wood players, "the Amazing Criswell." Criswell had become a local Hollywood celebrity with a TV show that combined his offbeat psychic predictions with the sale of a worthless diet supplement called "Criswell's Vitamins." He made a few appearances on *The Jack Paar Tonight Show,* and his odd, stentorian voice often delivered some of the bizarre narration that Wood used to frame his films. "Remember, my friends, future events such as these will affect you in the future" from

Plan 9 represents perhaps the worst bit of Ed Wood dialogue that Criswell ever, somehow convincingly, delivered.

In 1955, Nurmi appeared at a testimonial for Bela Lugosi hosted by Ed Wood. Although attracting horror legends like Lon Chaney Jr. (at a particularly low point in his life and career as he continued his losing battle with alcoholism), the real point of this "testimonial" was to raise money for and attract attention to *Bride of the Atom.* As with all his films, funding proved a problem. During the course of filming, angry actors had filed a complaint with their union and, even after finishing the film, Wood had no money to pay the costs of lab production so he could actually pick it up for distribution.

Nurmi later remembered that she attended the gathering with Riesner on an invitation from Forrest Ackerman. This may have been the first time Nurmi and Wood met, and Nurmi remembered thinking, "This little creep thinks I'm going to work for him." A picture taken at the event shows Wood standing beside Nurmi with a Cheshire grin while Nurmi affected a Garbo face in full Vampira regalia.

Nurmi's inability to find steady work in entertainment made her significantly more open to the little creep's desire to put her in one of his pictures. By 1956, she and her mother briefly lived together after Onni and Sophia had separated. Apparently, Nurmi's now 66-year-old father had met another woman. Divorcing Maila's mother, he remarried and moved to Lake Worth, Florida, with his new wife.

Sophia Syrjaniemi had likely come to see Nurmi on an extended visit rather than coming to live with her. Her son, Robert, was married and a manager for Oregon Egg Producers, one of Astoria's biggest employers. It is highly unlikely that Sophia would turn to Maila for help given her daughter's dire circumstances at the time. It's probable instead that she had simply come to visit her at a time when both found themselves at loose ends.

Whatever the exact circumstances, Sophia Syrjaniemi died in the summer of 1957 while visiting Maila, her ill health possibly made worse by the shock of her very recent and unexpected divorce.

Nurmi barely made reference to her family in any interview she ever gave. But even if she was as alienated from them as this suggests, the death of her mother, especially coming at the time that it did, dealt her a significant blow. Her TV career over and the small income stream that came from personal appearances dwindling, she received public assistance of about $13 a week in early 1957. Speaking about the time of Sophia's death, she described herself as feeling "stranded."

Under these circumstances, Ed Wood offering her a flat fee of $200 for a somewhat brief appearance in his film proved an offer she could not refuse. Nevertheless, even in her rather catastrophic financial situation, Nurmi aggressively defended the borders of her own dignity. After receiving the script, she found herself appalled by Ed Wood's complete inability to write dialogue or, indeed, to structure a narrative at all. Maila later told interviewer Rudolph Grey that it was because she had been "blacklisted" that "Ed Wood got me." She added that "If someone had said a year or two before that you're going to work for him, I would have said, 'You're mad, never in a million years.'" Her financial situation (she described herself not only as stranded but also "starving") more or less demanded that she take Wood's money.

Wood needed Vampira for more than the film. He hoped to use her to attract investors. Part of her work for Wood in 1957 involved attending cocktail parties meant to raise funds to shoot the film and pay the actors. Appearing dressed as Vampira, Nurmi remembered getting a tremendous amount of attention and, at the same time, almost no money being raised. *Plan 9* did have a number of small investors, much of the funding actually came from local Southern Baptist church leader J. Edward Reynolds. Reynolds, according to one of his ministerial colleagues Lyn Lemon, hoped to use the profits made from the science fiction flick to produce a religious film based on the life of turn of the century evangelist Billy Sunday.

The Southern Baptist Convention was, and remains, the United States' largest Protestant denomination. Despite its roots in the American South, the denomination has a strong presence in the Midwest and Far West. Deeply conservative in its mores, it also has a powerful proselytizing impulse. In fact, "witnessing for the gospel" almost functions as the primary ritual activity for most Southern Baptists. These variables led to some peculiar strings being attached to Reynolds's funding of the film.

Plan 9 carried its distractingly bad title because Reynolds had religious objections to the flick's working title, *Grave Robbers from Outer Space*. His religious concerns did not end there. Reynolds worked to convert members of the cast, including Wood himself. When he was finally convinced that, in Southern Baptist lingo, much of the cast had "accepted Christ," Reynolds pressed them to receive baptism by "full immersion," by being dunked underwater as a sign of "the new birth."

It's not clear that Nurmi actually took part in this rather cynical fundraising effort. Tor Johnson certainly did. The outsized, gentle giant known for pranks on the set actually pretended he was drowning during his baptism, much to the consternation and horror of the Rev. Reynolds. The pastor, who seems to have been utterly entranced with the movies, could be consoled by the fact that he received a producer's credit and had a cameo as, ironically, a gravedigger.

Nurmi had been set to work with Wood for only a single day on the project. In her own memory, however, she spent at least several days at a studio on Santa Monica Boulevard. The bargain-basement cost of the production meant that she did her own makeup, something Nurmi likely didn't mind given her own sense of having created Vampira in her own mad scientist's lab. She no longer had many of the costumes and materials she had

A promo picture for *Plan 9 from Outer Space*. Tor Johnson rises from the grave while Vampira and the Amazing Criswell bear witness. Ed Wood's orthodontist, who took Bela Lugosi's role after the star's sudden death, appears shrouded in a cape.

used on television, the chaotic nature of the last couple of years of her life leading to them perhaps being left at KABC or losing them somehow during the division of possessions with Riesner. Whatever the case, she found a version of the Vampira gown she had made famous, though she later said that the cut of the gown made it appear that she had "a hole in the crotch of the dress." Concluding that "nobody's ever gonna see this movie," Nurmi decided it didn't much matter.

Wood at first balked when Nurmi insisted that she would not speak a word of dialogue and instead play a kind of mute space zombie. Eager to draw on at least the memory of Vampira's once rising star, he relented. She would appear in the film as Vampira and would, in fact, create *Plan 9*'s most iconic image, arms menacingly extended toward the audience as she shuffles like some beautiful but dead thing to embrace us.

She did not speak but she did unleash her trademark scream of terror, aggression, and delight. According to several present on the set, the whole cast and crew broke into applause after her performance. It sounded as if Vampira had come back from the grave. But the woman whose scream had lit a dark fire in the secret places of the staid 50s had just portrayed her monster for the last time.

Plan 9 simply could not find any distributors, although, by 1959, it showed up on independent screens on the drive-in and grindhouse circuit. When it did appear, audiences embraced its amateurism with plenty of good-natured laughter. Nurmi remembered Criswell telling her that the film played in one of the tiny theaters on New York's 41st Street. Audiences apparently laughed uproariously at all the wrong places but came back for more, packing out the small grindhouse.

Plan 9, as everyone who has seen Tim Burton's *Ed Wood* believes, represents "the worst movie ever made." Wood, despite being a sympathetic character in many ways, symbolizes for most who have heard his name the very dregs of film production. His name and his infamous film have essentially become synonyms for hilariously execrable movies. It's probably not an exaggeration to say that the idea of some films being "so bad they are good" has its origins in Ed Wood's life work.

Much of Wood's reputation today does rest on Tim Burton's wonderfully realized and often heart-achingly biopic. Johnny Depp, always up for portraying the strange and outré in American pop culture, presents Wood as a sweet, charismatically enthusiastic lover of the movies who had every attribute necessary to become a great director . . . save talent.

Although an appropriate love letter to what was in the 1990s a mostly forgotten era, *Ed Wood* certainly gave audiences the wrong idea about where the quality of his films rank along the vast number of B-pictures being produced in the 1950s and 60s. Nurmi did not quite scrape the bottom of the barrel when she went to work with him.

Producer-director Jerry Warren might actually win the title for worst director of all time and perhaps even produced a few flicks that could take away *Plan 9*'s dubious honor. Warren served as owner, producer, and director for Associated Distributors Productions Inc., essentially tying together distribution and production of very bad films for small, busy theaters hungry for almost any kind of content. Deeply cynical about his own movies, Warren once answered the question of why he wouldn't inject a bit more creativity into his efforts by saying that "people aren't interested in anything good, they don't know and they don't care. Just give them garbage."

Not only was Wood perhaps not the worst of his kind, Nurmi never played the diva as Burton's *Ed Wood* suggests she did. Burton's film portrays Maila Nurmi (always called only Vampira) as enchanted with her own minor stardom, followed around by an entourage and unapproachable until she fell on hard times. Not only does the footage of her not sound or even really look like her, Burton's beautiful fantasy portrays her as the very epitome of the successful starlet, removed and arrogant. She was anything but and willingly posed for a picture with the man she considered an idiot at the very height of her short-lived stardom.

At the very least, *Plan 9* remains a beloved piece of film history because it suggests that rank amateurism can intertwine with such a deep love of the medium that something of the transcendent shows up amid the bad acting and the hubcaps used for flying saucers. Moreover, Nurmi's own appearance in the film, even though she clearly just needed the money, shows something of her own genius even as she refused to speak a word of the ridiculous dialogue. Eventually reaching a far wider audience than her television show, her tarantula walk through the graveyard became an icon of underground American culture and resonated with a pop-culture landscape overrun by graveyard women.

*****

Nurmi continued to work in B-pictures after the debacle of *Plan 9*, although the parts she played became smaller and smaller. Her career showed something of an uptick in 1959 when she appeared in an early exploitation film called *The Beat Generation* as a chanting poet. Filmed in the noir tradition, *The Beat Generation* told a lurid tale of "a Beatnik" who happens to be a serial rapist known to the police as "the aspirin kid." The assailant is pursued by an obsessed detective (whose wife has been raped), and the flick includes Beat coffeehouses, a chase scene in scuba gear, and, somewhat inexplicably, an appearance by Louis Armstrong portraying himself.

Ironies crowd like ghosts around Vampira's appearance in this film. She played a character that she had essentially aspired to become throughout her career. In the 1940s, she had lived out the experience that the male Beat poets of the 50s would write about. Unlike many of them, Nurmi followed the road without the privilege that accrued to Burroughs and Ginsburg on account of their parents' money and position in society.

Maila as Beat poet in *The Beat Generation* (1959), jazzing it up with Louis Armstrong.

Nurmi, moreover, had taken Beat to the small screen already. The performance art of Nurmi's television show mimicked the efforts of Burroughs and Ginsberg to create a new kind of vernacular art, to tap into streams of consciousness that could become streams of cultural transformation. Vampira brought to her gothic shadow play the same sense of mission, the same devotion to the weird as a source of social change that animated the dharma bums. Humor plus absurdity plus a deadly serious critique of the way things stood defined the style of Jack Kerouac, Maila Nurmi, and the rest of the Beat Generation.

But this film didn't celebrate the world that the Beats hoped to create. Instead, it incarnated every anxiety that middle-class Americans had about them, ranging from their alleged sexual profligacy to their tendency toward violence. The film's archetypal Beatnik is a rapist and murderer, and audience sympathies are firmly with the forces of law and order. An effort by major studio MGM to get in on the public appetite for sensationalistic exploitation, *The Beat Generation* isn't about the Beat Generation at all. The "square" mentality that informs it can be seen in the studio's inclusion of Louis Armstrong, representative of exactly the kind of jazz that Beatniks would not be listening to.

On the other hand, Maila Nurmi as a Beat poet makes every kind of cultural sense. She chanted up the darkness, and a deeply askew vision of postwar America, that the Beat Generation tapped into. If nothing else, her brief role in the film produced a still shot of her dancing and chanting while Louis Armstrong blows his trumpet that signals a powerful intersection of two generations of hip, one passé and one on the rise.

The roles Nurmi took in the era's B-pictures never rose above the level of *The Beat Generation*. In fact, they took a deeply bizarre turn at the beginning of the 1960s, bizarre even for her. In 1960, she had a cameo in the Albert Zugsmith screwball comedy *Sex Kittens Go to College* (also released under the title *Beauty and the Robot*).

Nurmi appeared briefly as "Etta Toodie," a professor with dominatrix tendencies, in this film that also starred Mamie Van Doren, Tuesday Weld, and Brigitte Bardot's sister, Mijanou Bardot.

Nurmi may have gotten this role because of her introduction to Mamie Van Doren during the filming of *The Beat Generation.* Universal Studios groomed Van Doren as their answer to 20th Century Fox's Marilyn Monroe. The studio insisted she drop her name, Joan Lucille Olander, and gave her a screen name they hoped would stay in the news. "Joan" was dropped in favor of borrowed "Mamie," mimicking Dwight D. Eisenhower's wife's name (she signed her contract with Universal on the day of the inauguration). They borrowed the surname Van Doren from the prominent poet Mark Van Doren, whose infamous son Charles won $129,000 on a rigged TV quiz show in the late 50s.

Mamie Van Doren and Maila had a great deal in common. In some respects, Van Doren had successfully followed the path that Nurmi had taken, at least for a while. Starting out as a model, she posed as a Vargas girl in 1951. Along the way, she had had some of the breaks that Nurmi missed. However, her career had gone into an eclipse by 1959, though was not on its way to a complete fade to black, as was happening to Nurmi. Universal released her in 1959, but not before she had become the primary star in a number of cult classics ranging from *Untamed Youth* (1957) to *High School Confidential* (1958).

During the 1960s, Van Doren's résumé became a bit more blue, as her appearance in *Sex Kittens* suggests. Released by the independent consortium Allied Artists Pictures with the tag line "You never saw a student body like this!," *Sex Kittens* actually told a fairly tame tale, despite the racy title. Van Doren plays Dr. Matilda West, who has "thirteen degrees and speaks eighteen languages," but also has a secret past as a stripper. These goings-on are made even more absurd with a subplot featuring a computer that runs the campus nicknamed "Thinko," which can pick both race horses and lottery numbers. "Thinko" was actually not a prop, but an early computer built by Westinghouse in 1937.

Nurmi's brief appearance in the film allowed her to reenact something of the bondage fantasy that had been at the heart of the Vampira narrative. In fact, it resembled the dominatrix schoolteacher skit she had once performed on her show with the disguised James Dean. Her appearance in the film likely gave rise to the rumor that she had appeared in "blue movies" during the 1960s. The original cut of the film promised more with the title than it delivered on screen. However, over the next decade, the film would be recut and shown in grindhouse theaters with a striptease dream sequence that included Thinko.

Sex Kittens would be the last film Nurmi appeared in using the name Vampira. This symbolized something of a shift in her own self-conception to some degree, but it has more to do with the fact that she was on the verge of disappearing into a long period of obscurity. Personal and financial horrors festered in the life of the queen of horrors, forcing her avant-garde representation of the living dead underground even as the world around her exploded in revolutionary social and cultural transformation. Vampira would not disappear. Soon all manner of goddesses of sex and death would walk the earth. But Maila Nurmi disappeared and lost control of the monster she had inhabited for so long.

*****

Career troubles came attended with personal difficulties. Nurmi's relationships with men continued to be disastrous. Having left Dean Riesner, she had married the 26-year-old actor John Brinkley in March 1958. Brinkley had a relatively obscure career playing various small roles in B-pictures and television's *Zane Grey Theater.* His marriage to Maila Nurmi lasted less than a year. In an odd twist, he had a small role in Roger Corman's 1959 *A Bucket of Blood*, a horror flick that borrowed from *The Beat Generation* by creating another murderous countercultural artist. The Cormanesque touch added an extra bit of the bizarre, with the murderer encasing his victims inside his "surprisingly lifelike" sculptures.

In October 1959, gossip columnists had Nurmi engaged to actor Carleton Carpenter and planning to marry right away. Carpenter later had a long-running career as a bit player on various TV series and made-for-TV films into the early 80s. Whatever the particulars of his relationship with Nurmi, they seem never to have tied the knot. In fact, not long after appearing in *Sex Kittens*, Nurmi married yet another television actor, Fabrizio Mioni. Eight years her junior, Mioni appeared in a number of 1960s TV staples ranging from *Bonanza* to *The Man from U.N.C.L.E.* His marriage to Nurmi also proved short-lived.

Maila Nurmi never established a longtime relationship with a male companion. Many of her attachments, since the early 50s, had been fleeting, though often not by her own choice. She brought horror into her relationships, at least for men transfixed by midcentury images of masculinity. Her interaction with Marlon Brando suggests that her persona proved as off-putting to his outré version of American machismo as to the man in gray flannel that wanted a combination of pin-up doll and housewife.

By the time Vampira took over late-night television, Brando already had *A Streetcar Named Desire* under his belt and was about to burn down the screen in his role as Terry Malloy in *On the Waterfront.* Their association went back to the 1940s, however, when both had been living in New York. Brando had already become a star on Broadway while Nurmi attempted to sell her art and, with little success, launch her own career on the stage. It is unclear how the two met, though it's possible they somehow made a connection through her short-lived experience with the Mae West show.

In an interview with author Peter Manso for his gargantuan biography *Brando,* Nurmi describes a night with Brando that involved looking at books, talking softly over candlelight, and getting into bed because "it was just bedtime. There was only one bed so we both fell into it. We necked a little and that's all. There was no screwing."

By Nurmi's own admission, she felt herself to be deeply in love with him. He was, she said, "such a poetic child" and "the first person I've met that's from my own planet" (an expression she also used for James Dean). Brando, however, clearly didn't return her affection. She admits that she saw "less and less of him" after their strange night together and even went so far as to claim that she left New York for California because of him, finding it too hard to live in the same city with him and never see him. This is a highly doubtful claim since, after all, her first move to L.A. coincided with her contract with Howard Hawks.

The two continued to be friends, remaining in touch after Brando himself came to Hollywood. She shared at least one dinner with Brando and his paramour Ursula Andress, about eight years before Andress became the ultimate island fantasy opposite Sean Connery in the Bond film *Dr. No*, and around the time the Swiss actress was rumored to have been with James Dean when he bought the car that ended his life. Brando and Nurmi would have several falling-outs. He seems to have dropped her right around the time her career went into complete freefall.

Brando's feelings for Maila tell us a great deal about her own personality and how it structured her portrayal of Vampira. He once told her, apparently because of her Scandinavian looks and demeanor, that she reminded him of "the woman who guards the ovens at Buchenwald." At the time Brando first met Maila Nurmi, friends and acquaintances described him as more or less wandering around New York looking for sex and having lots of it with everyone from wealthy socialites to underage girls to waitresses at Hamburger Hall, one of his favorite eating joints in the city. One acquaintance noted that he shied away from women who "had any dominance in them," and another described his most frequent prey as "little naïve girls" who were "essentially dumb." Maila certainly did not fit the bill. Brando moved on to what he thought were larger fields of conquest.

Albert Zugsmith, producer/director of *Sex Kittens Go to College*, seems to have been responsible for introducing Nurmi to Orson Welles, with whom she had one of her most interesting, and most shadowy, relationships. Zugsmith, known to his many drinking companions simply as "Zug," had done everything from managing TV and radio stations to serving as the attorney for Jerry Siegel and Joe Shuster in their unsuccessful 1948 lawsuit against DC comics over the profits from the character of Superman. He got into the motion picture business in the mid-50s, working no less than seven times with Mamie Van Doren. He frequently cast Nurmi in small roles, placing her in the Mickey Rooney flick *The Big Operator* the same year she appeared in *The Beat Generation*. Zug earned a reputation as an exploitation producer with films like *Teacher Was a Sexpot*, *The Private Lives of Adam and Eve*, and *Confessions of an Opium Eater*.

Although these titles suggest that Zug just liked to make junk celluloid, he's also responsible for the sci-fi genre masterpiece *The Incredible Shrinking Man* and worked with Orson Welles in a Jack Arnold–directed western called *Man in the Shadow* (1958). The two became fast friends, and Zugsmith passed along to Welles a script that became the basis for his noir masterpiece *Touch of Evil*. Zug symbolizes an era of high- and lowbrow coming together in Hollywood, the transition from the B-movie to the blockbuster with a bit of the art film thrown in for good measure.

A year after *Touch of Evil*, Zug produced *The Beat Generation*, and it is likely that Welles and Nurmi met during this time. The length and details of their relationship are unknown, though Nurmi claimed that he was the only man she ever traveled to spend time with. They may have actually met in one of the dressing rooms for

The Beat Generation. In a 1996 interview, Nurmi describes Welles as seeing her "scantily clad in a boudoir" and, looking her up and down, pronounced her "a magnificent carcass." She suggested that their relationship occurred during his separation and eventual divorce from Rita Hayworth, although this would place the relationship in the late 40s at a time when it's unclear when the two would have crossed paths. She added that that was "about all I have to say, I wouldn't want to talk about his giving me clap or anything."

Rumors have circulated for years that the two had a love child, and genre film historian David Del Valle has said that Nurmi admitted as much to him when they met at GlamCon, a convention of female genre stars, in the 90s. There's no corroborating evidence that this is the case, and, in fact, it's a story that Nurmi herself seems to have been responsible for promoting in her later years without much corresponding evidence.

Nurmi's marriage to Riesner seems to have lasted the longest of any of her relationships. Her willingness to marry fairly frequently in the late 50s seems to have been marked by an effort to hold on to some connection with a show business career rapidly slipping out of her grasp. Many of her unsuccessful romances were with industry people, younger men from the circles she moved in and hoped to continue to work in. But her marriage to Riesner had convinced her that she wanted to be more than, in her words, "a failed housewife." By the early 60s, she seems to have decided to go it alone.

By 1962, Nurmi's not particularly successful B-movie career began to circle the drain. In 1960, she had an uncredited role as yet another poet in the potboiler *I Passed for White.* Although she had performed her last several roles using the name Maila Nurmi rather than Vampira, the glamour ghoul she had created in darkness continued to haunt her efforts to find a new stage. She had lost control of her own story, and yet her identification with the character made her film appearances something of a novelty. In her last film appearance before almost 25 years of obscurity, she played an evil witch in a cheaply produced sword-and-sorcery fantasy called *The Magic Sword* (1962). Her character appears briefly and her features are plastered with hag-like makeup, making her unrecognizable.

In eight years, Maila Nurmi had gone from being a nationally recognized face and form to being hidden behind special effects makeup. She would not appear on film again until she began making cameos in underground films in the 1980s. Her star had not faded. It had descended into impenetrable darkness.

Two years later, three new television shows would become major hits and pass into the realm of iconography. In the fall of 1964 came the premiere of *Bewitched*, a romantic comedy sitcom with a very strong resemblance to the idea that Nurmi and Riesner had imagined during their marriage but never scripted or pitched. In the same fall season, a show called *The Addams Family* re-created Charles Addams's macabre family for TV, including a dark, curvaceous wife now named "Morticia," played by Golden Globe–winning actor Carolyn Jones. In 1964, Yvonne De Carlo played yet another vampire lady on *The Munsters*. Maila Nurmi was nowhere in sight.

*****

Nurmi's time working in B-movies came too soon. Genre films would eventually lay claim to all the prime real estate in American popular culture. By 1977, a monstrous killer shark and space tyrant "more machine than man" seized the American imagination. *Jaws* (1975) and *Star Wars* (1977) took traditional B-movie fare, outlandish creatures, and space opera and made them mainstream, transforming exploitation film into marketing and merchandizing empires.

"Blockbuster" essentially refers to very high-concept, genre material that once belonged in the drive-in and the grindhouse. Today, studios' summer releases are essentially one exploitation film after another, exploitation films with gigantic budgets that Corman and Wood never could have imagined.

Genre films remained completely disreputable, if popular, in the mid-1960s, and a résumé that included modeling, hosting a popular late-night show, and having bit parts in films considered beneath the notice of the rest of the entertainment industry offered Nurmi few prospects. Moreover, in her 40s when she made her appearance as a "hag/sorceress" in *The Magic Sword*, Nurmi would have been considered well past her prime by the standards of film and television.

So, she started over. Arts and crafts had always been important to her, going back to her childhood of drawing *Terry and the Pirates*–inspired art on lonely afternoons. Somewhere, most likely among the Finnish tradespeople of her youth, she picked up some minor skills in carpentry and construction. She began to work odd jobs, particularly for friends that she knew from the industry (though, not surprisingly, she never held a contractor's license). She described herself as "a lady linoleum layer" in the mid-1960s. She also reportedly took jobs cleaning houses, usually for various TV and B-movie personalities she had worked with at one time or another. According to Nurmi, she laid tile in Burt Reynolds's L.A. home. He grilled steaks, she claimed, and tried to seduce her.

Her artistic inclinations and something of an entrepreneurial spirit joined together in 1967 when she opened a shop on Melrose Avenue called Vampira's Attic. Here, she sold some of her own artwork, and it's likely during this period she began making the handmade jewelry she became known well-known for in West Hollywood and eventually on eBay.

Reports on what could be found at Vampira's Attic vary. Interviewers who spoke with her came away with the sense that it was a store that sold antique furniture or perhaps outré clothing or Nurmi's art plus the work of other local artists. Apparently, it was something of a rag-and-bone shop that sold a little bit of all of these things and stayed afloat in part because she remained a local celebrity. Her shop attracted customers who embodied the spirit of the times, including at least a visit or two from Grace Slick of Jefferson Airplane and the bandmates of Iron Butterfly.

By the mid-60s, the memory of Maila Nurmi as Vampira seemed to live only in funky West Hollywood (or WeHo) and among those who played some role in its scene. The counterculture had moved to the Sunset Strip after the Whisky a Go Go opened in 1964. In 1966, a demonstration against nightclub curfews had turned violent at a club called Pandora's Box, on the corner of Sunset and Crescent Heights Boulevard. Peter Fonda and Jack Nicholson, three years away from making the archetypal counterculture film *Easy Rider*, took part in the demonstrations that inspired the Buffalo Springfield tune "For What It's Worth." WeHo, a nearly perfect place to be weird, became Maila Nurmi's home for the rest of her life.

Vampira's star had utterly descended amid all of this evidence of social change. She had described herself and James Dean as "soldiers" in a war for the transformation of culture. He may have been remembered as the beautiful rebel without a cause, a prevenient symbol of youthful rebellion. She increasingly just became local color for WeHo, a place that already had its share of oddities.

When the wider culture did remember her, it was not always fondly. In 1963, Hal Humphrey's perennially grumpy *Los Angeles Times* column recalled how "a doll named herself Vampira and played hostess for old horror movies." She was not Maila Nurmi anymore, just "a doll" that this conservative commentator could use as "exhibit A" for his contention that "Los Angeles television is a nut incubator." Naming Vampira and several other local television stars, Humphrey claimed that "if those freaks had tried to extend their TV chicanery to any other city in the United States they would have been lynched or at least tarred and feathered."

Humphrey's comparison seems more than a little ill-chosen considering how common extraordinary violence in response to social dissent became in the 50s and 60s. Lynching was no metaphor in 1963 and, indeed, Humphrey made his joke just a few months before civil rights workers would be murdered in the midst of Mississippi's "Freedom Summer." Violent responses to the countercultural challenge became increasingly common as the birth pangs of a new kind of culture made America bleed.

Humphrey didn't exactly have a gimlet eye for the future. American culture took a decisive turn in the 1960s, and not only in the explosion of social dissent of the African American freedom struggle, second-wave feminism, and the gay- and lesbian-rights movement. Since the late 1940s, American culture shifted into a deeply gothic mode. The bats were in the belfry, old dark castles had come back into style, and the things that live in darkness began their slow crawl to the eyrie they inhabit today: the very heights of American entertainment culture.

Corman's 1960s Poe films embody the rise of the dark. AIP, the largest and most successful consortium of independent B-movie production, contracted with Roger Corman to produce a series of films using the titles of Poe tales. AIP would produce 13 of these films between 1960 and 1971, most with Corman at the helm. Many of these starred the new horror icon Vincent Price, whose career parallels the rise of the new American gothic sensibility.

This turn to the gothic continued through the 60s and 70s. The dark ladies who moved somnolently, fearfully, and often seductively through these films and television shows all depended on the image of Vampira. This dependence didn't mean that writers, artists, producers, and directors thought they needed the original. In fact, the only offer Nurmi received was another dubious deal from Ed Wood.

By the early 1970s, Wood primarily wrote and directed pornography. The adult film industry exploded in the 1960s, though it had a substantial foothold in American culture as early as the 1950s with so-called health films that appeared on New York's famed grindhouse district on 42nd Street. In the 1960s, some European films (most notably the highly controversial Swedish film *I Am Curious*) appeared in the United States only to face a number of state bans.

The Supreme Court ruled against these bans in 1969, leading to the explosion of adult film theaters and shops in the 1970s.

During the 70s, Wood churned out short pornographic features with titles like *The Cocktail Hostesses, The Undergraduate, The Dropout Wife*, and *Fugitive Girls (Five Loose Women).* In 1971, he cobbled together 60 minutes of porn with a horror theme called *Necromania*, featuring perhaps the first blowjob in coffin to be found in American cinematic history.

Wood called Nurmi at Los Angeles General Hospital during the making of the film. Earlier in the year, she had suffered an unexplained attack of paralysis and spent at least a few months in a wheelchair. Nurmi explained her physical limitations to Wood and, though he apparently didn't tell her the subject of the film, she told him she didn't particularly want to work with him again. Two weeks later, she remembered another call from someone whose name she didn't recognize but whom she described as "a beer guzzling type." Her caller explained that for "a hundred apples" all she had to do was lie in a coffin nude and allow a male actor to mount her and yell "Aaarow!" Maila told him that perhaps he should call Greta Garbo since she wasn't working either and hung up on him.

John Andrews, a friend of Wood's that appeared in several of his films, likely made that call. Andrews remembered Nurmi saying to him, "I've done professional suicide before, but I just don't think I should do this picture." Wood went ahead with the film and used a Vampira look-alike for the scene he had planned to shoot. The monster Maila had created was walking in all of the dark places of the earth as she became more and more obscure.

Only a few WeHo locals have memories of Maila Nurmi in the 1970s. Her stay in the hospital and the comments of a number of friends and admirers about this period in her life suggest that she was hounded by various health problems. But she remained a recognizable local character and continued to scrape by financially with her art.

David Del Valle, working in the late 70s at a tony Beverly Hills curio shop called Tiberios, remembers seeing her show up to speak to the owner wearing what he called "a strange combination of early goth, dressed in purples and blacks with spider rings and a cobweb necklace." She brought with her some silk ties and she spoke with Paul Tiberios, the owner of the store who, Del Valle remembers, seldom bought and sold things on consignment. Not only did he buy these, he asked her if he could purchase some of her handmade jewelry and, if so, if he could he place it at the center of his store.

Nurmi had clearly found her place in the memory of underground Hollywood. Vampira may have been especially appealing and gruesome to the dark edges of Tinseltown because she embodied some of the anxiety about female stardom that had become a part of the changing world of the movies over the last 30 years.

Maila understood her ghosts. She had modeled Vampira partially on Gloria Swanson's character Norma Desmond in *Sunset Boulevard*. The 1951 Billy Wilder masterpiece starred Swanson as an aging Hollywood waxwork, renowned in the age of silent films and all but forgotten in the age of the talkies. It's a macabre story, told in fact from the perspective of a dead man unlucky enough to have fallen into the shadow of Desmond's faded youth. Filmed at a 1920s mansion on Wilshire Boulevard owned by the Getty family, Nicolas Ray used the same haunted house four years later to film the empty pool scene in Dean's *Rebel Without a Cause*.

Wilder had originally wanted Mae West to play Desmond, believing that the aging sex symbol could bring to the screen the requisite camp, sexual energy, and threat that Desmond embodied. He had also considered Pola Negri, yet another of Maila Nurmi's models for Vampira. He settled on Swanson in part because of the astonishing intensity she brought to the role and because elements of her past actually mirrored the dark descent of Norma Desmond into madness.

Maila Nurmi found in figures like West, Negri, and Swanson a powerful sexual energy that upturned simple notions of the both the good girl and the dangerous vamp. She combined their campy sarcasm and sexual allure with the horror tradition and came up with a style that hit the sweet spot between terror and desire. It was arguably a spot too sweet, a cultural itch too strong. Television and film locked her away, not unlike Norma Desmond, in a haunted mansion. In urban legend, she had played Norma to James Dean's William Holden, vamping him into submission and a death that came even as audiences watched him perform on the set of the old crumbling Wilshire mansion.

Although managing to find new ways to be weird without her public stage, Nurmi experienced the 60s and 70s as decades of hardship and obscurity. Nurmi represented a powerful female sexuality that had tested boundaries in an era that believed in and depended on boundaries for national survival. The culture had been deeply intrigued with her and, at the same time, wanted no part of her. They sealed her away in Hollywood's old dark house. The macabre stories of dead James Dean made locking her behind these fusty walls all the easier.

Vampira soon walked free from this tomb. Like a horror queen in a Poe tale, she may have been buried alive but was anything but dead. She would haunt American culture in varied forms, insistently reminding it of a steamy darkness, an American wet nightmare.

Part IV

BURLESQUES

"Chase the costumes she shall wear"
—The Velvet Underground, "Venus in Furs"

Maila Nurmi tried to make another monster in the 1980s. She ended up creating another cult figure, though not by her own choice.

American loved a burlesque, loved to wear a mask, loved the play in the dark. Just as horror hosts had taken over America in the late 60s, a new horror host had taken over Los Angeles. Larry Vincent portrayed the character of "Sinister Seymour" for two local TV stations that carried his show *Fright Night*. Vincent (later portrayed wonderfully and hilariously by Roddy McDowall as "Peter Vincent" in the tribute film *Fright Night)* used early blue-screen technology to actually pop into the B-grade films that became his bill of fare. Vincent also used the trick of appearing in a small window to make a wisecrack about atrocious special effects or some unfortunate dialogue. Local audiences missed him enormously after his death in 1974.

In 1980, KHJ-TV Channel 9 hoped to bring the horror-host tradition back to Los Angeles and thought that the character of Vampira might be the way to do it. Maila Nurmi herself made an unexpected appearance at a screening of *Plan 9* in the same year to a huge, and hugely unexpected, audience response. Executives at KHJ had no plans for Nurmi herself to portray their new horror host. They apparently considered her too old at 58 (though male horror hosts tended to be in this very age group). They did want her aura attached to the project, since she obviously remained a local celebrity.

Nurmi claimed in later interviews that she never wanted to portray Vampira again. She thought of the character as being the age that she had portrayed her in 1954, a 30-something vampiress. Vampira should appear ageless, an old dark soul, but also could not be represented by a young, bouncy, and, to Nurmi's mind, naïve young woman. What she wanted, she told interviewer Michael Monahan, was the opportunity to "train a new girl" to become a Vampira, "beautiful, never older than her mid-1930s [*sic*]" but with "something contemporary" about her.

Nurmi never admitted that she did not essentially own the character of Vampira, an issue that became a major sticking point in a dispute with KHJ and the candidate they would choose to become America's horror host. She insisted that she held a kind of copyright to the character that she created, and it seems to have been the question of creative control over that character that led to the failure of her attempted return to television. Nurmi had no way of knowing that she would find herself caught in a cultural riptide that would prevent her from re-creating Vampira for much the same reasons she had been blacklisted in the 1950s.

Nurmi searched for the new Vampira in a period of backlash against some of the very demands for change in women's roles that had come in the two decades since she had left the stage. Susan Faludi describes in her 1991 book *Backlash* a culture that had begun to turn its back on some of the central claims of feminism before its successes in the early 70s had fully come to fruition. In fact, she found evidence in politics, pop culture, and in the editorial commentariat that the most conservative forces in American society had launched a counteroffensive against the gains of the women's movement.

Strong social dissent in the 1960s and 1970s had been met with an equally stiff response from conservative forces in American society. In some ways, America was no more ready for Vampira in 1980 than it had been in 1954. By the first year of the Reagan administration, the liberalization of divorce laws utterly transformed the demographics of marriage and family. Legalized abortion and access to contraception had given women more control over their bodies and health than at any time in American history, perhaps in global history. Since the Stonewall Rebellion of 1969, a gay- and lesbian-rights movement, much more public than the Mattachine Society had ever been, became part of the public discussion.

These social changes, and attempts at even more definitive social change, ignited a firestorm on the American right. Richard Nixon's successful presidential campaigns in 1968 and 1972 had strengthened the weak American conservative tradition that had been on the ropes since the election of Franklin Delano Roosevelt and the beginnings of the New Deal. Nixon's handlers put together a coalition of traditional Republicans who favored low taxes and a free hand for corporations with a new and powerful demographic: American evangelicals concerned that change in American society meant an end to traditional gender roles and what they described as a "decline in moral values."

Representations of women in television and film had fluctuated wildly and strangely with these conflicts. Pop media portrayed women, more than ever before, as creatures of sex and desire. But they seldom scorched the screen, as had the vamps of the silent era that Nurmi adored. Despite, or maybe because of, the critiques of second-wave feminism, female sexuality had become a national obsession. Such images continued to make women into objects of desire even as these same images represented a greater openness about sexuality.

The popularity of Farrah Fawcett symbolizes this shift that, in some respects, was not so much a shift at all. During the 1970s, Fawcett's deep-tanned, red-bathing-suit-clad body appeared on hundreds of thousands of walls in a poster that has become so well-known that it symbolizes the decade. Her coppery glow and feathered dark blonde hair became the epitome of 70s superstar sexuality, a character very different than the death-pale Vampira and her dark gothic imitators.

Meanwhile, Fawcett starred in the hugely popular TV series *Charlie's Angels.* In some respects, this may have seemed to represent a new day for women in popular culture. Action heroes rather than housewives, they combined fighting skills with basic cleverness to right a variety of wrongs. The show regularly achieved close to 60 percent of the Nielsen rating share, explained in part by 1976 not yet being the age of cable TV, but also a sign of its widespread popularity.

A number of feminist critics despised *Charlie's Angels*, calling it "jiggle TV." The year it premiered, 1976, had represented a high tide for second-wave feminism. The strength of the National Organization for Women reached its zenith in terms of membership and influence. The struggle for the Equal Rights Amendment to the U.S. Constitution seemed more than winnable. In the midst of this came Sabrina, Jill, and Kelly, who, critics noted, sometimes needed to fight crime in bikinis and went forth on their missions at the beck and call of the mysterious male voice of Charlie. They were "his" angels after all. Writer and pop-culture critic Judith Coburn compared this arrangement to a "pimp and his girls. Charlie dispatches his streetwise girls to use their sexual wiles on the world while he reaps the profits." The Angels seemed almost a parody of the calls by second-wave feminists for more meaningful pop-culture representations for women beyond the Miss America Pageant.

In fact, the Angels and Charlie's disembodied voice of male authority represented a barometer of both change and backlash against change. Media critic Susan Douglas sees it as the very symbol of a complicated era, a TV show that garnered the popularity it did because it "exploited perfectly the tensions between feminism and antifeminism." During the five-year run of the show, feminist activists struggled on the state level to secure the passage of the ERA. Equally committed conservative grassroots activists, many of them women affiliated with the Moral Majority and organizations connected with the emerging "Religious Right," worked against the ERA and to overturn the 1973 *Roe v. Wade* Supreme Court decision.

Conservative activism energized by religious fundamentalism became as much a part of the decade's cultural landscape as disco and bell-bottom jeans. Jerry Falwell, a highly influential Baptist minister who founded and became the primary voice of the Moral Majority, spoke stridently and with open and utter contempt about the women's movement. "I listen to feminists and all these radical gals," he once infamously said. "These women just need a man in the house. That's all they need. . . . They hate men—that's their problem."

Suddenly, it was not the powerful woman who evoked Dietrich and Garbo who began to take up cultural space. It was the bouncy, giggly, tanned blonde, frequently borrowing elements of Farrah Fawcett's look without the skills of the character that Fawcett portrayed on *Charlie's Angels.* Instead, pop-culture representations increasingly began to look like all those incapable women of the 40s pin-up mags who could barely keep their pants from falling off while attempting basic household tasks. Suzanne Somers portrayed exactly this kind of character for the hit network TV comedy *Three's Company* that ran from 1977 to 1984. Somers played "Chrissy Snow," whose snorting laughter came amid a welter of klutzy mistakes, malapropisms, and sexual double entendres the show's writers made her too dumb to grasp.

KHJ-TV decided its horror hostess needed to have the same kind of characteristics. Rather than a dark goddess of horror, 80s America would get a valley girl of horror, a male fantasy with no sharp edges, gothic jiggle TV. Vampira had to give up her stage once again.

*****

The desire of media execs to resurrect the horror host owed its impetus to a new kind of American horror culture, one that Vampira had played a crucial role in creating. Just as Maila Nurmi faded into obscurity, the 1960s became the era of the monster movie in American cultural life. This fascination, largely the preserve of adolescent boys, grew through the 1970s. Historian of horror David J. Skal describes what he calls the emergence of "monster culture" in this era, an obsession with the stable of monsters first created by Universal Studios. Soon, this love of 1930s horror had metastasized into a broader interest in all matters dark and dreary.

The horror host, scripted along the lines first imagined by Nurmi, had become a highly recognizable figure on the cultural landscape. The success of Vampira and the resonance of her legend into the late 50s laid the groundwork for this phenomenon, but new possibilities had opened up after 1958. In that year, Universal Studios released a package of 52 horror films to local TV stations labeled Shock Theater. This bounty of horrific celluloid made available films of generally higher quality than Vampira had ever been able to host, including classics like *Dracula*, *Frankenstein*, and *The Invisible Man*.

Local stations seized on this opportunity, and one Philadelphia station, WCAU, decided that their shock package needed a host. Producers contacted an actor named John Zacherle, who had portrayed a morbid undertaker named "Roland" in a daytime western series called *Action in the Afternoon*. The station wanted Zacherle to turn his character into a frightful and funny host for the "shock" films, and he did, with wildly successful results.

By the mid-1960s, most major American cities had a horror host. New Orleans and Detroit had the widely syndicated Dr. Morgus; Cleveland had the fright wig–wearing Beatles fan Ghoulardi. San

Francisco had Bob Wilkins, whose purposefully "square" demeanor in suit and jacket and horn-rimmed glasses enabled him to deliver his unforgettable slogan that simultaneously tapped into and parodied Cold War America's foreign policy: "Watch horror movies . . . Keep America strong!"

In this new cultural movement, the late-night horror host became what Skal calls "shamans, storytellers . . . anarchists, deconstructionists before their time." Vampira had set the tone for these midnight shamans, suggesting the idea that stories of death laced with comedy could become a source of cultural entertainment and, to some degree, cultural criticism.

Broadcasting terror and laughs to the children of the atom, the horror host made comedies about death at a time when the possibility of the mass catastrophe of a nuclear exchange became a part of everyday life. The kids who laughed at their horror hosts popping out of coffins and delivering macabre puns lived in the shadow of 1963's Cuban Missile Crisis and reflected their parents' fears that the American good life faced imminent destruction. While parents listened to news commentators and politicians speaking openly about "nightmare scenarios" as a regrettable but necessary element in American foreign policy, Shock Theater transmuted the anxiety that vibrated in the air into tales from the crypt and laughter in the dark.

Notably, the performance art of the horror hosts engaged in the same kinds of critique of American family life that had been such a crucial part of *The Vampira Show.* Marriage and family remained a constant theme in their skits. Roland, who had moved on to the larger market of New York City and started performing under the name Zacherley, spoke to his vampire "wife," a character never seen on screen but represented only by a single phallic stake. Baron Daemon, who did a kind of *Romper Room* meets Shock Theater for local New York City daytime TV, frequently mocked parents and introduced small children to gore and the macabre. Inexplicably, this low-rent Count Dracula also piloted a rocket ship.

The horror hosts not only modeled themselves on Vampira. They drew their material from the same well of cultural transgression. Their subversive laughter past the graveyard of the American experience echoed the dark work of other cultural critics that had influenced Nurmi.

Jack Kerouac had used horror, specifically his own deep fascination with Dracula, to create his homage/satire of American small-town life in the 1959 novel *Dr. Sax*. His "Count Condu . . . just risen from the coff of eve," embodied a dreamlike monster who wandered through the haze of Kerouac's imaginary town, part of the flotsam and jetsam of an American culture that had lost its way. Even the countercultural comic Lenny Bruce tapped into monster culture to make light of the American fetish of family and marriage. His bit "Beautiful Transylvania" imagined a nagging "Mrs. Dracula" and even went so far as to comment on Lugosi's well-known abuse of prescription drugs.

By the 1960s, Nurmi had helped shape the birth of monster culture and the idea that the macabre could be subversive. The combination of sex, death, and laughter she created appeared everywhere, although none of her imitators ever got the recipe exactly right. The baby boomers couldn't get enough, and entrepreneurs worked feverishly to tap into the craze for hilarious and sultry incarnations of blood and death, often creating what looks today like odd parodies of Nurmi's masterpiece.

Efforts to borrow elements of her image began almost immediately and continued for decades. Even mainstream stars attempted to soak up all the rays of Vampira's dark sun while it lasted. During the height of Vampira's popularity, actor Kim Novak appeared with her in public at least once. On that occasion, she posed for a photograph that unconsciously provided an archetype of American culture's schizophrenia about women in the postwar world. Novak, pert and blonde and fresh and soon to play a friendly witch opposite Jimmy Stewart in the 1958 film *Bell, Book and Candle*, sits beside Vampira.

Nurmi looks imperious, above and beyond it all, her umbrella shading her from the bright Southern California sun. The dark, frightening lady and the breasty blonde: America wanted a little bit of both but, arguably, decided to take the blonde home to mother.

Hopeful starlets joined Novak in trying to borrow a bit of Vampira's sexy, supernatural mojo. Jill Huntley, an aspiring model, appeared in several of her promo pics as a woman with a vampire that looks a bit like a mod Bela Lugosi. Huntley comes across more victim than vamp in these images from the mid-50s, though the pictures clearly try to imitate Vampira's combination of sex and death. Huntley, her stockinged leg fondled by the monster, ended up looking more like a joke without a punch line than the extended prank Maila Nurmi played on American culture.

In 1964, two major TV networks released monster comedies that included two variants of the Vampira image. CBS's *The Munsters* featured Yvonne De Carlo, who, before the collapse of her career, had played opposite Clark Gable in *Band of Angels* and portrayed Sephora in Cecil B. De Mille's *The Ten Commandments.* De Carlo starred as "Lily Munster," a typical postwar American housewife who also happened to be a vampiress. The producers of *The Munsters*, who had also been responsible for *Leave It to Beaver*, told De Carlo to play Lily as if she were playing Donna Reed.

Carolyn Jones portrayed a character much closer in both look and tone to Nurmi's undead temptress. Morticia Addams, dead sexy matriarch of ABC's *The Addams Family*, brought together Vampira's gallows humor with more than a little bit of her sexual innuendo. The network took Charles Addams's *New Yorker* cartoons as a direct inspiration for the show, just as Nurmi had borrowed them in the creation of her character. But TV's morbid family with vague supernatural connections had a bit more camp and a little less threat than Addams's creations implied. Still, a television show that encouraged the use of daggers, guns, and high explosives as household toys certainly incarnated more than a little of Addams's rebellious spirit.

Jones wore the same kind of tattered gown Nurmi had affected, transforming herself into a beautiful living corpse. She and Gomez Addams (who, like the actual Charles Addams, had a collection of medieval weaponry) are one of the first television couples to have an obvious, and obviously very hot, sex life. Moreover, unsuspecting (and possibly unwilling to notice) viewers received an introduction to an odd kind of necrophiliac sexuality. In almost every show, Gomez becomes uncontrollably turned on by the deathly paleness of Morticia's skin (and her willingness to speak to him in French).

Carolyn Jones did not attempt Vampira's shockingly tiny waist and the unearthly form that went with it. In fact, really none of her many imitators affected this particular element in her style. As a result, neither Jones nor De Carlo quite achieved the level of strangeness that overturned every element of postwar American domesticity as had Vampira. Perhaps most significantly, both came attached to a man and to a house. They may have been spooky housewives, but housewives nonetheless.

Pop-culture iconography that begged, borrowed, and stole from Vampira's image often seemed to segment her appeal. Either unable or unwilling to craft the mixture of feminism, humor, sex, morbidity, and threat she embodied, they tended to choose one element of the character to exploit. In the case of Forrest Ackerman's "Vampirella," all the elements but sex disappeared. What was left was a vampiress that incarnated Nurmi's politics of desire without the mockery and threat she used to satire sexuality. And she also came with tremendous amounts of cleavage.

Ackerman had known Maila Nurmi since her days as a struggling model but seems to have latched on to her soon after her star began to rise. For more than a decade preceding *The Vampira Show*, Ackerman had been a literary agent and tireless promoter of the horror and science fiction genres. He may actually be responsible for the term "sci-fi," a phrase he claimed he borrowed from the popularity of the "hi-fi." He probably did separate science fiction into its own catalog category for the Los Angeles Public Library in the late 1940s, at a time when everything from Shelley's *Frankenstein* to speculative science about rocketry to historical studies of witchcraft sat awkwardly together on shelves labeled simply "Improbabilia." He's best known today as the original publisher of *Famous Monsters* magazine and the curator of a 300,000-piece science fiction, horror, and fantasy collection.

Ackerman worked with the underground "comix" genius Trina Roberts to create the character Vampirella in 1969. Dressed in tiny and revealing bodysuits, her hair an undulating wave of black, the character combined horror and science fiction and sex. In the original iteration of the character, Vampirella comes from the planet Drakulon, where a race of vampires gorge themselves on rivers filled with blood. She's one of the lone survivors of this world and comes to Earth where she fights evil (including a member of her own race gone bad, Dracula himself).

Vampirella represented something new for comics. She not only starred in her own magazine but also became a horror host for the printed page. Ackerman and Roberts sold the original character to Warren Publications, a company that put out horror anthology magazines called *Eerie* and *Creepy.* Each of these anthologies had a horror host that introduced the black-and-white comic stories, not unlike Entertaining Comics' "Crypt-Keeper" or the late-night horror maestros that now populated the television landscape. Vampirella joined Uncle Creepy and Cousin Eerie as horror hosts for her own magazine beginning with *Vampirella* #1 in September of 1969.

Roberts and Ackerman created a powerful and enduring pop-culture franchise. Warren continued publishing it until 1983, when Harris Publications bought the rights. Although Vampirella dipped in popularity in the 80s and 90s, she has come roaring back with the early 21st-century interest in all things bloodsucking. Since 2007, Dynamite Entertainment has published one Vampirella series or another with some regularity. Despite her seemingly cartoonish sexuality and bizarre origin story, serious comic artists and writers have created their own versions of the character, including Kurt Busiek's 1980s iteration that parodied Ronald Reagan's most well-known slogan by calling the miniseries *Morning in America.* Creators have reimagined her interplanetary etiology several times and she's been given a more fittingly gothic and supernatural origin.

Vampirella might seem to have borne very little relationship to Maila Nurmi's creation. And yet, there's also no doubt that Ackerman drew his inspiration very directly from his former West Hollywood friend without ever giving Nurmi her proper due. Vampirella used the line "My name is Vampirella but you may call me Vampy." This borrowed directly from one of Vampira's stock lines. Ackerman appears in the 2006 Kevin Sean Michaels documentary about Vampira, and it's clear that he had a long fascination with her. It was during this interview that the aging bachelor remembered dancing with her in the early 50s and being able wrap both hands around her minuscule waist.

Fascination with her waist size and willingness to borrow elements of her character never translated into an effort to publicize the history of her character in *Famous Monsters.* His enormously popular magazine that long served as the Bible for late 20th-century monster culture seldom mentioned her, despite lengthy articles on every aspect of horror culture and a number of features on horror hosts. Zacherley, for example, got a cover story. It was as if the original horror host had never existed.

Ackerman seems to have had some level of awareness that he had borrowed Nurmi's ideas without much remuneration. This perhaps explains his coldness to her after their association in the 50s. In the last interview she gave before her death in 2008, Nurmi says that Ackerman gave her $25 in relation to the Vampirella character. It is likely that, during the difficult financial times she faced in the mid to late 60s, she did tell Ackerman that he could use her ideas. Still, Nurmi remembered, "He claims to have created that character, which is shameful and disgusting. He is not a very creative man, but is a very bright man for finding talent. He found many gifted people." She also recalled that "one day he dropped out of my life and pretended he had never heard of me."

Ackerman's $25 bought him a share in a comics and merchandizing empire. By 1972, Warren Publications marketed a "Full Color 6' Poster" of Vampirella based on the cover of *Vampirella* #19. For $3 (or $2 if you also enclosed $13.50 for a two-year *Vampirella* subscription), fans of the bloodsucking sex goddess could have six feet of her skin-ful form "on any wall or dorm door!" The character continues to generate revenue and fan interest and has become well-known enough that Vampirella is one of the pop-culture images most often confused with Vampira.

*****

Women had almost always been victims in the horror tradition. Fay Wray screaming her way through two hours of *King Kong* defined the role that women had played in horror before Vampira. In the monster movies of the 30s and 40s and the creature features of the 1950s, they had, with only one or two exceptions, played the role of endangered victim, sometimes protected by their men and sometimes protected by the monster.

Vampira's scream awoke another set of impulses. She had screamed with delight and with more than a hint of orgasmic pleasure ("Screaming . . . it relaxes me so!"). She had no fear of the monster: She was the monster. By the late 1960s, this evocation of sex and death had not only helped create Vampirella, it spurred the popularity of a new genre of vampire films. The sex-hungry female vampire, implicit in certain elements of the genre since the 19th century, suddenly took over the macabre imagination of film audiences.

Vampires as monsters are almost ridiculously Freudian in their construction. It's a monster that can enthrall its victims, lives by penetration with phallic fangs, and replicates itself through an exchange of bodily fluids. Homoerotic elements in vampire stories issue from its very origins. Lord Byron's friend and physician John Polidori had produced a novella called *The Vampyre* in 1819 that grew in part from his fixation on his famous patient and confidante. In the 1870s, Sheridan Le Fanu's *Carmilla* told a forthrightly lesbian tale in the Victorian era that, with a wink and nod, kept some of its naughty bits under the covers. In 1936, Gloria Holden portrayed a vampiress that seduced her female victims in scenes as scorching as the new Motion Picture Production Code allowed in *Dracula's Daughter.*

A number of different elements made for the lesbian vampire renaissance in the late 60s. The emerging gay- and lesbian-rights movement made public discussion, if not acceptance, of diverse sexual identities more common. In the years following the Lavender Scare and the suppression of the Mattachine Society, a growing political consciousness resulted in a much more public face for gay life. The Stonewall Rebellion of 1969, in which patrons of a gay bar in New York City's West Village fought back against continued police harassment, marked a new beginning for the gay-, lesbian-, and transsexual-rights struggle.

The same era saw studios test censorship laws in both Britain and the United States. Hammer Studios had been mixing sex and horror since the late 50s and would use the lesbian vampire theme to open new territory, essentially baiting censors to try to stop their hugely successful films. In the United States, the birth of independent films and grindhouse cinema opened the door for a revolution in filmmaking that allowed for the exploration of all manner of gritty themes, alternate sexualities among them.

The 1970s became the golden age of the lesbian vampire flick. Between 1970 and 1974, at least 20 films in the British and American market made the Sapphic vampire its central theme. Hammer Studios released what essentially constitutes a lesbian vampire trilogy with *The Vampire Lovers* (1970), *Twins of Evil* (1971), and *Lust for a Vampire* (1971).

Although these films unleashed harems of female vampires onto the pop-culture landscape, they are strikingly different from Nurmi's peculiar creation. In general, both vamps and victims are driven by their lusts rather than driving the lusts of their viewers. Although many of the vampiresses are portrayed as aristocratic figures (not unlike Vampira with her monocle and old-world demeanor), none of them seem to have any personal agency.

The lesbian vampire craze of the 70s, without exception, depended on its pornographic appeal for male viewers. The films may have been built on male anxiety about the figure of the lesbian and perhaps of feminism more generally. But these films also staunched this anxiety by making lesbians into objects of male desire. Andrea Weiss, a media critic who has written about the portrayal of lesbians in film, notes that the lesbian vampire almost always appears as a traditional object of heterosexual male desire rather than as a "butch" figure. She notes that lesbian sex scenes in these films tend to assume a male voyeur, sometimes even featuring a male character in the film, watching. Some of these movies are even constructed as narratives told by a male "vampire hunter" who destroys the dangerous lesbian bloodsucker in the end.

One of the stranger films in this subgenre, and one that encapsulates America's racial obsessions in this era, directly borrowed Nurmi's character name even as it focused on a very different character. In 1974, British New Wave director Clive Donner made a film originally called *Vampira*, though it was released as *Old Dracula* in the United States (in hopes of building on the success of the cult classic *Young Frankenstein*).

Vampira used little from the mythos Nurmi had created other than the name and the idea of alluring vampire women. The uproarious narrative features an aging Dracula attempting to bring his lost love, Vampira, back to life. He hopes to accomplish this by draining the blood of a castle full of Playboy bunnies. However, since one of these nearly nude women is black, his lost love comes back to life as an African American woman. Comfortable with blood drinking but not an interracial relationship, Dracula tries to turn her white and ends up being bitten by the black Vampira, a bite that transforms him into a black man.

Donner, best known for directing Woody Allen's first produced script, *What's New Pussycat?*, may have heard the name of Nurmi's character only in passing. He may have had no knowledge of *The Vampira Show* or even the existence of Maila Nurmi. Regardless, it's altogether fitting that a film spoofing American conventionalities about sex used the name Vampira.

Sexuality and the female vampire has remained a cultural obsession. In the 1980s, *The Hunger*, starring Catherine Deneuve and Susan Sarandon, became something of a classic of lesbian film. HBO's *True Blood* has frequently employed all manner of homoeroticism with the lesbian vampire taking a backseat to various gay male subtexts.

Like so many burlesques that borrowed bits and pieces of Maila Nurmi's character, these sex-starved female vampires borrowed only the outward lineaments of Vampira. Most strikingly, these films take their sexual content incredibly seriously, even if today we find them laughably inane. Made primarily for the pleasure of male viewers, they mostly employed the "what would women do without men" notion that had become a fetish in the 40s and 50s with that era's "women in prison" and "private school girls" pulp novel fantasies. Even when the genre tried to spoof itself, as in Donner's *Vampira/Old Dracula*, male viewers laughed primarily at the buxom and not very bright women that populated the screen. The real Vampira had always been in on the joke. And the joke was always on us, not her.

Efforts to cash in on the idea and image of Vampira during the 60s and 70s often had more entrepreneurial directness. Nurmi received a letter in the summer of 1967 from Verne Langdon, vice president of Don Post Studios, about the possibility of creating a Vampira Halloween mask. The letter, dated August 23, suggests that Langdon had recently visited Vampira's Attic and spoke to her in person about "doing a life mask impression." In fact, the correspondence suggests that they had made plans to make just such a "life mask" the following week.

Don Post has been called "the father of Halloween" because of the enormous number of rubber masks his company produced in the 1960s, an important part of the growing popularity of Halloween. Ackerman's *Famous Monsters* became one of the primary forums for selling these masks. Warren Publications had difficulty attracting traditional advertisers, given that the magazine seemed to represent only adolescents with a parochial interest in monsters, who would have little interest in buying a new brand of soap or toothpaste. So, *Famous Monsters*' back pages had become a catalog of monster products. Don Post's "Super Frankenstein" rubber mask became one of the most popular of these products. Don Post Studios also produced the William Shatner ("Captain Kirk") mask that, spray-painted and deathly white, became the iconic and terrifying harlequin of the supernatural serial killer Michael Myers in John Carpenter's 1978 film *Halloween*.

Famous Monsters did market a Vampira-like mask in the 1960s, and it's to be hoped that Nurmi had some income stream from Don Post Studios for these reproductions of her image. It's been impossible to determine whether this is the case, and it's likely that she received a onetime "rights" fee rather than anything resembling royalties off the mask's sales.

She almost certainly received nothing from a marketing effort by Hanna-Barbera, famed animation and merchandizing empire responsible for *Scooby-Doo*. Produced through "Ben Cooper Famous Faces Costume & Mask," the company sold several versions of a "Vampira costume" in the late 70s and early 80s. All made use of a mask with eyebrows and a facial structure recognizably and undeniably of Maila Nurmi's Vampira. In one version, she's a sickly shade of green, suggesting a witch-like character. In another, she's simply and clearly the dark vampire lady from the 1950s.

The strangest aspect of this costume is how it captured something of Vampira's sensuality and attempted to market it to, as the box itself says, "8 to 10 year old" girls. The vinyl costume that accompanied the mask outlined the curvaceous waist of a porn star in a red costume. Although not showing any cleavage, large breasts and a plunging neckline make it an open question whether or not very many parents ever allowed their children to wear this incarnation of Vampira for Halloween. Notably, the Ben Cooper company chose not to portray Vampira's rather alien-seeming narrow waist but instead chose a version of the female form much closer to the "jiggle" values of 70s portrayals of women.

All of these vampire women and dark ladies are burlesques. Whether transforming the female monster into a Sapphic predator or a macabre housewife or simply a Halloween costume, all of these images had a hint of the dance hall, the seduction of the viewer with a bit of naughty fun, an ultimate sideshow blow-off where less was delivered than promised. The American sideshow tradition had gone into decline by the 1930s and 40s, many of the "freak" exhibits on Coney Island closing down in the years after World War II. But the idea of the carnival image that titillates and disturbs lived on and increasingly found its focus in dark ladies, dark comedy, and dark promises of a cultural return of the repressed.

The dark ladies of camp drew from Vampira, often very directly. But they also drew from a new idea in American culture, the notion that laughter in the dark had a kind of subversive quality. So much of postwar America had played it safe. By the 1960s, with an explosion of cultural dissent, playing it camp became more and more common.

The Beats laughed knowingly at middle-class mores, but their sense of irony owed as much to the "lost generation" of the 1920s and 30s as it did to the emerging sensibility of countercultural rebellion. Being "campy" went further than the Beats in its refusal to take oneself seriously and, by doing so, calling into question the very nature of seriousness. It went beyond laughter and mocked itself for its tendency toward mockery.

Susan Sontag captured the idea best in her 1964 essay "Notes on 'Camp,'" which described a sensibility that was "something of a private code, a badge of identity, even, among small urban cliques." She gave a few examples of what she meant, including the Brown Derby restaurant and "stag films seen without lust." Camp, she claimed, was bad taste freely indulged in, not only for the purpose of humor but to call into question the very notion of taste.

Sontag believed that the aesthetic sensibility of camp resonated primarily with the postwar gay male subculture that had emerged in the 1940s and 50s; indeed, she writes that "homosexuals more or less invented camp." She also insisted that camp and its enjoyment had no particular politics. Their purpose, she wrote, is to "dethrone seriousness" and not to substitute some other program to replace the ways things are with the way things should be.

Camp had seemingly won the day. Its sensibility blended perfectly with the 1960s feeling that you "shouldn't trust anyone over 30." Parody had become one of the primary modes of social expression. When Yippie leader Abbie Hoffman said in 1968 that "sacred cows make the tastiest hamburger," he captured the spirit of the era.

The creation of camp emerged close to a moment when at least an element in American culture became deadly serious. In a 1969 speech, Richard Nixon had referred to what he called "a silent majority" of Americans that allegedly represented his true constituency. In fact, Nixon had a point. A segment of middle-class America (though not a true majority of Americans) had been deeply disturbed by the social protest movements of the 1960s and by a counterculture they viewed as repulsive and immoral rather than a new wind of progress blowing in.

But the wind blew, whether they liked it or not, and carried with it more than a little laughter. Sontag's pronouncements, about how camp dissolved the world that was, in favor of a world that could be, may have been primarily the preserve of artists and intellectuals. But those artists and intellectuals would shape a culture that mocked, protested, and laughed at the values of postwar America.

Plenty of families sitting down with their TV dinners and foldout trays to watch TV in the late 60s and 70s may not have known about the highfalutin discussion of camp and subversion, but they saw ABC's *Batman* series with Adam West and Burt Ward, which functioned as a send-up of squares who talked about "truth and justice" and celebrated villains like Cesar Romero's completely bonkers portrayal of the Joker. And America had experienced Ken Kesey's "Merry Pranksters," who somehow blended frontier American spirit with the desire to mock the middle class at every opportunity. Meanwhile, the kids were watching *The Bride of Frankenstein*, James Whale's rather outré comedy about death, on Shock Theater when they should have been doing their math homework.

All of these diverse cultural conflicts and crosscurrents lay behind what became Maila Nurmi's war against an attempt to create a new Vampira. American culture had become a subversive burlesque, a sideshow with a sense that performing cultural identity always means some level of love and theft. KHJ-TV and Cassandra Peterson were clearly far from the first to borrow, or steal, her image for entrepreneurial purposes. The reasons Nurmi decided to fight back on this point are perhaps not very complex. In the 1980s, she saw the chance to reclaim her stage, to resurrect the character that she had created and to come back in all her subversive glory. That chance was being taken away from her, she suspected, for the final time.

*****

KHJ-TV first contacted Nurmi in 1980, noting that her local fame in WeHo seemed to be enjoying a brief renaissance because of the rediscovery of Ed Wood Jr., who had just died two years earlier. They made her a producer on a new project, though it is unclear what her remuneration was supposed to have been. The station obviously wanted to make use of her name rather than actually give her any creative control. Conflict between Nurmi and the station erupted almost immediately.

At least one rumor has it that Nurmi wanted Lola Falana to become the new Vampira. This would be entirely possible, as Falana's career and background would have helped her shape the kind of powerful female character Nurmi wanted to see on the screen. The Cuban musician had exploded onto stage and screen in the late 60s, working with Sammy Davis Jr. and starring in spaghetti westerns and a number of action films directed by African American directors (often unhelpfully labeled "blaxploitation"). But despite the wattage of her star power, it is highly unlikely that a major market station would have, even in 1980, chosen a woman known as "the black Venus" to become its new horror host even if the original horror host had chosen her.

A better-sourced story about Nurmi's conflict over the re-creation of her character comes from David Del Valle. In 1987, Del Valle introduced Nurmi to Martine Beswick, a British star of the Hammer horror and sci-fi films *Dr. Jekyll and Sister Hyde* and *One Million Years BC*. Beswick had subsequently achieved greater fame as a "Bond girl," having appeared in both *From Russia with Love* and *Thunderball*. Nurmi referred to Beswick as the woman who had appeared in those "deliciously sexy horror films" and wanted to meet her, in part, to tell her that back in the early 80s she had wanted her to become the new Vampira.

Beswick seems to fit the profile Nurmi wanted for the new Vampira. Dark-skinned like Falana, she had portrayed characters both seductive and dangerous. What's most interesting about both of these women is that Nurmi had clearly decided that the new Vampira had to cross the color line in some way. Although her own creation had been purposefully deathly pale, she probably had become aware that America needed a new kind of shock to its system that only a black woman performing the macabre could provide.

Channel 9 wanted more fun and less controversy and refused Nurmi, essentially locking her out of the creative process. Nurmi could perhaps have had more influence over the direction America's new horror host might take had she stayed and worked with the other producers. But this looked like another blacklisting to her, and she left. KHJ selected the blonde and buxom Cassandra Peterson as their new horror host, "Elvira." She would become almost an immediate sensation.

Ironically, Peterson actually shared a great deal in common with the woman who made her into a nemesis. Like Nurmi, Peterson also fled small-town life (Colorado, instead of Oregon) and had a brief career in Vegas where, again like Nurmi, she met a much older Elvis Presley. She had had some contact with gay male subculture when, as a high schooler, she worked as a dancer at a local gay bar. Peterson shared Nurmi's concern for animal rights, later becoming a PETA spokesperson. She had had a number of bit parts in larger films, including a small role as a showgirl in the Bond flick *Diamonds Are Forever*.

Very much unlike Nurmi, though, her invitation in 1981 to become a horror host began a three-decade career that brought her both wealth and fame. Also unlike Nurmi, the character she created, or that was created for her, had none of the subversive, aggressive power of Vampira. She was a valley girl in goth drag.

In the early 80s, the valley girl became a recognizable trope in American popular culture. Based on a stereotype of young, upper-class white women from the tony San Fernando Valley suburbs, the image of the valley girl incarnated materialism, lack of intellectual curiosity, and utter superficiality. "Valleyspeak" became so widespread in popular culture that it has become a relatively stable element in American English, especially what linguists call the high rising terminal that tends to transform statements into breathless questions ("So, anyway, we were like, at the mall?").

Peterson's horror host persona grew from the valley girl. The macabre has a stronger link than might first appear to this phenomenon, and Peterson successfully picked up on this. The valley girl has a bit of an edge to her, a subculture that may be about going shopping but that shops in an America increasingly uncertain about its own materialism. A few years before the 1983 film *Valley Girl* made the figure a permanent part of teen romantic comedy and a highly recognizable cultural force, George Romero made the mall the new American haunted house in *Dawn of the Dead*. Showing the fate of a group of survivors holed up in America's ultimate symbol of consumerism, Romero forever linked death and shopping, consumerism and wasted lives, death and the department store.

By the late 80s, the idea of the valley girl became identified with the growing fascination with morbidity. In 1988, Winona Ryder and Christian Slater starred in *Heathers*, a gruesome landmark in teen culture. *Heathers* introduced us to valley girls in order to kill them off in hilarious fashion, nodding along the way to James Dean, noir films, and an obsession with death that lay at the heart of youth culture during a period of atomic saber-rattling in the Cold War.

In 1992, the feature film *Buffy the Vampire Slayer* introduced a valley girl as a "chosen one," anointed with the power to slay demons and vampires. Cheerleader Buffy has no desire to accept this task since, like any typical valley girl, she just wanted to "graduate high school, go to Europe, marry Christian Slater, and die." She took up the stake and her destiny, and, though the film had little success, screenwriter Joss Whedon used it as source material to create the TV show that became a pop-culture phenomenon.

The show would not create a goth heroine (at least at first), but instead linked goth elements with exactly the kind of teen culture produced out of the valley girl craze.

Peterson picked up on this element in popular culture when she wed goth image with valleyspeak. Furious with KHJ for even considering this transformation of Vampira's image into something she wrongly read as silly and superficial, Nurmi sent the station a cease-and-desist order after taping for the first show began and insisted to anyone who would listen that the station had "stolen" Vampira from her. Thus Nurmi began a nine-year legal battle with the station and eventually with Cassandra Peterson herself.

Nurmi did not have the full story and probably would have appreciated some of its macabre ironies. Peterson had wanted a very different direction for the character she created, and originally suggested to station managers that she adopt the look of Sharon Tate's character from *The Fearless Vampire Killers.* Voluptuous, but without a hint of gothic, its wasn't what KHJ wanted to see (and they perhaps worried that this image could cause some audience consternation given that most Americans identified Sharon Tate with the 1969 Manson murders).

The character she did create joined the valley girl with a punk haircut and presented America with a vampire lady that joked more about her own cleavage than the horror movies shown on screen. She played a parody of herself, rather than taking Nurmi's approach of playing a parody of America's expectations for women. In some respects, her soaring popularity fit perfectly with the 80s backlash against the women's movement, especially the conception of feminism as frumpy and neo-puritanical. Elvira was all sex and silliness, even a silly kind of sex.

Cassandra Peterson had found a formula that sold in a way that Vampira never had. *Fright Night* transformed into *Elvira's Movie Macabre* and she went from being a cult figure to the head of a merchandizing empire. In the mid-80s, it was possible to purchase

Elvira comic books, calendars, and look-alike wigs, and, in 1988, to see the film *Elvira: Mistress of the Dark*. It's not too much to say that she had become America's horror host, the first truly national figure to take on the role over an extended period. She remains so recognizable today that almost any expression of goth culture leads outsiders to reference Elvira. Most of the earlier dark ladies of television, including Maila Nurmi's Vampira, have been subsumed under her image in the popular mind-set.

Following the truly massive success of the Peterson brand, Nurmi focused her legal battle on the broad frontiers of the Elvira empire. Her lawyers specifically charged Peterson with having violated the Lanham Act, the major federal trademark law established in the United States in 1946. In *Nurmi v. Peterson*, her complaint alleged that Peterson had, "in creating character 'Elvira,' used certain props, clothes, and mannerisms similar but not identical to 'Vampira' character." In this basic contention, Nurmi was right. Elvira did use more than a few macabre props first introduced by Nurmi. She even ended her broadcasts wishing viewers "unpleasant dreams," not at all unlike Vampira wishing her late-night audience "bad dreams, darlings."

Of course, every horror host since Zacherley had done much the same. Moreover, a number of precedents in the entertainment industry had made Nurmi's hopes for a favorable settlement fairly unlikely from the start. In a decision issued by the California District Court in March 1989, the court ended no less than five series of claims issued by Nurmi and a claim against Peterson for punitive damages. Peterson also sought sanctions against Nurmi for "frivolous" efforts to appeal the findings of lower courts.

John Skerchock's fan biography of Vampira claims that Nurmi substantially damaged her own case by frequently failing to make court appearances. This has the ring of truth about it, as Nurmi had become increasingly reclusive since the early 70s, even as she tried to make something of a comeback. The court pretty clearly decided *Nurmi v. Peterson* on more meaningful grounds. Nurmi's claims had no real substance.

Nurmi's complaint alleged that Peterson had "created a new character that resembled the Vampira character." This in no way violated the Lanham Act. Peterson had not used Vampira's "likeness" but, as the court's decision pointed out, "likeness" had generally been interpreted in such cases "to mean an exact copy of another's features and not merely a suggestive resemblance." The court further argued that a broad interpretation of "likeness" would "freeze all rights to certain props, clothing, or other qualities surrounding a character with this first person to portray the part." This led the court to the quite reasonable conclusion that this would "greatly inhibit the development of the entertainment arts." It would mean, essentially, that since Bela Lugosi wore a cape to portray Dracula, no other actor ever could wear one without legal sanctions.

Nurmi probably already knew all of this. In fact, it's fairly obvious that elements of her character had been copied before in the endless echo chamber that constitutes American popular culture. Suing the creators of *The Addams Family* or Forrest Ackerman for his creation of Vampirella would have made a great deal more sense. But what drove her in this was not simply that Elvira had become another dark lady that stole a bit of her show. Her opportunity to re-create the character had likely enthralled her, and that ability had been taken away in a studio executive's shell game that surely reminded her a great deal of what had happened to her in 1956. It surely felt like yet another blacklisting.

Peterson, for her part, went on to make stacks and stacks of money off the character of Elvira. She also claimed that she had never heard of Vampira before she found herself being dragged into court. This is a bit difficult to credit and points to exactly the kind of dismissive attitude that caused Maila Nurmi to pursue litigation with some enthusiasm.

Vampira may have lost her national stage, but she remained a powerful figure for an American underground that actively resisted the cultural influences of Reagan-era America. In both the goth and punk movements, Maila Nurmi, now into her 60s, influenced, often very directly, the shape of these subcultures.

It's as hard to define goth as it is to uncover its incredibly diverse cultural origins. For most people, it's mainly a set of images that might include wearing Doc Martens, listening to Joy Division alone in your dark and cavernous room, or engaging in elaborate absinthe-preparation rituals while reading Shelley's poetry and Neil Gaiman's *Sandman* series. It was all very easy to poke fun at. *Saturday Night Live*'s "Goth Talk" featured goth prince of darkness Azrael, "forlorn" because of his mall job at Cinnabon. The "Goth Kids" of *South Park* parody captured elements of the subculture that real goths immediately recognized and laughed, yes laughed, about.

Others in the United States have had a much more negative response to goth kids (and elder goths). The American media helped to ignite a moral panic about goth culture after the 1999 Columbine shootings, suggesting a widespread and somewhat satanic "trench coat mafia." Kids dressed in black had already been targets of bullies since the movement became widespread in the United States in the 80s.

In West Memphis, Arkansas, in 1994, a rogue local justice system tried and convicted three teens for the brutal murder of two young boys based on nothing more but fear of the three young men's goth interests. Damien Echols, Jessie Misskelley Jr., and Jason Baldwin, better known as the West Memphis Three, spent almost two decades in prison even though the only evidence offered against them was that they wore black T-shirts, listened to heavy metal, and read Stephen King novels. Although forensic evidence essentially cleared them by 2007, they were not released until 2011.

Although it's a subculture built out of all kinds of diverse cultural materials, Vampira stands as godmother to the goth movement in the United States. All goths had a sense of morbidity, and all goths, or at least lots of them, had a sense of humor. The last point may seem a bit surprising to outsiders, since the goth sensibility seems all about pondering death while the other kids are off having fun. But, in fact, as Liisa Ladouceur points out in her encyclopedia of goth culture, there's a sense of subversive laughter behind every black cloak and vampire role-playing game. Born in the shadow of the bomb, goths of all ages are part of a subculture that parodies death and made dry comedy out of things that weren't supposed to be funny. The way that goth kids found themselves treated in schools and households across the nation shows that the culture recognized this dangerous element in goth culture, its ability to question the way things were "supposed" to be.

Vampira pioneered the laughter that surrounded horror and death. Her imperious power of making fun of American culture influenced the dark ladies who came later. She's visible today in the women of all of the goth subcultures, especially in the heavily tattooed female fans on the horror convention circuit that mimic her style. And almost every goth girl out there, consciously or unconsciously, tries to be her. Or at least create the same kind of macabre burlesque she pioneered. Ladouceur calls Vampira the template for "campy, sexed-up femme fatales," and she is that. It's impossible to imagine the imagery of the goth movement without her.

Nurmi's relationship with American punk and postpunk is both more tenuous and yet also a more direct part of her biography. Her role as a local character in WeHo led to a brief revival of interest in her in the punk scene. In fact, punk culture provided her with some of her very last public performances in the 1980s.

Punk exploded out of the simmering anger of unemployed youth from working-class backgrounds in Margaret Thatcher's England. The Sex Pistols and the early Clash are the incarnation of thrashing revolt against both the escapist puffery of pop music and what many kids saw as the starry-eyed idealism of the 60s coming to nothing in the materialism and militarism of the 80s. In the United States, punk had its beginnings in a scene that developed around CBGB, a club on Manhattan's Lower East Side.

The Stooges, the Ramones, and Television inaugurated American punk on the East Coast. The West Coast soon followed with a style labeled "postpunk" or sometimes "hardcore," and a scene that included Black Flag, the Circle Jerks, and the Minutemen. Punk bands and their followers shared a relationship unlike anything in popular music, with shows advertised by hand-drawn and mimeographed flyers and bands acting as their own agents, publicists, and roadies. "We jam econo," as the Minutemen famously put it.

Although Hollywood during this period earned a reputation as the incubator for hair metal or glam bands like Mötley Crüe, much more was happening just off the Sunset Strip. The Anti-Club on Melrose Avenue became perhaps the premier underground hardcore club in 80s L.A., regularly featuring bands like Black Flag, the Descendents, and some naughty boys who would become the Red Hot Chili Peppers. And Maila Nurmi.

By the mid-1980s, Nurmi had long been a well-established bit of local color in WeHo. Vampira's Attic on Melrose went out of business in the mid-70s, profits unable to keep up with rising rents. Maila wrote to horror journalist Robert R. Rees that too many patrons seemed to think of the shop as "an antique museum rather than a shop" and simply weren't buying anything. She lived in a series of cheap apartments, only barely managing to keep up with exponentially rising property values through sales of her memorabilia and holding down jobs at local establishments such as a Finnish restaurant, where she worked as a hostess in the early 80s. She lived as cheaply as possible, once renting a room above a garage and living in sections of WeHo considered déclassé by even the hippest of gentrifiers.

The Anti-Club hosted a "spoken word night" during the week, part of the origins of the slam poetry movement that echoed the Beat Generation's fascination with impromptu verbal performance.

Vampira became an important symbol for hardcore and postpunk culture. Her influence can be seen in the 1999 zine *Gutter Trash*, one of many D.I.Y. efforts that thrived in West Coast punk culture.

Notably, Nurmi had started sporting a pixie cut reminiscent of how she wore her hair for the 1959 film *The Beat Generation.* Dharma bums seemed to be hitching rides across the old, weird America once again.

Nurmi became the star of Anti-Club spoken-word night, not by cashing in on Vampira, but by evoking old macabre Hollywood. She read, night after a night, from a manuscript (since lost) she had been writing about Tinseltown in the early 50s, the time when things were about to go bad, but when James Dean was still alive and the young crowd at Googie's laughed at the aging stars and starlets over at Schwab's, plotting a new world that would be born from the death of the studio system. Everyone present seemed to grasp something of what she was talking about, while feeling the pathos that Nurmi herself embodied with her fatal connection to Dean, the boy king that never lived to see the revolution in moviemaking, in teen culture, in American culture that his rebellion without a cause helped to body forth. For the young, body-pierced, Mohawk- or crew cut–sporting crowd at the Anti-Club, it must have been like sitting down with Norma Desmond to watch some of her old pictures. Ghosts cluttered the stage.

These monthly readings seem a bit out of character for Nurmi at this stage of her life. Maila once described herself in an interview as a "half recluse." In the last two decades of her life, she seemed to sometimes seek the stage again, only to run from it. In some ways, this had been her approach to the world since the early 60s and the end of so many of her dreams. She had something to give to the world that the world sometimes seemed to want and sometimes seemed to reject, like an inconstant lover.

Nurmi dealt with this the only way she could, by withdrawing from the world whenever it seemed as if it was about to reject her or mock her or ignore her. She continued this pattern in the 80s when she suffered some kind of embarrassment at the hands of the Red Hot Chili Peppers. Not yet a household name, the band had a following in WeHo as their musical acumen combined with an unabashed desire to be as obscene as possible in public. Nurmi, who could be suddenly and shockingly puritanical, described the band as "those guys who appear naked with socks on their penises" in an *Entertainment Weekly* interview in 1994. She obliquely alluded to how the band had interrupted one of her Anti-Club readings. "That was the end of it," she recalled, and remembered that she swore to never try to regain a literal stage again. "I said I'd never face a live audience again," she remembered, "except with a loaded machine gun." She never did.

In one of the dark ironies that seemed to mark Nurmi's life at every turn, the 90s seemed more willing to give her a stage than any time since the 50s. Elvira's merchandizing empire may have seemed to be taking up all the cultural air in the room, but the world Vampira had helped create, the meditations on darkness and death, vibrated under the surface of American culture.

It was in 1994 that director Tim Burton (known best for *Beetlejuice* and his darkly bizarre reimagining of the Batman mythos in two films) used Rudolph Grey's oral history of Ed Wood's career as the source material for a major motion picture. Johnny Depp starred as Wood and Martin Landau gave a bravura performance as the badly aging, drug-addicted, deeply lovable Bela Lugosi. In *Ed Wood*, Burton somehow managed to find the sweet spot between making fun of Wood and giving his rather absurd efforts at creative production their due.

Although Vampira appears only in a few scenes, they are particularly memorable moments, and actress Lisa Marie plays her at her most imperious. The film became a cult hit that also created plenty of mainstream fans, and interest in Vampira, and Maila Nurmi, grew.

Ed Wood made connoisseurs of 50s underground culture interested in Nurmi's paintings, something she had kept up with throughout the 70s and 80s. Her work began to fetch higher prices because of the connection with the film. In November 1994, *Entertainment Weekly* did a very brief piece on Nurmi, calling her "the original scream queen" and suggesting, correctly, that "if these are good times for sexily cheeky bloodsucking freaks, the mother of them all—Vampira—isn't getting her due."

She wasn't. But she was also more visible to the public than she had been in four decades. She even had another brief film appearance spawned by the interest in Burton's biopic. In 1998, she had a cameo in the knowingly absurd *I Woke Up Early the Day I Died*, a film directed by Aris Iliopulos that featured everyone from indie film icon Christina Ricci to Tippi Hedren, best known for her starring role in Alfred Hitchcock's *The Birds*. Based on one of Ed Wood's screenplays, Nurmi had only a few moments of camera time. Today, it's almost impossible to locate a copy of this already forgotten film. But she was being remembered, even though the world didn't know what to make of her any more than she knew what to make of it.

Nurmi's inglorious departure from the Anti-Club hadn't even ended her influence on punk. In the late 80s and early 90s, Nurmi worked with a local garage punk band that called themselves Satan's Cheerleaders. The band became well-known locally in the "garbage punk" scene and had Nurmi appear on two of their EPs, *Genocide Utopia* (the cover of which features a martial-looking dominatrix version of Vampira) and another release, one side of which simply has Nurmi giving a spoken-word performance about her meeting with Elvis.

Jane Satan, the guiding force behind Satan's Cheerleaders, remembers that the band had Nurmi in the recording studio for really only one day to perform on the EPs. She had been writing a spoken-word tribute to James Dean that the Cheerleaders would back up with their busting-surfboards-meets-punk-thrash sound.

Nurmi, almost at the last minute, decided she didn't feel right recording anything about Dean. Someone from the band suggested that she write up something quickly about her encounter with Elvis, and they would turn the EP into a "Tribute to Elvis" album since the time was close to the tenth anniversary of his death.

Although an Elvis tribute may seem a counterintuitive choice for a punk band, West Coast punkers, especially of the goth punk variety, had been heavily influenced by rockabilly. Vampira not only related the story of her meeting with Elvis but also recorded a track in which she screams, moans, and sighs his name while the band thrashes in the background. The Cheerleaders released the album on gold-colored vinyl, in part a commemoration of Elvis's gaudy Las Vegas persona.

Satan's Cheerleaders had the closest association with Maila Nurmi, but another goth punk band came to be identified most closely with Vampira. The Misfits, a band whose skeletal symbol has become synonymous with the subgenre of horror punk, represent another example of how Nurmi's gothic sensibility seeped into the culture. The original incarnation of the band lasted for about seven years with lead singer Glenn Danzig and bassist Jerry Only as the consistent personnel. In 1983, they planned to release a studio album called *12 Hits from Hell* that would contain a tribute to her called simply "Vampira." The song eventually appeared on *Misfits Collection I*, and Only briefly met her when the owner of a WeHo record store called Vinyl Fetish gave him her address.

The Misfits are only the most well-known of a number of bands in the 80s that fused an appreciation of underground 50s and 60s horror culture with thrashing guitars and an unmistakable rockabilly beat. The Groovie Ghoulies from Sacramento and, of course, Satan's Cheerleaders from L.A. shaped this strange musical experiment in cultural archeology while Rocket from the Crypt, out of San Diego, carried it forward into the 1990s. Certain elements of "gothbilly" or "hellbilly" music (incarnated most obviously in both the music and films of Rob Zombie) owe their origins to these bands. Maila Nurmi and Elvis Presley could never have imagined that the time they spent palling around in Las Vegas symbolized a future fusion of the worlds they were making.

Nurmi's association with the L.A. punk scene of the late 80s embodies the changing political atmosphere for American feminism that itself had a musical component. Many young women who came of age in the 70s and 80s began to define themselves as a "third wave" of historic feminism. Open to and savvy about popular culture, they viewed themselves as celebrating sexuality in a culture that feared female sexual agency.

Third-wavers adopted an ironic style toward elements of popular culture that had enraged second-wave feminism. Camp proved especially congenial to them. The tendency of camp to defang seriousness and mock the "natural" way of things dovetailed with the hottest new theorists in women's studies programs across the country. More importantly, it fit perfectly with the sensibility of a generation of young women who would invade every traditional male preserve of privilege with an ironic smile on their faces.

Even rock and roll got a visit from third-wave feminism. Bands like the Raincoats, the Slits, and Bikini Kill mocked not only the cock-rock masculine edifice of pop music but second-wavers' sometimes puritanical leanings. *Bust* magazine, founded in 1993, sounded like a wank mag but spoke to this generation that wanted to "bust out," celebrate sexuality, and mock every patriarchal anxiety about women's bodies and women's independence. *Bitch* magazine came along soon after, taking back a malicious term and cleansing it, making it about being heard and speaking out and having a loud and strong voice. Subversion had a smile, and Vampira's screams and laughter made sense in a way it had not in the 1950s.

In so many ways, it seemed like Maila Nurmi's time had come. And she was nowhere to be found.

Postscript

NIGHTMARE SCENARIOS

Around the time *Dig Me Later, Vampira* first premiered on KABC, the April 5, 1954, cover of Newsweek magazine captured mid-century American schizophrenia. The cover featured two young women driving a convertible, the car covered with bumper stickers that boasted of all the destinations they had visited.

The look shouts prosperity, excitement, postwar America's bacchanalia of consumerism, and a world that could now be beautiful after years of Depression and war and atrocity and horror. And yet, cutting across this image appeared the title of the issue's major story: "THE BOMB: WHAT ARE THE ODDS OF SURVIVAL NOW?" The article concluded that if you lived in an American city, the odds against you were a million to one.

But the cover seemed ask, "If we are all going to die anyway, who wouldn't want this new world of beautiful and fast and shiny things?"

The "duck and cover" campaign began in the United States in 1951, driven by civil-defense concerns that Americans feel safe even if the atomic age meant that they were decidedly not.

The short film strip, shown in classrooms throughout the country, featured Bert the Turtle hunkering down under his own shell and encouraging children to do the same, getting on their knees and covering their heads if early-warning sirens released their terrifying whine. In the event that these systems failed to detect the oncoming attack, they were told to duck and cover upon seeing a bright flash "brighter than anything, brighter than the sun."

There's no evidence that anyone responsible for putting together the campaign considered it effective protection from the apocalyptic holocaust of atomic war. Its creators hoped it would serve as a palliative, perhaps more for parents than children. Young 1950s families that felt their government had everything firmly under control would be unlikely to question the country's foreign policy in this age of American empire.

Bela Lugosi and Ed Wood sat and watched *The Vampira Show* in Lugosi's modest suburban home. Lugosi thought that her appearance on the cultural radar screen meant that gothic horror had made a comeback. He was also excited by Universal Studios' recent release of *Creature from the Black Lagoon*, a sign that the studio had not forgotten its monsters, and even releasing it in 3D. Lugosi dreamed of a new, colorized version of *Dracula*, 3D bats flitting around him in the textured darkness.

Horror historian David J. Skal tells us that Lugosi encouraged a fan campaign of letter-writing to Universal's production executives calling for just such a film. He wanted a legacy untarnished by press reports of his morphine and methadone addiction.

But he died with a decidedly mixed legacy as an actor. Everyone remembered his 1931 horror classic. But everyone would also remember his involvement with Ed Wood's absurd productions, particularly after Martin Laundau's Academy-Award-winning performance in Burton's *Ed Wood*.

He never got the chance to make a real comeback. American horror fans wanted gargantuan things rising from seas and coming from space, radioactive horrors like Godzilla that could crush the world they had built beneath its feet. As Skal writes, "an enveloping cloak was no longer an image of dread. But a mushroom cloud was."

America woke up screaming.

"Duck and cover" and its friendly turtle mascot gave the children of the 50s nightmares rather than calmed their nerves. Laura Graff, a young student in New York City, remembered the Board of Education issuing dog tags to her and her friends so their bodies could be identified in the event of an atomic attack. She later surreptitiously watched a late-night show "not meant for children" that showed an America wrecked and ruined after a nuclear exchange. She went to bed with images of people melting while they slept.

In August 1974, Gerald Ford became the 38th president of the United States. In his inaugural address, he promised Americans that their "long national nightmare" had come to an end. Ford obliquely referenced the Watergate scandal that had brought down his predecessor, a scandal that had shown Americans a darkness underneath its most honored institutions.

He could have easily been referencing how the social conflict of the 1960s pulled the country to pieces or the conflict in Vietnam, America's "living room war" that had sent home more than 50,000 body bags and tens of thousands of physically and psychologically mutilated veterans. Or he could have been describing the continuing tensions of the nuclear age. By the early 70s, the intercontinental ballistic missile (ICBM) and the nuclear submarine had made possible the delivery of warheads to almost every patch of U.S. and Soviet soil, destroying human civilization in a single apocalyptic roar.

But, Ford promised us, the nightmare was over.

In 1979, the Office of Technology of the United States Congress issued a report called "The Effects of Nuclear War." The report imagined four scenarios. Ranging from an "accidental" nuclear exchange whose effects could be limited, it also contemplated a full-scale nuclear exchange with the Soviet Union. That scenario, the "nightmare scenario," estimated the immediate death of 70 to 160 million people. Radiation sickness and environmental collapse would follow. The extinction of humanity seemed the likely ultimate outcome.

In the same year, the goth punk band Bauhaus released "Bela Lugosi's Dead." Regarded as a seminal moment in the origins of goth music, Bauhaus turned classic monster-movie imagery into a parable about death. The past had not only died, it had come back as a living corpse even as the bats left the bell tower and the virgins had been bled.

Bela Lugosi was, in fact, long dead. But something still rattled around in the darkness.

In 1980, Ronald Reagan's presidential campaign captured American optimism and the deeply held belief in American exceptionalism with the TV ad "It's Morning in America." Reagan served two terms, furthering American imperial ambitions in Latin America and the Middle East through CIA subversion, gunrunning, and outright military intervention. He also played a dangerous game of brinkmanship with the Soviet Union that could have melted everything in flames.

Reagan projected a sunny image that seemed to join with a cult of the 50s that emerged in American culture. Some young men in the 80s dressed conservatively in polo shirts and chinos, sweaters wrapped around their shoulders like characters from an Archie comic. Teen comedies embraced materialistic values; *Ferris Bueller's Day Off* and *Risky Business* suggested that wrecking the family sports car represented the height of existential tragedy.

The Soviet Union fell, world markets boomed, some declared the end of history in the sense that its former intractable conflicts had been replaced by liberal democracy and capitalism as the wave of the future.

Kurt Cobain sat in his bedroom listening to the Melvins and Scratch Acid and planning to let out a long, tormented scream, but people in the world outside shopped till they dropped and were pretty sure they would win if they died with the most toys. The biggest political issue of the 90s had to do with cum on a cocktail dress. Maybe things were not so scary, America dreamed.

*****

By the late 1990s, Maila Nurmi knew she would never have a stage again. But she seemed more than content with this and had made her life about other things. Vampira continued to live on, but in some ways very much without Maila Nurmi.

Ed Wood accounts for the increasing fan fascination with her. As she approached the end of her life, cult magazines expressed occasional interest, and she built friendships with some of the writers that seem to have delighted them while making her incredibly nervous. When horror fanzine writer Robert R. Rees attempted to get in touch with her through mutual acquaintances, she would not allow him to speak to her directly and only accepted letters through trusted emissaries. She did not give out her mailing address.

Mike Black, a writer for the L.A. punk zine *Gutter Trash*, had a similar experience in the late 90s. Although he visited with Nurmi frequently and ate with her at several local WeHo spots, Nurmi never allowed him to come into her apartment. After one of their outings, he mentioned that he needed to use the restroom and, in his words, "She didn't let me into the house but directed me to a little alley near the house where I took a piss."

Nurmi's reticence partially grew out of a lifetime of watching people disappear. Into her 80s by the early 21st century, she had almost no contact with anyone from earlier periods of her life. Her ex-husbands had died and in any case had been out of touch with her for four decades. She reconnected with her niece, Sandra Niermi, though it is hard to say how close they became during these years. Nurmi never had any real connection to her brother, Robert, or to any extended family, for close to half a century.

There was more to her reclusive tendencies than a fear that intimacy wouldn't last. Since the 1950s, she had been the target of stalkers, usually psychologically damaged men who found it impossible to deal with the dark sexual energy of the character she had created. This began when she was attacked in the streets of L.A. in the mid-50s and continued long after she had left the public spotlight. At least one deranged stalker sent her terrifying letters that dwelt on how he was "fattening up a cat" to sacrifice in her honor. He later left a dead cat on her doorstep, an incident that not only frightened her but also left this lifelong animal lover crying uncontrollably when describing what had happened to interviewers years later.

Maila Nurmi held herself partially responsible. She believed to the end of her life that she had unleashed a dark creature by creating Vampira, summoned up something so powerful that it shook the foundations of American culture. She was right, perhaps especially to men unable to deal with how Vampira embodied both sex and power and lashed out at her in rage. She once told filmmaker R. H. Greene that she didn't envy the Hollywood elite their fame and money. She envied their electric fences.

The second half of the 20th century hurt Maila Nurmi in almost every way it knew how. Internet commentators, bloggers, and anonymous posts in forums sometimes speculate that Nurmi may have been bipolar manic-depressive. Diagnosis via gossip is appalling and also completely unhelpful in understanding anything about her. The celebrity commodity culture had stolen from her what she had created and abandoned her, refusing to recompense her. Friends had drifted away, many of them because they had come seeking the glow of fame that had faded. The violent and insane had threatened her. There's no need to seek more explanation for her behavior. She had every reason to cut herself off from a world that had claimed to love her but never really had.

But she never truly disappeared, and she certainly didn't want to be forgotten. Maila Nurmi willingly talked with almost anyone that contacted her up to the very end of her life. Reading through accounts of reporters, fans, and the curious who tried to form a connection with her during these years, a template of her relationship to the outside world begins to emerge. An enthusiastic fan that has learned about her through the *Ed Wood* film makes contact with her. She meets them at various cheap WeHo diners and restaurants (she seems to have especially liked Sizzler, though she always warned her dinner companions that the french fries would ruin their skin). They listen to stories about James Dean and Ed Wood. They ask very little about Nurmi herself or even *The Vampira Show*. After a while, they disappear from her life.

A young Finnish reporter, Tomi Hinkkanen, formed just such a relationship with her in the mid-90s. Hinkkanen wrote a moving tribute to her in 2011, describing "My Saturdays with Vampira," a friendship that seems to have lasted several years. He contacted her for a program for Finnish television (it's unclear if this was ever produced) but became for a time her regular dining companion at Sizzler.

Hinkkanen describes a friendship in which Nurmi kept certain, well-defined boundaries. Although the reporter seems to describe an increasingly close friendship, he also wrote of how "many a Saturday, Maila and I sat on the pavement in front of her apartment, talked and fed the pigeons." In other words, she never allowed Hinkkanen to go into her apartment either. Then, rather suddenly, he dropped out of her life or she dropped out of his . . . "for one reason or another," he writes. He read about her death in the newspaper 13 years later.

Animals, on the other hand, became her closest companions. In the last two decades of her life, she not only spent a lot of time feeding pigeons but also seems to have made pets of more than few of them, taking them into her home and naming them. In what must have been a sometimes-hostile domestic situation, she played mother to innumerable cats over the years as well. She also had a beloved dog named Bogie, who may well have been the best friend she ever had. She seemed inconsolable about his death even years after.

A few articles and biographic sketches of Maila Nurmi refer to her as an "animal rights advocate," but I have been unable to find any hard evidence of this fact. She may have been involved with a local shelter on some level (probably as a frequent adoptee of strays). It is not clear that things ever became more political than that, and she certainly was not a vegetarian (interviewers often found themselves at an unnamed and very cheap burger place near her house). Still, in her seclusion she found a solace with animals that human companions never seemed to have given her.

Her seclusion never became total. The continued interest in her generated by Tim Burton's film ensured a steady stream of the curious and the admiring, especially in the 1990s. Mike Black, on his three visits with her, claims to have crossed paths with the head of the Finnish consulate coming by to bring Nurmi a newspaper clipping about her from her birthplace, a hopeful documentarian who wanted to make yet another biopic of Ed Wood, and an unnamed member of Satan's Cheerleaders who brought her a compilation CD.

She made feints at the world in these years and then disappeared. She continued to show up at a number of small, local horror conventions, though memories of her from these events seem sparse. It's easy to imagine that her strange, new half fame troubled her, based as it was on her link with Ed Wood and not for the character she believed so important to American popular culture.

Maybe this is why the self-portraits began. Or rather, the portraits of her other, secret self, Vampira. She had been painting and drawing since the 1930s and her love affair with *Terry and the Pirates*. But in the last decade of her life, she seemed to want to paint Vampira, over and over again.

Many of these images feature her in the incarnation of Vampira that appeared in *Plan 9*, arms outstretched, about to grab us and do God knows what. One fan purchased a portrait called *Vampira Stalks You* that directly referenced the famous graveyard scene from *Plan 9*. She was delighted that people wanted them and frequently sent along letters and signed photographs to anyone who purchased them.

She worked from still photographs, tracing out the past. "I add a little graveyard earth to the board," she told one friend. She probably lied about this but did it for the fans. It's exactly what we would have wanted her to do.

*****

James Dean wanted to make a horror movie. Once, in a high school play, he played Frankenstein's monster in a spoof called *Goon with the Wind*. In the final months of his short life, he and William Bast worked on a screenplay of a new version of the Jekyll and Hyde story. As Calvin Thomas Beck writes, it's incredible to think of Dean portraying this two-sided double. After all, every character he ever played explored the terror of identity, the possibility of two worlds crossing in one person and blowing up a little universe. Maila had thought they would be doubles, twin soldiers in the war on American conformity. But he abandoned her. Then he died.

Soon after his death, Maila Nurmi took a train to Indiana to visit his grave, one of the very few trips she ever made outside of California after her move there in the 40s. On the train ride, a much older Maila Nurmi remembered, she had stolen a sugar bowl and claimed that a young James Dean, riding the rails with his dead mother's body in 1940, had also stolen a sugar bowl on a train. We aren't required to believe her to feel that everything is connected, because we make things connect and these links create what we like to call history.

She died on January 10, 2008. Her seclusion from the world had come to mean that only a few close friends checked on her regularly.

The woman who had a photo spread in *Life* not only died alone, her body lay in the county morgue, unclaimed, for three days. Friends and admirers put some money together to claim it.

In fact, Maila Nurmi didn't receive a proper burial until later in the spring. On April 5, 2008, friends and supporters held a benefit for her burial at the Steve Allen Theater on Hollywood Boulevard. For $10 a head, the interested and curious could hear a set by the "zombie-friendly comedian" Dana Gould and music provided by the Ghastly Ones, one of the many "spooky surfer" bands born in the wake of the Misfits, the Cramps, and Satan's Cheerleaders.

In 2009, friends, fans, and hangers-on laid to rest what was left of the corpse of Maila Nurmi in the Hollywood Forever Cemetery. An etched image of one of her most famous TV images appears on the headstone. A web stretches behind her, strange and complex like the web of her life, while she stands as she was in 1954, morbidly shaped and alien, the original vampire lady. "Hollywood Legend," the stone lies.

In the year of Nurmi's death, Stefani Joanne Angelina Germanotta released the album *The Fame,* later remixed and rewritten as *The Fame Monster.* The story of Germanotta's early life seems similar to Nurmi's. She began her career in New York, in a kind of neo-Beat scene that included playing gigs at places like the Bitter End and the Mercury Lounge in the Village and on the Lower East Side.

She worked for a while as a go-go dancer in the burlesque revival, fascinated by the idea that the display of her body could mean power instead of oppression. A true child of third-wave feminism, she embraced the idea that she could celebrate her sexuality and that this would undermine the patriarchal strictures the Catholic Church had tried to force her to embrace. A former student at the Convent of the Sacred Heart School, she often performed in a thong as she became increasingly attracted to the glam rock of Queen and David Bowie.

Lady Gaga has embraced the gothic and used it to make a statement about the acceptance, indeed the celebration, of sexual minorities. Her fans are "little monsters" and her concerts are "Monsters' Balls." Like Vampira, she regularly reconstructs the appearance of her body, creating alien and otherworldly designs. She's more straightforwardly political than Vampira ever became, outspoken and generally consistent on LGBT issues. At the same time, her immense wealth and global recognition give her a stage she's unlikely to ever lose completely. She can afford to be outré. Indeed, that's her whole act.

It's too much to say that there would have been no Lady Gaga without Vampira. But it is true there would have been no Gaga and no Madonna and no sense of irony to upset the boundaries of what America thought was real without the movement Vampira represented and embodied. She made the darkness talk, and it said things no one had ever said, or screamed, before in American history.

Almost a century lay behind her. She had channeled all the terrors of a world that dreamed of death into and through a bizarre satire of the 1950s female form. The 1950s had not wanted her, and she came into her own just as she disappeared from the world.

Two documentaries have tried to capture elements of her life while her appearance on tattoos, T-shirts, and other memorabilia at horror conventions across the country continues to grow. *Vampira: The Movie* appeared in 2006, not long before her death. She allowed director Kevin Sean Michaels to interview her, in her home, suggesting that the personal boundaries that she sometimes drew for herself did not extend around Vampira. She believed Vampira would live on, in other incarnations, an idea that crops up in many of her final interviews.

More recently, R. H. Greene produced what may be the definitive documentary look at her life. *Vampira and Me* premiered in 2012 at the Los Angeles Film Festival and was released on DVD in late 2013. The subtitle calls her "The first goth, the last icon" and rightfully emphasizes her contributions to everything from punk to hipsterism. Greene managed to uncover more archival footage of Vampira than fans ever knew existed, two new kinescopes. These new materials enabled him to fully re-create her brief moment of fame in the 1950s and gave her more of a chance to speak in her own voice than any other representation of her ever has.

Efforts to say something meaningful about her, including my own, feel like efforts to capture her. Most of the fans who have sought her out, either just to get her autograph or to write a book or to make a movie about her, have wanted something of her mojo. She seems to have sensed this, and it helps explains her reticence toward the world. She knew we wanted something but doubted it was her. She asked fanzine writer Robert R. Rees if he thought of her as a "highway across the veil to James Dean and Bela Lugosi."

She does take us behind a veil to a moment that America changed. The romance of James Dean is the romance of a time lost and an opportunity missed. Vampira channels that fixed temporal point, the moment after World War II when many Americans thought that a new and beautiful and prosperous world had opened its vistas. Vampira, and a handful of others, knew it was a world of nightmare scenarios, knew that the next half century would continue to be about death. Laughter and a scream was the best response to a frightened and tranquilized postwar world, a world that needed her desperately and didn't know it.

In one of the stranger interviews that Maila Nurmi gave in her final years, she compared Vampira to Lilith, a demon goddess from Jewish mythology and folklore with roots in the ancient Near East. In much of this folklore, Lilith is Adam's demon-lover, a satanic competitor for Eve. "That's who Vampira is in another incarnation," she insisted.

When I first read this comparison, it seemed strange and inexact. If anything, Vampira seemed to have a more powerful aura than an ancient mythological construct. Moreover, it seemed like more of the metaphysical pap that Maila Nurmi always seems to have felt some attachment to—psychic links, mystical dreams, other incarnations.

The more I have pondered it, however, the more it seems that Nurmi captured something very important about her own cultural meaning in that statement. Since the 19th century, poets and artists have come to see Lilith as a powerful symbol of the feminine principle set against the patriarchal traditions of the Abrahamic religions. Lilith became important in third-wave feminism for this reason, leading to, for example, the Lilith Fair music festival. Lilith captured the spirit of wild rebellion and sense of irony that went along with that movement. Vampira embodied exactly this spirit of whimsical destruction, a real-girl power.

She revealed something important about Vampira in this interview, but also something very important about Maila Nurmi. She reflected on how frequently close-up shots of her screaming in *Plan 9 from Outer Space* have been used to represent her. Nurmi said that the irony of her scream in that moment is that she was ready to hit her mark and unleash her trademark scream but, just at that moment, the camera startled her and unleashed the scream for her, tore it out of her. "That's better horror than when the monster goes 'boo,'" she reflected. "When the monster is frightened," she said, "the monster is out of control. That is dangerous."

Maila had created a monster that was dangerous. She may have been scared herself much of the time. So she decided to turn that terror into something beautiful and powerful.

Her following has grown. The curiosity *Ed Wood* aroused has transformed into something more affectionate and even obsessive since her death, as if she really became a dark goddess of horror when she herself crossed the veil. Her fan base has a fanatical online following, with a Tumblr and a Facebook page with thousands of followers. Most interesting of all, a kind of vernacular art has grown up around her image. On the craft and vintage sellers' site Etsy, it's possible to purchase everything from screen-printed T-shirts to portraits to "saint's" candles in which the face of Maila Nurmi takes the place of the Virgin Mary revealing her sacred heart.

I have one of the latter. The artist included a note that reads "In Vampira We Trust."

It's as if we know that this ragged lady in the shadows actually helped make the world we live in, walks still in our own nightmare scenarios, laughs at us in the dark.

The sculptor Thomas Kuntz captured something about her that she would not have feared or derided or been ashamed to have someone capture. Kuntz first learned about Vampira and her story during the 90s when she made an appearance at L.A.'s Cinema Cafe, one of her rare outings in that era. He immediately became fascinated with her and her story.

Kuntz has sculpted and machined numerous images over the years, crossing the line back and forth between performance art and fan art. Part sculptor and part illusionist, his work sometimes feels like a clockwork from a steampunk novel rather than anything we're familiar with in relation to commercial fan art. Deeply interested in the 18th-century science of automata, his sense of the human form and its possibilities made him a perfect artist to represent and befriend the woman who created Vampira.

Poly-resin statues have become significant commodities in American geek culture, serving a purpose not dissimilar from saint's statues in traditional Catholic culture. Often highly expensive since they are made in limited numbers, statues of comic book heroes and villains, movie monsters, and nerd culture icons often fetch high prices on eBay and through distributors like Sideshow Collectibles and Bowen Designs. Kuntz worked for the latter, a company that generally created sculptures of popular comic book heroes. He also experimented with much more interesting projects, building what some called "garage kit" sculptures of obscure characters from the silent film era.

Kuntz's 2001 sculpture of Vampira clearly grew out of his admiration for Maila Nurmi. In the image he crafted, she's not the cardboard and mute monster of the Ed Wood film. She's not vaguely pornographic, as are many pop-culture statues of female characters. She's a dark goddess of horror, an image that seems to step out of 1954 into the present. She looks directly at us, glares at us really, the moment right after her scream has relaxed her so and she's about to give us a night full of delightful terrors, America's horror host in the every sense of the idea. Of all the film stock used and the ink spilled over her story, it is one of the images that most fully embodies what she meant to American culture.

Unlike many of those who passed in and out of her life, Kuntz remained close to Maila Nurmi from the early 90s until the time of her death. "She was a mentor and muse," he says, and he served as a pallbearer at her funeral.

On January 15, 2008, the AP carried Maila Nurmi's obituary. The meaningful confusion of her with the dark goddess she created continued: "TV's Vampira, Maila Nurmi, dies at 85."

Nurmi would have liked most of the obit. It did not dwell on her association with Ed Wood. It described her life as a young woman in the Village and a bit about how she made her way to Hollywood.

Sadly, it spent a paragraph on her war with Cassandra Peterson and signaled to readers that they should recognize her because actress Lisa Marie had played her in Tim Burton's *Ed Wood*.

The article quoted Heather Saenz, who seems to be one of several friends who checked in on her over the years. Saenz and her husband, Bryan Moore, had been local characters in Hollywood who, in 2005, recruited Nurmi to serve as grand marshal in a procession of hearses that the Petersen Automobile Museum organized as a publicity stunt.

The story quoted Bryan Moore as saying that "Funeral arrangements are pending. Nurmi has no known surviving family."

Thomas Kuntz crafted this amazing image of Vampira at the height of her dark powers. An image from her niece poses the statue with James Dean, her "fellow soldier." Courtesy of the Clatsop County Historical Society.

Of course, she did have family that survived her, at least a niece who has worked hard to preserve her aunt's legacy. It's a measure of how far Nurmi had disappeared into the shadows of cultural memory that so little of her personal biography remained a matter of record, making even an accurate obituary hard to write.

She created another kind of family whose influence has continued to grow. From the moment she unleashed her first scream, she gathered around her the fascinated and the enthralled who joined her in her love affair with sex and death. All the morbid dark ladies of the past half century have been dressing up like Vampira. The now hundreds of horror conventions that meet yearly all over the country remember her as tattooed and cos-playing women, and sometimes men, concoct the same unearthly cultural potions she did.

The goddess of horror's dark sun throws its long shadows beyond the world of monsters and monster fans. Wherever camp becomes protest, whenever performance art becomes political, indeed wherever conventionality about sexuality and gender and death itself are turned into a punch line, Vampira's orgasmic scream of delight echoes in the background. Her life, the broken and sad and lonely part of her life, shows that oppressive systems are never funny. But the art she birthed out of her own darkness remind us that oppressors don't get the last laugh.

The world forgot Maila Nurmi and the monster she made. We have the chance to remember her. But not everyone would even agree we should. Wasn't she, after all, a minor character in our cultural cavalcade? A "cult figure" like dozens of others who become a focus of fascination for their followers but whose lives really offer us little more than the pleasures of eccentricity?

Why do we need cultural icons? Why do we love them and sometimes hate them? They seem to exist to be lampooned, tabloid-style, and to become centers of controversies that don't matter. Female icons are particular targets, their personal and artistic decisions mocked and punished with giggles from the audience, from us.

It's a bitterness against life that would seek to make fun of Maila Nurmi. This is not to say that it didn't happen. Not a few of the magazine articles and interviews I used for this account descended into the attempt to create a freak show, to draw out her possible mental instability, or to mock her beliefs about psychic powers, reincarnation, or her idea that she could communicate with James Dean and Marlon Brando beyond the veil of death. We seem to like our female icons to be weird, and we seem to like to punish them for it as well.

But for most of her fans, most of the family her monster made, she poses a series of questions, questions about what we want our collective history to become. Nurmi made Vampira to have a conversation with us, a conversation we can still continue, even if Nurmi herself is gone but Vampira lives on, like the undead goddess she is.

The girl who drew comics, the glamour model, the hatcheck girl, the vamp and the vampire, Sister Saint Francis, the dark goddess of horror, the aging recluse. These seem like tarot card images, archetypes alive in our collective psyche that Maila Nurmi had the strength to render to the world through her own body.

Folk artist Danielle Jenkins created the image of Vampira on a saint's candle in which the dark lady melds imperceptibly with the Virgin Mary, bearing to the viewer her sacred heart of suffering. Of course it's kitsch, and of course our love for every cult figure gets called kitsch when we want to separate the suffering it requires to create a symbol that lives in the world from the ravages of one's own life.

Vampira is going to haunt you, so it would pay you to seek out her ghost and get to know it. Learn to live with her. Her face swims in every film that allows the weird and the wanton to shriek and stir, urges you to refuse to believe the stories that the straights and the phonies want to sell you. Her scream echoes, and the light of her darkness does not go out. She wants you to join her midnight ramble.

A Note on SOURCES

Maila Nurmi's life might seem an odd window through which to observe several decades of American cultural history. She chose to live her life in the shadows. It was Vampira, not Maila, who held the stage. She often answered questions about herself and her personal life with misdirection, opacity, or the outright lies that complex personalities often find necessary and useful.

The usual archival materials frequently mined by historians offered clues but little in the way of answers. My archival research centered mostly on her early life and the a-lot-harder-to-get-than-you-would-think newspaper accounts.

I hope what follows will allow readers and Vampira fans to at least find the trails that I did, even if they promptly get lost on them. I want to give special attention to those sources and people that proved especially helpful in reconstructing Maila Nurmi and her times, and to express gratitude to the scholars whose careful work has helped me reconstruct several incredibly complex eras through the life of one dark lady.

I should note that the work of David J. Skal, especially *The Monster Show: A Cultural History of Horror* (1993), as a major influence on my overall interpretive approach. Skal's encyclopedic knowledge of the horror tradition in America and Europe, and his ability to blend good cultural history with a real love for his subject, suggested to me many years ago that my own love of monsters could be turned into a "serious" subject. I owe him and his work immeasurably and will never forget the first time I read his dauntingly excellent book.

Its also difficult to imagine this book without Sam Kashner and Jennifer MacNair's very well-researched, and very fun, *The Bad and the Beautiful: Hollywood in the Fifties* (W.W. Norton, 2002). This extraordinary book provided me with material on everything from 1950s LA geography to a history of scandal rags to the story of organized crime and the movies. A wonderful book in its own right, it perfectly captures the era that made Vampira both possible and impossible.

SOURCES

INTRODUCTION

Several primary sources proved especially useful to my effort to recreate a sense of the official culture of the 1950s. Elmer Henderson's address says a great deal about how fears of communism entwined with almost every aspect of life in the 1950s and appeared in *JAMA* 1950 (143 (9): 783–789). J. Edgar Hoover's *Masters of Deceit* (Pocket Books, 1958) remains a kind of landmark of the decade's paranoia.

Magazine ads provide the basis for my discussion of the role of the housewife and 50s consumer goods as images of the self. Most of the images I used are in my personal collection and came from magazines such as *Look*, *Time*, and *Life* from about 1948 to 1962.

The work of several historians informs a great deal of my representation of the 1950s that appears here. Elaine Tyler May's *Homeward Bound* (revised edition; 2008) offered the first definitive study of the 50s ideology of domesticity. I have also borrowed throughout the book from three important collections of essays on the Cold War simply called *The Culture of the Cold War* (John Hopkins University Press, 1996) and edited by Stephen J. Whitfield. The quotes from Peter Kuznick and James Gilbert come from the introduction to *Rethinking Cold War Culture* (Smithsonian Books, 2010). Some of the material on the representation of lesbians in postwar American comes from Donna Penn's essay in *Not June Cleaver: Women and Gender in Postwar America, 1945–1960* (Temple University Press, 1994).

Lynn Spigel's excellent *Make Room for TV* (University of Chicago Press, 1992) provided the statistics I used in this section showing the spread in television's popularity and my basic interpretation of that medium's early years. Anecdotes and details about early television throughout my book are borrowed from her voluminous research.

I found two cultural studies of the Cold War useful throughout: Beatriz Colomina, Annmarie Brennan, and Jeannie Kim's collection *Cold War Hothouses: Inventing Postwar Culture, from Cockpit to Playboy* (Princeton Architectural Press, 1994) and Alan Nadel's *Containment Culture: American Narratives, Postmodernism, and the Atomic Age* (Duke University Press, 1995). A number of my reflections on the era are also informed by Margot A. Henriksen's *Dr. Strangelove's America: Society and Culture in the Atomic Age* (University of California Press, 1997).

PART I: BAD GIRL

My research on Maila Nurmi's background was aided enormously by the work of Clatsop County Historical Society archivist Liisa Penner. Penner wrote an excellent article on Maila Nurmi, her Finnish background, and her family history in the winter 2008 issue of the *Clatsop County Historical Society Quarterly*. She also helpfully answered my questions and put me in touch with other local sources.

Ella Hill, a friend and neighbor of Maila Nurmi's during her teenage years who still lives in Astoria, happily spoke with me and filled in as much detail as she could about Nurmi's childhood.

Several books proved useful in describing the life and politics of Finnish immigrant communities, especially A. William Hoglund's *Finnish Immigrants in America: 1880–1920* (University of Wisconsin Press, 1960), Michael G. Karni's *Strangers in the Land: The Experience of the Immigrant Finns* (Center for Immigration Studies and the Immigrant Archives; University of Minnesota, 1974), and Peter Kivisto's *Immigrant Socialists in the United States: The Case of Finns and the Left* (Fairleigh Dickinson University Press, 1984).

Two books helped me very much in describing cultural attitudes toward women early in the century and the "white slavery panic." The key book on the latter is Brian Donovan's *White Slave Crusades: Race, Gender and Anti-Vice Activism, 1887–1917* (University of Illinois Press, 2006). Janet Staiger's *Bad Women: Regulating Sexuality in Early American Cinema* (University of Minnesota, 1995) helped me trace the changing trajectory of bad girls and provided the interview with Theda Bara on the nature of "the vamp," an idea essential in making sense of Maila Nurmi's creation.

Many of the articles I used for this section, including "Vampire When Ready" from *People in TV* and much more obscure pieces like Aline Mosby's "Beautiful Blonde from Lapland Is TV's Most Terrifying Queen" from the May 15, 1954, *Beaver Valley Times*, came to my attention only because of a wonderful Vampira fan forum on Yuku called "Our Favorite Horror Hosts" in the classic horror forums. Though not especially busy in recent years, it still contains a wealth of materials on Vampira, almost constituting a digital archive of media coverage of her time as a local L.A. star.

Although I had to double-check a number of facts in John Skerchock's enthusiastic fan biography *Vampira*, I made use of it to fill in a number of gaps and to try to establish a basic timeline. I also quote from Rudolph Grey's *Ed Wood: A Nightmare of Ecstasy* (Feral House, 1992) on Nurmi's first interaction with Bela Lugosi. Grey's book proved useful to me throughout and is a highly recommended oral history not only of Wood's career but also of the exploitation film genre in general.

Maria Elena Buszek's *Pin-Up Grrrls: Feminism, Sexuality and Popular Culture* (Duke University Press, 2006) illuminated not only the world of midcentury pin-up art but also how historical representation of women intertwined with these representations. Buszek's work also kept me on the lookout for subversions and rebellions as I looked at this once much maligned art form.

My description of the history of pin-ups comes from several sources. A Taschen Press collection called *1,000 Pin-Ups* contains just that, with images from Harrison Publications from the 1940s through the 1950s of both cover images and photographic spreads. A sense of what a midcentury "Spook Show" might have been like came from a digitized *Tops* magazine found on an online fan site here: www.creepymagic.com/spooksters/silkinispookshow.html (accessed April 29, 2012).

PART II: BONDAGE

Several articles from the *Los Angeles Times* proved helpful in unraveling the story of Nurmi's firing from both KABC and KHJ. Walter Ames, a real fan of Maila Nurmi's, documented elements of her rise and fall. The story of KABC's publicity stunt gone wrong appears in the story "Singer Asks for $100,000 for TV Trick" from June 1954. John Skerchock's fan account of Maila Nurmi's life, Vampira Unauthorized (self-published, 2010) includes a complete copy of "Vampira's Witty Slayings."

Gay and lesbian life in postwar America has become an important area of study. I used Robert J. Corber's *In The Name of National Security: Hitchcock, Homophobia, and the Political Construction of Gender in Postwar America* (Duke, 1996). On Hay, see the biography by Stuart Timmons, *The Trouble with Harry Hay* (Alyson Publications, 1990).

Barbara Norfleet's *When We Liked Ike: Looking for Postwar America* (W. W. Norton Company, 2001) offers the reader a first-person stroll through the 1950s and its attitudes about sex and family in the shadow of the bomb. John Wertime's memoir *Improbable Love: My Secret Affair in the 1950s* (Printemps Press, 2011) offers an even more personal, if very idiosyncratic, reading of 1950s ideas about sex and relationships.

My discussion of *Bizarre*, and of individual images, comes from another Taschen Press collection called simply *Best of Bizarre* (2001). It includes Willie's earliest efforts in 1946 and images and text from the magazine between 1948 and 1951.

Several works proved essential in navigating the intricacies of early bondage culture and its meaning. Anne McClintock's article "Maid to Order: Commercial Fetishism and Gender Power" offers an excellent brief analysis (www.english.wisc.edu/amcclintock/writing/Maid_article.pdf). The broader historical context of bondage and its relationship to the Victorian era can be found in McClintock's landmark book *Imperial Leather: Race, Gender, and Sexuality in the Colonial Contest* (Routledge, 1995). Anne Creadick's book *Perfectly Average: The Pursuit of Normality in Postwar America* (University of Massachusetts Press, 2010) tells the bizarre story of "Norm and Norma" and helped me explain what made Maila Nurmi's body sculpting such an act of rebellion.

Quotes from Maila Nurmi in this chapter come from Greene's film *Vampira and Me* and from an article by Finnish reporter Tomi Hinkkanen titled "My Saturdays with Vampira." David Dalton's *James Dean: The Mutant King* (Chicago Review Press, 1991) and William Bast's controversial memoir *James Dean: A Biography* (Ballantine Books, 1956) provided more material about Nurmi and Dean's relationship, "the night watch," and the controversy surrounding Vampira after Dean's death.

PART III: B-MOVIES

I've pieced together the relationship between Vampira and Liberace from a *Los Angeles Times* article from April 9, 1955, scattered photographs, and her comments in interviews (she told the story of spitting in an audience member's face only in the late 90s). Darden Asbury Pyron has a gigantic biography of Liberace called *Liberace: An American Boy* (University of Chicago Press, 2000) that allowed me to talk about his career and audience reception. Sadly, it has no details to share on Liberace's relationship to Maila Nurmi.

The story of the circumstance under which she met Elvis is somewhat controversial. Film fan magazine *Outré* did a well-researched article that included photographs of Vampira and Liberace (issue 27, n.d.) and full details on her meeting with Elvis. On Satan's Cheerleader's *Tribute to Elvis* EP, Maila Nurmi told a slightly different story that seemed to downplay the Liberace connection. I have gone with the account of Mike Weatherford, who also interviewed Nurmi for the story in *Outré*.

Scattered accounts of her public appearances in the *Los Angeles Times* helped fill in her increasingly shadowy life after her career spiraled, including short articles or advertisements on the following dates: March 29, 1955; May, 18, 1956; June 14, 1956; November 14, 1956; and February 28, 1957.

Almost all of my discussion about the exploitation flicks that Maila Nurmi appeared in comes from secondhand accounts or IMDB.com. Nurmi spoke very little about these experiences, other than the filming of *Plan 9*. Here, Grey's *Nightmare of Ecstasy* became my guide.

There are two exceptions to this. *The Magic Sword* (1962) can fairly easily be located on DVD, though, as I described, Nurmi appears only briefly and in bizarre makeup. I did manage to purchase a bootleg copy of *The Beat Generation* from a cult film enthusiast in Toronto.

This era in Nurmi's life, especially her exploitation career, gets some good attention in Calvin Thomas Beck's indispensable

Scream Queens: Heroines of the Horrors (Collier Macmillan, 1978). Based on interviews and written before her cult status, Beck captured elements of her life and importance missed by eager interviewers in the 90s.

The history of exploitation flicks has been well covered in Blair Davis's wonderful book *The Battle for the Bs: 1950s Hollywood and the Rebirth of Low-Budget Cinema* (Rutgers, 2012). Most of my discussion of the changing nature of Hollywood at this point in Vampira's life comes from her work. Roger Corman's autobiography, *How I Made a Hundred Movies in Hollywood and Never Lost a Dime* (Random House 1995) provided not only information about his career but also numerous details about the era that allowed for guerrilla filmmaking such as this. A shameless self-promoter (this is why he's been so successful), Corman also writes without illusions and with a desire to say something true and meaningful about his life and times.

On Brando, and his relationship and comments on Maila, see Peter Manso's magisterial biography *Brando: The Biography* (Hyperion, 1995).

David Del Valle is one of the great fanboy historians, and his *The Del Valle Archives* blog is well worth your time if you love horror and science fiction fandom. His August 18, 2012, entry, "Vampira, Orson, and the Whole Damn Thing," is invaluable because it gives a window into Nurmi's life during a period mostly hidden from view (delvallearchives.blogspot.com/2012/08/vampira-orson-and-whole-damn-thing.html).

PART IV: BURLESQUES

The place to begin when examining the horror host phenomenon is Michael Monahan's *American Scary: Conversations With the Kings, Queens and Jesters of Late-Night Horror TV* (Midnight Marquee

Press, 2006). Monahan loves and understands the genre, and his interviews, including his interview with Vampira, are an amazing archive of television and horror history.

The excellent work of several scholars of media and culture informed what I had to say about representations of women, and how women chose to represent themselves in the 70s and 80s. I don't know how you manage to be authoritative, funny and quirky, and give a detailed history of feminism right up to the day before yesterday in 170 pages, but Deborah Siegel manages it with *Sisterhood Interrupted: From Radical Women to Grrls Gone Wild* (Palgrave, 2007). Much of what I have to say about third-wave feminism draws on her work. Meanwhile, I learned about the cultural politics and controversy that swirled around *Charlie's Angels* from Whitney Womack's "Reevaluating 'Jiggle TV': *Charlie's Angels* at Twenty-Five" in Sherrie A. Inness's *Disco Divas: Woman and Popular Culture in the 1970s* (University of Pennsylvania Press, 2003). Andrea Weiss's *Vampires and Violets: Lesbians in the Cinema* (Penguin, 1992) has a chapter on the lesbian vampire subgenre.

Although pretty heavy in terms of critical cultural theory, Pamela Robertson's *Guilty Pleasures: Feminist Camp from Mae West to Madonna* (Duke University Press, 1996) guided me in my thinking about sexual personas, gender, and camp styles in the 20th century. The chapter on West is invaluable. My only complaint is that Maila Nurmi did not get her due.

There are several good documentaries and oral histories of West Coast punk available. I found a chapter from historian Bradford Martin's *The Other Eighties: A Secret History of America in the Age of Reagan* (Hill and Wang, 2011) most useful in terms of placing hardcore (and related genres) in political and cultural context.

R. H. Green has an excellent interview with Jane Satan about her band's recording session with Maila Nurmi. The Satan's Cheerleaders EPs on which Vampira's voice appears are out there but hard to find and much valued by collectors.

Although I am a Vampira partisan, it's hard not to sympathize with Cassandra Peterson's position (though impossible to feel sorry for her, given her massive multimedia success). John Skerchock reprints the full decision of the California District Court in the matter of *Nurmi v. Peterson*. The horror film fan magazine *Fangoria* interviewed Nurmi in 1983 (allowing her to give a kind of oral history), and this contains perhaps the most detailed description of the Elvira controversy. *Fangoria* also gave KHJ-TV program director Walt Baker a few lines to give the station's side of the story (*Fangoria* no. 30, 1982, 26–29).

POSTSCRIPT: NIGHTMARE SCENARIOS

Some of my thoughts on Maila and her cult status are drawn from R. H. Green's more than praiseworthy *Vampira and Me.*

The full congressional report "The Effects of Nuclear War" can be found here: www.fas.org/nuke/intro/nuke/7906.

Tom Hinkkanen published his story on Maila Nurmi for the *Finnish Times* on October 5, 2011. Mike Black published part of his interview with Nurmi in the L.A. punk zine *Gutter Trash* (no. 4, 1996). The author has a copy of the mimeographed issue in his collection.

I received the much sought-after and rare statue of Nurmi by Thomas Kuntz from Sandra Niermi, Maila's niece, for far under current eBay prices. Thomas Kuntz spoke with me over the phone briefly, something that was a real honor for me.

Horror fan magazine *Rue Morgue*, a true bellwether of horror and neo-goth culture, published "The Last Interview with Vampira" in its April 2008 issue, with interviewer Alexander Anastasio. Its very fitting that this magazine, so much a part of the culture that Nurmi created, published this piece.

The obituary I quote from, "TV's Vampira, Maila Nurmi, Dies

at 85," appeared in the *New York Daily News* on January 15, 2008. A comment on the website opined, " a pioneer . . . in media history . . . a very attractive performer."

She deserved more.

ACKNOWLEDGMENTS

Writing the acknowledgements for this book has been more difficult than with any other project. This has come very easy in the past but this work felt at times like it was done in isolation with a lot more obsessive scribbling and lonely brooding than normal, even for me.

Looking back, I realize this is not the case at all. There are not only people to thank. There are people who created this book in a way I did not.

I'd like to first mention the willingness of people like Jonny Coffin, Sandra Niemi, Ella Hill, and Thomas Kuntz to speak with me, even if sometimes very briefly, about their friend and muse. If a full biography of Vampira is ever written, they are keepers of the flame and the place to begin. My only wish is that time and distance had not made it impossible for me to get to know them better. I hope this will change.

And, though I have not had the chance to meet or speak with him yet, this work could not have happened in the same way or with the same depth without the film documentarian R.H. Greene. His

2012 film *Vampira and Me* and more recent work uncovering the relationship between Vampira and Disney's 2014 *Maleficent* leave all of those who love her in his everlasting debt.

It's impossible to imagine this book coming to full fruition without Sheri Holman. Her friendship has been a constant source of inspiration for my work and her own interest in Vampira, described in the "Foreword" to this book she generously provided, helped me to see the compelling cultural forces that Maila Nurmi unleashed. Moreover, her utter devotion to the craft of writing that has found expression in a series of award-winning novels pushed me to find a truer voice than I have before. Whether dealing with the uncertainties of Skype across coasts or drinking sake in a basement bar in Manhattan, Sheri willingly has used her time with me to help me to do the work I needed to do to make this book possible.

Through Sheri, I also got to meet one of my writerly heroes, Christopher Bram. Author of *Father of Frankenstein* (later to become *Gods and Monsters* and the Academy Award winning film of the same name), has long been an idol of mine. His interest in the life of James Whale helped drive my interest in the forgotten genius whose life I have tried to explain and celebrate.

Even troubled loners like me need good friends. My life-long friend and companion Alan Richard continues to be one of my biggest cheerleaders in life and writing and that has been true for this book as well. Doryjane Birrer has become a wonderful movie-going companion as the number of B-grade blockbusters and bottles of wine we have consumed on Saturday afternoons continues to climb. Tammy Ingram likes to make clear to me that she has no interest in horror, monsters or "spaceships" but she does drink with me regularly and this means more to me than she knows. Nina Kushner lives too far away and is very busy breaking new ground in the study of gender and sexuality but our long comradeship and love for one another frequently makes dark clouds part for me.

Authors often have as complex a relationship with their agents as patients have with their analysts. I'm lucky that my relationship with Deirdre Mullane is simple, straightforward and good. She shaped this project as much as she helped sell it and has helped me to reimagine the way one goes about writing a book. She believed in Vampira when not everyone did and worked some magical matchmaking that could not have been more perfect.

Speaking of which, my publisher, Counterpoint /Soft Skull, has done more than any I have ever worked with to make this a better book than it was when they received it. Editor Dan Smetanka believed strongly in the project and the book itself but also made some suggestions, after I had "finished" in my own mind that helped me rethink some essential points and rewrite what seem to me now to be crucial passages. His devotion to books and authors make me feel good about the future of both those things.

Others at the press have been attentive and helpful, saving me from a number of errors and mistakes. Kelly Winton has overseen the editing process in expert fashion while my copy-editor Matthew Grace did extraordinary work and proofreader Mikayla Butchart combed over final proofs. I appreciated their close work and their enthusiasm for the book. Any mistakes that remain are most assuredly my own.

And speaking of enthusiasm, I have been overwhelmed with Megan Fishmann and Sharon Wu's support at the press and eagerness to get the book out there to readers.

Colleagues, as well as students and former students at the College of Charleston, often had very direct influence on this book. Rich Bodek's support for my research and writing has been unfailing. Phyllis Jestice has become a great friend as well as my new department chair and has rooted for my work on 20th century American cultural history more than any sword-collecting medievalist should be expected to.

CofC alum Sharon Pobe McAlister and I probably have deeper conversations via text about everything from movie monsters to

Marxism that many people ever do in person. James Boast's work on gay and lesbian life in mid-century America pushed me toward some important books on the topic whose findings helped me make more sense of Vampira's Los Angeles. Frank Martin is my horror film companion and, if we are lucky, his incredibly innovative ideas about the genre will make it to the screen. Christina Butler is both one of my most beloved friends and my contractor, a wonderful combination indeed. She's also one of an infinitesimally small number of people for whom I'd attend a wedding.

The section of this book that deals with third wave feminism simply would not have been written without the work, and inspiration of Emily Farrier. We have been friends now longer than we were professor and student and I hope she knows how very much that, and she, means to me. Her texts about life in New Mexico and Joss Whedon are always a treat and, my God, I actually receive things from her in the mail written in her own hand, which, these days, seems like an almost supernatural occurrence. I want to thank her for letting me play Giles to her kickboxing Buffy.

Through much change and difficulty, Beth Phillips has been the one utter certainty and unfailing support in my life for many years now. She contributed to this book in a more direct sense of being a constant reminder and my best example of what creative, independent and strong women are. Like Maila, I cannot get over the strangeness of the world and, without Beth's love and support my link to it would be tenuous at best. I can never repay her for this kind of trust because it's beyond what most people in this life get to enjoy. But I do want her to know how deeply grateful I am for receiving from her the best gifts anyone has ever been able or willing to give me.

About the Author

© LESLIE McKELLAR

W. Scott Poole, who teaches at the College of Charleston, has written widely about American history, horror, and pop culture, including most recently in his award-winning history, *Monsters in America*, which received the John G. Cawelti prize from the Popular Culture Association and was named among the "Best of the Best" by the AAUP for 2011. *Monsters* received nominations for the Bram Stoker and the fan-sourced Rondo Hatton Classic Horror Awards. Poole is a regular contributor to *Popmatters* and his work has appeared in the *Huffington Post*, *Religion Dispatches* and *Killing the Buddha*. He has been a guest speaker at Authors@Google and has collaborated on films for the History Channel, PBS, and, most recently, the Banger Films project, *Satan: The Movie*. He blogs at his website www.monstersinamerica.com.